George Mackay Brown

was born in Stromness in the Orkney Islands in 1921. He studied at Newbattle Abbey under Edwin Muir and read English at Edinburgh University. He has published many books including plays, poems, novels and collections of short stories. Edwin Muir described his work as possessing 'a strangeness and magic rare anywhere in literature today'.

Apart from his years of study on the mainland, George Mackay Brown has scarcely left Orkney, and the imagery and history of the islands have been the inspiration for all his work.

His most recent novel, *Beside the Ocean of Time*, also published by Flamingo, was shortlisted for the 1994 Booker Prize.

GEORGE MACKAY BROWN

Vinland

Flamingo
An Imprint of HarperCollinsPublishers

Flamingo
An Imprint of HarperCollins*Publishers*
77–85 Fulham Palace Road,
Hammersmith, London W6 8JB

Published by Flamingo 1995
9 8 7 6 5 4 3 2 1

First published in Great Britain by
John Murray (Publishers) Ltd 1992

Author photograph by Gunnie Moberg

ISBN 0 00 654618 8

Set in Times Roman

Printed in Great Britain by
HarperCollinsManufacturing Glasgow

To Surinder Punjÿa

Contents

I

Vinland

1

There was a boy who lived in a hamlet in Orkney called Hamnavoe.
The boy's name was Ranald. Ranald's father had a small ship called
Snowgoose. Ranald's father – his name was Sigmund Firemouth – did
not like the land or anything to do with it, such as ploughs or horses or
barns. Sigmund Firemouth was only happy when he was at sea,
adjusting his sail to the wind, going from one port to another with a
cargo, and, sometimes, passengers.

Ranald's father had been given the name Firemouth because of his
violent language when anyone or anything crossed or displeased him.
Then he would fly into a sudden rage, and shout and strike the table
with his fist. Even his wife Thora was afraid to say a wrong word to him.

The boy Ranald went white in the face, and trembled, whenever his
father was in an ill-humour – for example, when his cargo was safely
stowed on board and he could not put to sea because the wind was
contrary.

Sometimes *Snowgoose* ventured to a Scottish port, like Leith or
Berwick, with a cargo of salted fish or smoked fowls. Once she had
even gone as far as Grimsby.

But mostly her voyages were eastward, to Norway or Denmark, and
then she would return with a great cargo of wood, for wood was scarce
in Orkney, there being no trees to speak of. Men in the islands liked to
build their houses of wood rather than stone.

One day in early summer Sigmund Firemouth returned from the bay
where his ship was anchored. He was well pleased. The loading of the
cargo had gone well; the sailors were eager to be off. The wind was in
the right quarter.

'We leave with the next tide,' said Sigmund to his wife. 'We're going to a place I've never been to before, Greenland, with a cargo of grain and Scottish timber.'

'Greenland,' said Ranald's mother, 'that sounds like a nice place.'

'It's called Greenland', said Sigmund, 'because it's the most fertile and delightful place in the world. Greenland has only recently been settled. Families are flocking there from all over the north. Especially the Icelanders. Well, what do you expect – the Icelanders live among glaciers and gales all the time. I'm looking forward to this Greenland voyage.'

'If it's so fertile and green', said Thora, 'why do they need a cargo of grain and timber?'

Sigmund's face flushed and he struck the board with his fist. 'What do you know about it, woman?' he shouted. 'Mind your own affairs!'

As always, his rage quickly died down. By the time he had supped his bowl of porridge and ale, he was in a mild mood again.

He went to the door and licked his forefinger and held it up. Yes: the light south wind was still blowing. And he could tell by the look of the clouds that presently the wind would freshen. They might well have a fair wind, with a touch of east in it, all the way to Greenland.

To his son he said, 'Now boy, how old are you?'

'Nearly twelve,' said Ranald.

'Then you'll soon have to make up your mind what to do. You can't sit with the other boys at that monk's bench learning to read and write forever.'

Ranald said nothing. He was afraid to open his mouth. He disliked the sea. Even in a small row-boat he felt uneasy and squeamish.

His mother was kneading dough at the table. There would be new loaves for supper. His mother paused. She looked anxiously from father to son.

Sigmund went on, 'Of course reading and writing, and learning to count, will be a great help once you take over *Snowgoose*. I won't last forever. I had rheumatism bad last winter, from all that sailing in rain and gales. In three or four years maybe, you'll be taking over command of *Snowgoose*, boy.'

'That he won't,' said his wife quietly, setting lumps of dough on the griddle.

'Did you say something, woman?' said the skipper. 'Or was it the whisper of peat ash in the fire?'

2

'Ranald will not be going to sea,' said Thora. 'Our son Ranald is going at plough-time next spring to work on his grandfather's farm. His grandfather had no son, only five daughters, and I'm the oldest of them. The old man looks to Ranald to work the land of Breckness after him. Everything at Breckness will be Ranald's. So, to Breckness the boy will go when the oxen are yoked. And that way, beginning at plough-time, he'll learn every stage of farming through the year, right round to the reaping of the corn and harvest home.'

Normally Thora was a quiet woman. She had spoken in a torrent of words, knowing that it had to be said, and quickly, before the tempest broke.

But Sigmund the skipper when he spoke at last, said quietly, 'Boy, get ready to sail in the morning . . .'

2

First day out of Orkney, between Fair Isle and Sumburgh in Shetland, Ranald was wretched with seasickness.

But then, beyond Unst, he found that he was enjoying the ship and the sea.

The five seamen thought it good to have a boy on board.

Sigmund his father said nothing. He sat at the helm in sun and rain, occasionally shading his eyes northwards.

At night they stretched out for sleep under a canvas awning, except for two men who kept watch always, taking turns.

Three days and nights passed, of gray sea and empty horizon.

A dense clot of fog lay to westward one morning, with round summits piercing through.

'That's Faroe,' said Lund the seaman, splitting some fish they had caught and washing them in a wave that surged cold and green against the hull. Lund hung the fish on a spit over a little fire amidships.

The smell of the cooking mackerel made Ranald very hungry. He had hardly eaten since *Snowgoose* had sailed.

Now he ate heartily with the crew.

Over the meal, Sigmund the skipper accused one of the sailors of falling asleep on watch. Before the sailor, called Krak, could say a word in reply, Sigmund struck him a violent blow in the face, so that Krak's nose gushed blood.

The rest of the meal was eaten in silence.

It seemed Sigmund was in an ill-temper because the strong south wind had blown them off course somewhat.

Then Sigmund said to his son, 'You, boy, have been idle long enough. I notice that you can eat your share of fish. Tomorrow you'll do some work, cast a line for fish or help Grigor with the sail.'

Krak managed to suck the fish-bones clean though blood from his nose was still flowing.

That night Krak kept watch beside another sailor called Hwal who sat at the helm.

Ranald, on the verge of sleep, heard Krak say, 'I could kill the skipper for hitting me without a cause.'

'That would be bad luck for the ship and the crew,' said Hwal. 'Sigmund is a hard man, but a good skipper.'

'I would kill him with pleasure', said Krak, 'but that his son Ranald is a joy to us all. I think my nose is broken.'

'It seems more crooked than it was, indeed,' said Hwal.

Then Ranald slept.

He woke to hear a cry from Hwal. 'Land ahoy! A snow mountain! Iceland!'

3

For most of a day they were busy unloading part of *Snowgoose*'s cargo at the port of Reykjavik.

Merchants came down to bargain with Sigmund. They argued long and urgently. At last Ranald got tired of their narrow calculating eyes and their fingers touching sacks and money-bags, and he wandered past barking dogs, and a group or two of inquisitive women, and children who pointed at him and jeered.

On he wandered, amazed at the burning mountain and the ice-covered mountain and cornless fields. Iceland was very different from the green low islands of Orkney.

Down at a bay he saw quite a big ship being got ready for sea. The sailors were being ordered about their tasks by a tall handsome man, who didn't need to shout like his own father to get things done. Instead, the sailors went about their work with great cheerfulness, stowing sails and provisions. A few of them even sang.

The ship was called *West Seeker*.

The skipper of *West Seeker* noticed the boy above the shore, and gave him a pleasant greeting. 'You're a stranger in Iceland,' he said. 'Welcome, boy. My name is Leif Ericson, from Greenland. We have bought this big ship here in Iceland. What we want to do is sail west as far as we can. We leave at sunrise.'

Ranald said his father Sigmund Firemouth had a ship too, and they were on a voyage to Greenland, but they had been blown somewhat off course and here in Iceland his father was doing some buying and selling and bartering. The *Snowgoose* and her crew would rest for a day or two before sailing on west.

'We will see what ship will get to Greenland first,' said Leif Ericson, '*Snowgoose* or *West Seeker*.'

Now the seamen of *West Seeker* were carrying on board barrels of ale and boxes of salted whalemeat and bread still warm from the ovens.

Ranald heard a distant shout. He knew his father's voice. He ran back to the quayside.

His father's face was like a furnace with anger. The Iceland merchants were packing their goods on to small shaggy horses. The sailors of *Snowgoose* stood in the stern, all looking away, and their faces were white.

Ranald went up to his father.

And his father struck him, again and again, first on one side of the head and then on the other, till the boy's skull was seething and singing like a hive of burning bees. But Sigmund hit him with the open palm, not with the clenched fist that had broken Krak's nose.

'Who told you to wander away out of sight!' cried Sigmund. 'Don't you know, this island is full of thieves and scoundrels? What would I say to your mother back in Orkney if the Icelanders did you harm? Answer me. I wanted you here, at the quayside, to see how business is done as between shipowner and merchant. Or rather – as today – to see at first hand what scoundrels some merchants are . . .'

He threw the boy from him. He turned to the ship. 'What are you standing there for, idle!' he shouted. 'Put all those grain sacks back in the hold. We're going to Greenland at once.'

The group of sailors in the stern broke up. They went about the reloading slowly and silently. They growled among themselves. One or other turned from time to time to look furtively at their smouldering skipper, who stood alone at the head of the jetty, his fists trembling.

The sun went down. The first star glittered.

The sailors of *Snowgoose*, one after the other, crept under their blankets. There was no banter and singing that night.

Leif Ericson's *West Seeker* stood out for sea, at first light.

As soon as Iceland could no longer be seen, Leif gave the summons for breakfast.

As Wolf the cook was tilting an ale barrel to fill a pitcher, he heard a stir and a cough. There, among the ale barrels, shivering and blue in the face with cold, he found the boy Ranald Sigmundson, a stowaway.

4

Leif Ericson took it as a good omen that a boy should be on his ship.

'We all have beards, black or red or gold, it will not be too long till those beards become thin and gray, and then death is not far away. This lad from Orkney is a token that our voyage will have a happy and light-hearted outcome . . .'

Leif welcomed Ranald among the sailors, and they all took to him, and saw to it that he lacked for nothing in the way of food and comfort.

Ranald thought that *West Seeker* was a happier ship than *Snowgoose*. The men liked Leif Ericson and respected him. They brought their differences to him – a dispute over dice throwing, perhaps, or the name of a passing bird, the exact lineage of the kings of Norway – and they always accepted Leif's verdict.

At night they sang after supper, round the fire. Always, before sleep, they would discuss what they would find at the world's end, further west than any ship had sailed before.

'I think', said Trod the carpenter, 'we will strike the flank of Stoor-worm, and Stoor-worm will be angry and he'll turn on us and devour us at one gulp.'

The sailors laughed at that, and Trod was angry.

'You won't laugh so loud', said Trod, 'when you're stuck in Stoor-worm's throat, ship and all.'

'What's Stoor-worm?' said Ranald.

Trod said seriously to Ranald, but in a whisper, for now the sailors were throwing a dice and one, a bit drunk, was singing loudly, that Stoor-worm was the great dragon that girdled the whole world and held earth and sea together.

Leif Ericson, at the helm, said nothing.

The next morning they ran into heavy seas, with driving rain and flying spume. And then Ranald found that he was enjoying the great waves, and being flung from side to side of the ship, wielding a bailing pan, emptying the sea back into the sea.

In the afternoon the gale moderated, and the cook, a man called Wolf, got the fire lit and made a meal, but the sailors complained that the broth and the meat were too salty, and the sailor called Swale who had the keeping of the sails and cordage, was so displeased that he threw his half-gnawed meat bone at Wolf.

Wolf growled deep in his throat and would have gone for Swale.

But Leif said the food was over-salted because of the spindrift that had sifted into the ship from the crests of the big waves.

That night they began to discuss once more what they would find at the end of the voyage.

'What we will find is this', said Fiord, an elderly Norwegian, 'a mighty torrent into which the ocean empties forever, one vast thunderous cataract, and this end-of-the-world waterfall will take *West Seeker* and hurl us all into eternity.'

Trod's eyes bulged and his mouth opened.

'It's nothing to dread,' said Fiord. 'Nothing in this to make your face so gray, Trod. Better that than withering away in a shut-bed, an old toothless man. Why else do you think I've come on this voyage?'

Swale the sail-maker laughed sarcastically. 'If that is so', said he, 'if the ocean empties itself in mighty surgings and torrents over the last ledges in the west, why is the sea not empty? Where does all the water come from?'

Fiord could not answer that. First he looked confused, then he tried to look wise and patient, then he shook his silver-streaked beard and was silent.

There was a sailor who had been taken on the cruise not so much because of his sea-wit as because he was a good singer and reciter of ancient verses. His name was Ard. It was thought that in the end Ard might become a passable poet. He got drunk nearly every night over supper, though on the whole he tilted fewer ale horns than the other sailors.

Now, on the verge of tipsiness, Ard began to improvise a chant about the mystery of water, that comes in many beautiful shapes, raindrop, pool, stream, well, river, lake, enchanted prisoner in a snowflake, dew, marsh-water, ocean . . .

At that point Ard the poet's tongue thickened and the ale horn clattered out of his hand and he fell forward. He would have nose-dived into the fire if the sailors hadn't dragged him out and laid him under his sea blanket.

Leif Ericson said he didn't know what they might find at the end of the voyage.

'But first', said Leif, 'we must call at Greenland, at my father's farm there, with this cargo of Norwegian timber and tar. There is a great shortage of wood for building boats and houses in Greenland. We will get a good welcome from my kinsmen in Greenland.'

Ranald thought this strange. Had not his own father said that Greenland was a fertile well forested place?

Then it was time for the crew to turn in, all but helmsman and watchman.

Ranald was awakened at first light by a shout from Swale, who was the watchman that night. One by one the sailors stirred and yawned and shook themselves free of their blankets.

They saw, in the first glimmer of morning, boards floating on the sea, and a mast tangled in a sail, and a barrel and a broken oar.

'It seems', said Leif Ericson, 'that some ship came to grief in that storm, Greenland-bound.'

As he said this, Leif did not look at Ranald.

A broken curve of wood drifted past, and Ranald saw a snowgoose carved on it. It was a part of the prow.

The men on *West Seeker* gathered up the fragments of wood from the broken ship, but they allowed the piece with the carving on it to float past.

Then Ranald knew that his father and the sailors on *Snowgoose* were all drowned.

He felt such a stirring of the sources of sorrow inside him that his hands and his mouth shook.

'You should weep,' said Ard the poet. 'Then you'd feel better. It's a good thing to weep sometimes.'

'No,' said Ranald. 'Only women weep, and children. Now I'm a man and a seafarer.'

5

After Leif Ericson had settled all his affairs in Greenland, and given orders about his farm and fishing boats, and loaded *West Seeker* with the best provisions, he bade his friends and family farewell.

Ranald was given many presents by the Greenlanders. They were much taken by his eastern words and accent. Many of them thought that such a young lad should not venture so far into the unknown.

Ranald would have liked well to have stayed with those kind people. But Leif said, 'The salt is in his blood now, there will be little rest for him.'

So *West Seeker*, after careening and a coat of tar, was launched. With a fair southeast wind she stretched a westward wing.

One night the watchman heard mighty crashing and thundering. 'Rocks ahead!' he cried. All the crew woke up. The noise increased, ahead of them – a chaos of shaken water.

The old Norwegian Fiord said they were approaching the torrent at the world's end.

Trod the carpenter shook so much that his teeth chattered. 'The Stoor-worm is getting ready to have us for his breakfast.'

Then the sea thunders diminished. Leif Ericson said there was nothing to be afraid of: it was a company of whales trekking north.

Sure enough, by first light they saw frail fountains on the horizon northwards. The whales were seeking pastures among the ice floes.

The wind swung round into the west for three days and the ship made slow progress.

'Now we will see', said Leif, 'if the raven will be a help to us.'

On board *West Seeker* they kept a raven in a wicker cage and they gave him little food. The bird glared out at them from the bars of the cage.

Now Leif opened the door of the cage and the raven, after trying to snatch Leif's finger off, flew out and up over the mast. It climbed higher and higher, pausing now and again to swing its eye round the always growing horizon, then it went up another gray step of air. When it was so high that all Ranald could see was a fluttering dot, it seemed to linger there for a longer pause. Then suddenly it leaned westward like an arrow, and at last was lost in a cloud.

'That', said Leif Ericson, 'is a good sign. The bird is smelling worms and berries in the west.'

That put heart into the sailors.

Now the wind had dropped, and they were lingering becalmed in a stretch of blue sea.

The men unsheathed the oars and rowed westward eagerly, singing as they bent and stretched rhythmically on the rowing-benches.

'Crows sing better,' said Ard the poet. 'Besides, it's a bad ballad. On the far shore, if we get that far, I will make a proper poem, one fit to be recited in the king's court in Bergen.'

Wolf the cook made soup in an iron pot over the fire. From time to time two rowers would ship oars and sup a bowl of fish broth beside the fire.

Still the calm brooded on the sea, as if the northern ice had enchanted the whole universe.

They had never seen such brightness in the star-wheel as on those still nights.

One morning, just at sunrise, when the sailors, sleepy and grumbling, were fitting oars into rowlocks, Leif Ericson said, 'Be quiet, all of you! Listen!'

The ship fell silent. All they could hear was the light slap of sea against the hull.

Then, as often happens at dawn, there came a stir or two of wind, then sea and air were becalmed once more.

'There's land ahead,' said the skipper.

The heads of the rowers swung westward. The horizon was empty.

Now the oarsmen began to grumble. Their shoulders were sore! They had cramps in their calf-muscles! They were free sailors, friends of sail and wind, not bondmen who were doomed to grunt their lives away at this salt mill!

But old Fiord from Norway told them not to be fools. Leif Ericson had ears as keen as a wolf.

Later that morning, Ranald, sitting on the stern thwart, saw a flurry of seabirds ahead, squabbling over a hidden shoal. Then, after that tumult subsided, he heard a sighing, a thin shredding murmurous thread, far in the west.

An hour later, at noon, Leif Ericson suddenly strode from his station at the prow of *West Seeker* to the stern. He took the steering oar from the languid hand of Trod, who was helmsman that watch. He pointed ahead with his free forefinger.

Once more the sullen oarsmen swung their heads westward.

There, along the horizon, loomed a low headland.

The men cheered. They fell on the oars as if the sea was a great harp. *West Seeker* surged on.

Late that afternoon, the keel touched sand. Leif Ericson vaulted ashore first. He went on his knees and kissed the new land.

Then, one by one, the sailors waded ashore, laughing.

Ranald came last.

First the sailors secured the ship. Then they lit a great fire among the rocks, and Wolf the cook hung chunks of whalemeat on a spit, and he put salted rabbit and mutton in the iron pot to make soup.

Instead of tapping the ale barrel, Swale tore the top off with famished hands. 'For', said Swale, 'I've drunk nothing but salt for the last month, I think.'

So the sailors ate and drank heartily on the grass-links above the sand, and most of them were soon drunk.

'Now', said Wolf, 'it's time for Ard to recite a poem about the voyage.'

But Ard was lying drunk on the tide-mark, and a seal was looking at him gravely.

'Pull the poet higher up the sand', said Fiord, 'before the flood tide stops his mouth for ever . . .'

Leif Ericson did not eat or drink much. He sat against a big rock and made marks with charcoal on a piece of parchment, making a rough map of the coast.

From time to time Leif got to his feet and walked to a low hillock and his eye wandered slowly over the landscape.

Ranald, who was afraid of drunk men, kept close to Leif the skipper.

'Good,' said Leif. 'There are springs of fresh water. Abundant woodlands. We will not lack for fish or fowl or deer. There, and there, and there, we can build the houses.'

Then he said, 'Those fools won't be fit for much work in the morning.'

Leif said to Ranald, 'We must sail back to Greenland in the spring. We can't make a settlement here without women and horses and sheep . . . It seems to me that this new-found-land is a far more promising place than Greenland . . . Our people will live here and prosper, I think, for many generations.'

Then Leif returned to the fires and ordered the men back to the ship for the night.

11

'I do not think', said Leif, 'that any people live in this place at all. I have seen none. But they may be forest dwellers. It is better for us to sleep on shipboard, till we know for sure.'

The sailors grumbled but one after the other they heaved on to their feet and went staggering down the sand and splashing through the shallow sea, and somehow or other they heaved themselves, or were hauled, into the ship.

Two men lifted Ard the poet aboard.

'Now, boy', said Leif to Ranald, 'it's time for sleep.'

Ranald was long in sleeping. He shuttled over and over in his mind the events of that day. What would they call this land? Would he ever see Orkney again? Would the raven forgive them and fly back to them?

He could not sleep. It was hot in his sleeping bag. All around him were drunken snores. Leif Ericson was asleep, stretched out along the steering-bench.

Ranald was the only watchman that night.

He walked to the prow and looked out to the darkling shore. The sun had been down for an hour.

Ranald saw a movement on the shore. Was it an animal? His eye quickly accustomed to the darkness. It was too tall for a dog or a wild pig. It was a boy!

The boy stood for a long time looking at the ship.

It was likely that he saw Ranald outlined against the stars.

The boy raised his hand, palm spread outwards: a greeting.

Ranald put both hands out to greet the boy across the narrow fringe of sea.

Then the boy fluttered his hand like a bird, and turned, and was lost among the rocks and dunes.

6

When Ranald woke next morning, he saw that all the crew were leaning over the side of *West Seeker*, gazing shoreward.

Ranald got up and looked too.

There were about twenty men on the shore, and among them the boy who had greeted him last night.

Now there was a prolonged discussion on shipboard about how things would turn out.

Some of the men on the beach were armed with spears and bows.

They had black lank hair and eyes like black stones, and most of them had faces painted yellow and red and white, and the man who seemed to be their chief had feathers stuck in his hair.

'That man's grandmother must have been a bird,' said Wolf.

But nobody laughed at that.

Swale thought the seamen should go ashore, armed and shouting, 'Because', said he, 'our axes and swords are superior to their wooden weapons, and we would make a quick end of them.'

But Leif Ericson said they should wait awhile yet. What good would it do, if they killed all those people? There must, said Leif, be settlements in the forests, and all they would gain would be the enmity of the forest tribes.

Soon after Leif had said that, the chief of the shore dwellers made a sign to his men, and those who had spears and arrows laid them down among the rocks.

'I take this for a good sign,' said Leif.

Then the chief threw back his head and gave a long ululating call like a great bird. The call went on echoing between the dunes and the sea.

'That was a sound of great beauty,' said Ard.

'It was a summons to his cut-throats to come with their knives,' said Wolf. 'Hold on to your weapons.'

In a short while other men appeared on the shore with painted faces and noses like hawks and eyes like coal, and they were carrying loaded baskets.

Leif, who had a sharp eye, saw that the baskets contained salmon, and haunches of venison, and bunches of small fruit.

'Now it's plain,' said Leif. 'They want to give us a peace offering. We'll go ashore now. What shall we give them? Bring a few drinking horns, the horn with the wrought silver rim for the chief. Bring a few skins of ale and one or two goat cheeses.'

Then Leif let himself down into the sea and began to wade ashore, and the others after him. Ranald came last.

Ard the poet refused to leave the ship.

'Don't let our gifts get wet,' said Leif. Two sailors were carrying the ale skins, the goat cheeses, and the drinking horns.

'We'll hold on to our axes,' said Wolf. 'That's more important.'

Leif Ericson and the chief of the painted people met at the tidal mark. They greeted each other gravely. The chief put his hands together in front of his face and bowed.

13

Then he made a sign and the young men who were carrying the baskets laid them at Leif's feet.

Then Leif signed to his gift-bearers. Without much ceremony they flung down the ale horns, the ale skins, and the cheeses at the chief's feet.

The chief held up a swollen ale skin and shook it. He was at a loss to know what to do with it.

Then Leif showed how the mouth must be opened and the head tilted back and the unstoppered ale skin squeezed till a thin swift line of ale issued and struck against the palate.

The chief pulled out the stopper and squeezed the skin. Then he had at first a look of disgust on his face, but a short time after he smiled, and then he broke into laughter. It was like the sound of a small torrent over rocks.

Then the chief handed the ale skin to the young man standing beside him, who drank also, and laughed, and so the skin went from mouth to mouth till the skin was empty.

Then the chief indicated that Leif and his men should accept his gifts.

Leif plucked one of the small fruits and put it in his mouth. He bit on it, and it was sweet. 'Grapes,' he said.

But Fiord the Norwegian said that was impossible – no grapes could be grown so far north.

Now the forest people had opened a fourth and fifth ale skin and were beginning to drink recklessly.

One young man began to prance about on the sand.

'I think', said Leif, 'ale is a new thing to them.'

Now the forest men were all laughing, and some were throwing their heads about.

Even the boy that Ranald had greeted the night before had wet his mouth from the ale skin. He came now to where Ranald was standing on the sea verge. He cupped sea in his hands and threw it over Ranald, laughing.

Ranald kicked sea into the boy's face.

And they laughed, circling round each other, scattering water.

Higher up the beach, first one of the forest men reached for his spear and began to shake it, making the long ebb and flow of the bird-call in his throat. Then a second man took his bow and held it up to the sun, and yelled.

'I think they should not drink more ale,' said Ulm the head oarsman on the ship.

'This is becoming dangerous,' said Wolf. 'See how white my knuckles are about my axe.'

'They will perform a war dance now,' said Leif. 'It is an honour that they are doing us.'

The forest men formed themselves into a line and began to disturb the sand, going up and down, dancing.

From time to time they threw back their heads and yelled.

One of the warriors turned in his wild whirling and found himself face to face with Wolf. He raised his spear and thrust his painted face close against the cook's.

Then the sun flashed on a steel blade. There was a smashing of bone and the thud of a body on the sand, then from the head of the fallen dancer blood gushed into the sand.

The dance stopped.

Leif said, 'I think it is time for us to be getting back to the ship now.'

As the sailors clambered aboard, arrows fell singing among them and stuck quivering into hull and mast.

The sail-maker got a graze on the arm from an arrow. Nine drops of blood issued from it.

Ranald was struck on the neck by a stone. He turned. The boy he had laughed and played with an hour before had flung the stone.

'Wolf', said Leif, when they had set up a shield-wall against further woundings and bruisings along the ship's side, 'I do not know what I should do with you. I know what you deserve, to be bound and weighted with a stone and dropped overboard. But then we would have to make our own dinner, and nobody does that as well as you.'

'They were going to have us for *their* dinner,' said Wolf. 'I should be thanked for saving you from that.'

'It is some great fool like you, Wolf, that will bring the world to an end,' said Leif.

When they had gnawed the last bone round the fire and licked the grease from their knuckles, Leif looked out over the shield-wall. The shore was empty.

The moon shone on the silver rim of the ale horn on the sand, and on the scattered globes of sweet fruit that Leif had called grapes.

'I think', said Leif, 'we will not make a settlement here, but further south, beyond the next headland and the next.'

15

Later he said when the men were getting ready for sleep, 'The grapes of this country are delicious, and would, I think, make a good wine, and so I will call it Vinland.'

7

Further south beyond the two headlands, the sailors cut down trees and began to build three log houses.

There was no sign of any forest people in this place, which was more fertile than the place of their first landing.

'I think we have scared those skraelings so badly they won't attack us again,' said the sailors. ('Skraelings' was their name for the forest folk, meaning 'savages').

But still, until the cabins were built, a few of the sailors thought it prudent to sleep on board.

They lived well for the next few weeks. The sea abounded in fish. Flocks of birds flew overhead and their arrows brought down many of them. The forest swarmed with deer. Those sweet berries were everywhere in profusion. Wild corn swayed in the wind.

'Now', said Leif Ericson, 'I know we have found a bountiful land. Life here will be much easier and pleasanter than at home in Greenland. We will establish ourselves here, and then once everything is secure a few of us will sail back east. We can't go on living without women, and a few kinsfolk that we can trust, and seed corn and oxen and cattle. I think in the end it will come to this, that all Scandinavia will envy us Vinlanders for our resoluteness and good fortune.'

The seamen agreed whole-heartedly with what their skipper had said.

They laboured cheerfully to cut down the trees and make dwellings.

They lived well on the forest fowl and the immense cod swimming beyond the headland. From a broad river that was there they netted salmon.

Ranald helped with the logging and the building and the hunting.

Leif Ericson said to Ranald, 'When you are older and stronger, hard work will be expected of you. I know this, that boys love to range freely in the country of their imagination, and there they are captains and jarls. So don't overstrain your body now with dragging trees.'

So Ranald spent many golden afternoons wandering through the woodland, or along the shoreline.

One day Ranald walked through the forest. The trees thinned, and he found himself on the open prairie, with only a tree here and there. A great river flowed, singing a hundred songs.

As Ranald walked towards the river of the salmon, he was aware of a stirring in the branches. He looked, A redstone face with black eyes was looking at him through the leaves. It was the boy he played with on the beach of the landing.

Once more Ranald held out his hands in greeting. A bird seemed to whirr out of the tree towards his hand. It fell from his wrist into the grass, quivering. Ranald saw that it was a bone knife. Drops of blood fell from his wrist.

Ranald turned and ran back through the forest. He did not stop till he came to the clearing where the men were thonging logs into the roof with hide ropes.

Wolf was making a stew over a big fire.

'Such a white face!' said Leif. 'What's wrong, boy? Is there a bear after you?'

Then Ranald told Leif Ericson what he had seen. The house builders leaned from the half-made roofs to listen.

Ranald showed them his wrist. The blood had stopped flowing, but there was a new red-crusted scar.

'Life here might be more exciting than we thought,' said Leif.

Then he ordered the builders back to their work.

Wolf rubbed some herbs between his great hands, smelled the juice, and threw the herbs into the bubbling pot of stew.

That evening, while the men were eating, Leif Ericson ordered three men to take turns keeping watch.

Nothing was heard by the watchmen all night but the song of multitudinous leaves and the murmur of sleepy birds.

Some of the men said they would rather sleep on board ship that night. They were mocked by the others. Two men closed with each other, raging, fists rising and falling, till Leif dragged them apart.

'Whoever wants to', said the skipper, 'can sleep on board. There is no shame in that. The skraelings could as well steal alongside in their skin boats and attack by water. While a man draws breath, there is no such thing as safety. We should be glad of that, for danger puts an edge on our enjoyment of things.'

In the end about half the men chose to sleep on *West Seeker*, and the others slept beside the fires on shore.

Ranald slept beside the fire.

Wild dogs howled all night under the moon.

In the morning, after breakfast, the men were busy felling trees and sawing logs and fitting roof-beams, when the whole forest gave voice, in one prolonged ululation, and a shower of arrows fell among the huts, and a company of skraelings ran at the sailors with spears lifted.

Leif Ericson had taken the precaution of ordering each man in the crew to have knife and axe near to hand, so they were quick to stand face to face against the young skraeling warriors. An axe can deliver two quick blows for each slow swing of a spear. The skraelings stood their ground for a while, but in the end they fled back into the forest, shrilling.

'Those are not coward cries,' said Leif Ericson, 'they are challenges, they are a promise of bigger skirmishes to come.'

At that, many of the sailors looked dismayed.

'We will hang on yet for a month or two', said Leif, 'and see what is to happen. It may be, those warriors were sent out to probe out any weaknesses. Now that they know how strong and resolute we are, they may think twice before they come back. All the same, from now on it will be well to set watches of six men through the night instead of three.'

From that night most of the men chose to sleep on shipboard.

But Ranald slept always beside the fire.

There were no more skraeling attacks on the Greenlanders.

But after supper each night, the men spoke longer and longer, their faces flushed with ale and flame-shadows.

Ard recited the ancient poems, over and over.

'Those verses', said Fiord the old Norwegian, 'make me homesick.'

Then Ard told the story of the giant maidens, Fenia and Menia, slaves of the King of Denmark. The king had a magic mill called Grotti, that would grind out for him whatever he wanted. But the mill Grotti was so huge that the stones could only be turned by the mighty arms of Fenia and Menia. The mill ground out so much gold that the king was the richest man on earth. But an enemy of Denmark, a sea king, came when the regal palace was sunk in sleep and darkness, and prevailed on the giant girls to grind out warriors, and so before morning the royal palace of Denmark was dripping with blood instead of gold and pearl and diamond. The sea king took the mill Grotti, and Fenia and Menia, and sailed off west. At that time the sea was as fresh as raindrops or mountain streams. The sea king ordered a mighty feast to celebrate his triumph, so his cooks had a busy time roasting swine and cooking salmon in pots. Also the ale horns went round. 'The meat and fish', said the half-drunk king, 'are savourless. Bid the girls grind salt.' So the mill Grotti spewed out salt, so much of it that the ship sank and the sea king and all the crew with it, and also Grotti and the giant girls. This foundering occurred in the Pentland Firth between Orkney and Scotland. There, on the sea bottom the mill Grotti still lies, endlessly churning out salt. And that is the reason why sea water is salt . . .

One by one, while Ard was telling the story of the magic mill Grotti, the sailors nodded off to sleep.

But it was unquiet sleep. A few of them lying near Ranald spoke in the darkness.

'I am very lonely in this place,' said one.

Another, 'I am missing my dear wife Freya.'

A third, 'I don't want to die on a foreign shore.'

A fourth, 'I'm afraid of the skraeling with feathers in his hair.'

A fifth, 'We're sailors, not foresters or house builders . . .'

But in the morning they all set to with a will to finish the houses of the first settlement.

They kept, each man, axe and dagger beside the building tools.

Now Ranald wandered more along the shore than into the forest.

One day, in his wave-dallying walk, he came across a scattering of shells on the sand. He knew at once that it was no random wave-strewment of shells, but rather a deliberate pattern set by a human hand. It was in the shape of an arrow and a spear. The arrow pointed at the ship *West Seeker*. The spear pointed at the little cluster of houses above the shore.

Ranald heard a stirring in a tussock among the dunes.

The face of the skraeling boy was looking at him through the grasses. There was no laughter in that face.

Ranald told Leif Ericson what he had seen.

Leif said he must say nothing about that to the sailors.

8

One morning, one of the watchmen did not come to the breakfast fire.

They looked for this man, called Valt, and went deep into the forest. There was no sign of him.

19

The other watchmen had heard or seen nothing to alarm them. But one, Audun, had heard the whirr and flight of a strange bird – so it seemed to him – at midnight, at the outpost where Valt had been standing on watch.

'I think Valt must have been lured away by a skraeling girl in the form of a bird,' said Leif.

The men said little all that day.

They planed and hammered, making doors for the houses. But now they put less vigour into their work than they had done.

Fiord said, 'Many a pigsty back in Norway has a better door than the door Vrem is making today.'

The sailors laughed, but the man who was thonging the door timbers bit his lip.

'I'm a sailor, not a carpenter,' said Vrem.

Next night, those allocated to watch seemed reluctant to go to their places after sunset.

'I did not know', said Leif Ericson, 'that I had children on this voyage scared of the dark.'

The six watchmen went to their posts.

One of the group of houses had been built close to the edge of the forest. It was a well built dwelling and Leif Ericson had chosen it for his house, and had slept there for many nights, but now all the sailors including Leif slept on board *West Seeker*.

At midnight a cry was raised on the ship, so loud that all the crew woke up.

The look-out in the prow pointed ashore. Leif's house was dappled here and there with flames and shadows. As they looked, suddenly the house seemed to shudder as if some red beast had broken loose inside. For a while the roof-tree stood black among the flames, then it crackled and fell.

'Well,' said Leif, 'if I'd been at home tonight, I wouldn't be so cold as I am standing here on this deck now.'

In the morning the men went ashore.

The watchmen did not come out of the forest to greet them as usual.

'If we keep losing men like this,' said Leif, 'we'll have trouble manning our ship.'

They found one of the watchmen deep in the forest. His hair had been removed from his skull.

'Bjorn won't be needing Bula to comb his hair again,' said Wolf.

20

'If the skraelings were looking for Bjorn's brains,' said a sailor called Ulbrid, 'they needn't have gone to all that trouble. I could have told them how stupid Bjorn was.'

The seamen laughed, but the roll and the ring and the recklessness were out of their laughter now. They laughed like old men beside gray embers.

The dead man, Bjorn, had indeed been rather stupid, and he had been so vain of his long golden hair that at the commencement of every voyage his wife Bula had had to wash it thoroughly in fresh water and afterwards comb it till the comb sang through the bright flood.

But in spite of being slow-witted and vain, Bjorn had been a good seaman and so laughter-loving and open-hearted that he had been well liked at every fair in Greenland and on every voyage he took part in.

Now they carried the body of Bjorn back to the shore and made a funeral pyre and burnt it.

'Nor will we leave Bjorn's ashes here to be dishonoured,' said Leif.

Leif had a clay jar fetched from the ship, and Bjorn's ashes were put into the jar and sealed.

'Now Bula his wife will have him back,' said Leif. 'She will build a howe over this urn. We will not tell her about how the skraelings stole his hair.'

None of the house-builders seemed eager to pick up their adzes and hammers that day.

At noon Leif Ericson gathered all the sailors about him. He said, 'We have found this land. It is a rich bounteous place. We will not be leaving it.'

At those words, shadows fell on the faces of all the men.

'I think, though,' said Leif, 'that we will not make a settlement in such an unlucky place as this. Things have been wrongly done here. We will sail further south. I feel that the land will be even more fertile beyond the next headland, and the next and the next, sailing on south towards the sun.'

Still the sailors looked doubtful. There were murmurings and shakings of the head.

'But first', said Leif, 'we will sail back to Greenland. The ship must be overhauled and reprovisioned, and more sailors enrolled. When we come back, to the valleys and forests south from here, we will have our women with us. We will have harps and honey-hives and horses. We will try to live in friendship with the skraelings. We did an evil thing

21

when we broke their dance of welcome. When we return we will know
how to give them gifts, and how to receive the gifts they offer us. It may
be, there will be perpetual peace between us Norsemen and the
Vinlanders.'

The sailors wrinkled up their noses. One or two of them spat into the
fire.

'But now', said Leif Ericson, 'we will make the ship ready for the
journey east.'

At that, the men raised a great cheer.

'This voyage of ours will be famous,' said Leif. 'Many times the story
of it will be told over winter fires from Iceland to Ireland.'

Then the men busied themselves to stock the ship with venison and
salmon and the wild sweet berries that grew in such profusion. They
filled their casks with river water.

Ard made a poem for Bjorn that night.

Now, Bjorn, may the savages
Keep your bright hair,
A tumult of gold among their bones and feathers,
A wonderment to them.
We bear back to Greenland, Bjorn,
Your heart, your hands strong
For tree-hewing, oar-hauling,
Sowing barley in broken sillions.
Bula and the six bairns
Will build you a howe
Between the barn and the beached boats.

Next morning they raised anchor, and as soon as the wind began to
blow from the northwest they stretched the sail and were soon making
good way eastwards.

Ranald looked back at the shore.

A dozen skraelings had come out of the forest and were standing
among the dunes watching their departure.

The skraeling boy had climbed to the top branch of the tallest tree.

9

On the voyage back to Greenland, Leif Ericson often had Ranald
seated beside him at the helm of *West Seeker*. He gave Ranald

instruction on navigation and the management of ships. 'There is only one constant star in the sky, the northern star, and that star is the sailor's friend always. But there is a great wheel of stars that swings nightly from east to west, and good sailors learn to read that map, and so they can hold a true course. There are five wandering stars that go like tinkers or like pilgrims among the star-towns, and we become acquainted with their ways too. There is always the mystery of the moon. Does the moon touch some pulse in our blood? I have noticed that the moods of seamen alter with the changing moon. Many a sane sober man says strange things under a full moon. I have known men of few words utter poetry at such a time. I tell you this, Ranald, it is a foolish skipper who sets out on a voyage under a waning moon. His ship might end on a rock or vanish forever in a sea-fog. The moon rules the tides of ocean and so there is little doubt in my mind that the blood in our veins and the ocean-streams are kin to each other.

'There are nights at sea when there is no star chart to steer by, because of a cloud cover. Then a good skipper must have all his senses alert.

'Touch, smell, taste, sound, sight acquire an extra keenness. The skipper can hear, miles away, the smallest wave-wash on a dark cliff. A pulse goes through him, there is a cross current, or the mid-ocean surge has given way to a land-swell! Then he must be vigilant. The cry and flight of a petrel, crossing the prow quickly, tells him that there is land in this direction or that. The slightest smell borne on the wind, seaweed or ice or nettles, tells him this and that. What his senses tell him, in those subtle ways, might make the difference between wreckage and a prosperous voyage.

'There's little sleep for a skipper on a night when the sky is covered. How happy that skipper is when he sees the first gray of dawn in the east! But the greatest joy is this, when in the thick darkness a rag of cloud is torn away, and a star shines through! Then another and another star, until they form a familiar cluster, a sure constellation, under it he can steer the ship confidently.

'This morning you see, boy, that there are bits of ice in the sea. This to me is a strange matter, and not altogether to my liking. I have been this way a dozen times, in this latitude, and only this time, and the time before, have I seen these floes and bits of broken iceberg. We must not think of the sea as constant and unchanging. Slow pulsings go through the elements of sea and land – so slow that only a man with gray in his beard may observe them. It seems to me that this northern curve of the world may be growing colder. And if the sea has ice in it, then we may be sure that the lands round about are growing colder too, and soon the roots that nourish men and beasts may be frozen. Then it will be a hard time for the Greenlanders. I think this cold time will not come next year, or in the next hundred years. But I think our great-great-grandsons will think it no bad thing that Leif Ericson found out fertile places in the west, in Vinland.'

They sailed on with a good wind on the starboard beam. On the fifth morning out they saw the early sun flashing from the mountain tops of Greenland.

At that sight the sailors raised a great cheer.

But presently the wind dropped, and they had to take to the oars, and there was a good deal of grumbling.

A whale surfaced close by and sent a great fountain skyward from its blow-hole, and made *West Seeker* rock in its wash, then it sank into the depths again.

Wolf said it was a great pity they couldn't kill the whale. Then they wouldn't need to worry about dinners all next winter.

'It's a good thing', said Leif Ericson, 'that there are still some creatures too big and strong for the greed of men to compass.'

'But I think it will come to this in the end', said Leif later, 'that men will devise weapons to kill even the greatest whale. The skraelings, that we thought so savage and ignorant, were wiser than us in this respect. They only killed as many deer and salmon as they needed for that day's hunger. We are wasteful gluttons and more often than not leave carcasses to rot after a hunt – a shameful thing. Did you not see what reverence the Vinlanders had for the animals and the trees and for all living things? It seemed to me that the Vinlanders had entered into a kind of sacred bond with all the creatures, and there was a fruitful exchange between them, both in matters of life and death.'

Then Ranald saw a shore, and houses above a sea-bank, and a group of people standing among the rocks.

And presently he saw the familiar faces of the villagers, and heard their welcoming voices.

10

Ranald stayed all that winter in Greenland. He was well liked by the villagers, and as Leif Ericson said, 'You have twelve mothers, all the women here want to take you under their wing.'

Ranald stayed at Leif's farm. They were glad to have him there. At home at Breckness in Orkney Ranald had learned to herd cattle and to feed swine. At his grandfather's farm he had learned to ride the horses.

There was one horse on the farm that had been a foal when Leif Ericson set out for Vinland. Now it had become an intractable animal, so that none of the farmworkers could handle it. The name of the horse was Hoof-flinger.

'It was a promising horse,' said Leif Ericson to the farmhands. 'You have insulted him in some way. Horses are proud and sensitive. You have punished him when you ought to have praised him.'

The farmworkers said they had treated Hoof-flinger in the same way as the other horses.

'But Hoof-flinger was a special colt,' said Leif. 'I intended him to race against the best horses from the other villages at the harvest sports.'

Hoof-flinger had broken out of the paddock and had been roaming free on the mountainside for a month. Whenever Hoof-flinger saw a man approaching, he would fling up his hooves and whinny and go galloping away among the snow patches.

'I'll go and have a word with the horse after breakfast,' said Leif to Ranald. 'You can come with me.'

Leif and Ranald walked among the foothills and at last they saw a beautiful horse grazing in a meadow, high up. Leif and Ranald were walking quietly but Hoof-flinger got wind of them, and he whinnied and flung up his hooves and ran round and round in the meadow.

'It will be hard to throw the rope over the horse and bring him down,' said Ranald.

'It would be an insult to a horse like this', said Leif, 'to tame him with a rope.'

Leif stood back then and let go a whistle on the wind. Almost at once the thunder of hooves fell silent. The horse turned, trembling, and looked across at the man and boy.

'We will go and have a word with him,' said Leif.

When the horse saw them coming he began to back away, but Leif continued to speak to him, and Hoof-flinger seemed to recognize Leif's voice from far back when he had been a foal running beside his dam in the paddock.

He stood between two rocks, trembling, ready to turn and gallop off at the first unfriendly sign.

'Now', said Leif, 'I will speak to him. You wait here.'

Leif walked right up to Hoof-flinger. The horse waited with one hoof raised and the wind sifting through his mane.

Leif stood right beside him. The horse curled a black lip and his eye blazed. Then Leif spoke a single word into the horse's ear, and at once the horse nuzzled his head into Leif's shoulder and Leif's hand was in his mane, and it seemed that the man and a horse had known each other since the beginning of time.

They walked back to the farm together, all three.

Hoof-flinger soon began to show almost as much affection to Ranald as he did to Leif Ericson.

The horse suffered Ranald on his back, then he would thunder off across the meadow, with Ranald holding on to his neck. Once the horse swerved to avoid a rock, and then Ranald was thrown, but the ground on the other side of the rock had a clump of marigolds growing through a wet patch, and Ranald came back to the farm plastered with mud and marigold petals, with the horse following.

Hoof-flinger did not suffer rein and bridle gladly, to begin with. 'But', said Leif, 'we must race him against the Westlanders at the harvest sports. The Westlanders boast far and wide how their horses have always outpaced ours in the races. We will see what Hoof-flinger will do for us.'

Ranald was told to ride Hoof-flinger against the Westland horses at the harvest sports.

The Westlanders laughed when the harvest festivities took place and the horse-race was called and a horse they had never seen before stood at the starting line with a boy astride him.

Their own horses and riders were famous throughout Greenland.

Horses and riders from other villages in the north were there too, but they were thought to have little chance against the Westlanders.

The starter blew on a horn and the horses were off. The course was a wide circuit of three miles. At first Hoof-flinger lagged behind. He had never been in a race before, and the sight of the strange horses seemed to upset him, but even more the yells and cheers of the crowd put him off his stride.

Half-way round the track Hoof-flinger was behind.

Ranald bent over and whispered into the horse's ear. White clouds were being driven on the wind across the summit of the mountain.

Ranald murmured again to Hoof-flinger. At last he spoke a word Leif Ericson had taught him to say – a secret word that only a few men knew in the business of horse-rearing.

At once the boy was aware of a great surge of power under him, and the pulse of the hooves on the links quickened.

Soon Hoof-flinger had overtaken one horse, then another and another. Ranald was fleetingly aware of surprised or agonized faces of rivals now beside him, now falling behind.

Still Hoof-flinger increased his stride, and they swept past a cluster of horses, then a group of two, then an urgent and solitary horse with foam flying from its lips. At last there was only one other horse in front of them, and that was the famous champion of the Westlanders, a horse called Wavebreak, ridden by a young farmer called Sven Nialson. All the Westlanders had said that Wavebreak was certain to win.

And indeed the horse was well named, for he was sea-gray in colour, and now he stretched his neck like a wave in a westerly gale, and it seemed that the rhythm of the open ocean possessed him.

'Now', said Ranald to Hoof-flinger, 'think of the high cloud, think of our mountain torrent.'

Ranald could see the finishing post and the crowd waiting.

Sven Nialson was suddenly aware that he was being challenged. He threw one wild astonished look over his shoulder, then he dug his spurs into Wavebreak. And that brave horse, goaded and driven too fiercely, stumbled and lost his stride, and when Sven Nialson looked up again he saw Hoof-flinger rearing up in victory beyond the finishing post, and the Eastlanders with happy faces helping Ranald to dismount.

'Well ridden,' said Leif Ericson. He put a silver piece into Ranald's hand.

That night much ale was drunk in the booths, and though there had always been fighting at the harvest sports between the Westlanders and the Eastlanders, on this particular night there was more than the usual amount of overturned ale horns and blood-splashing and broken bones.

Sven Nialson rode home immediately after the race. His famous horse Wavebreak was never seen again. Dark whispers went abroad as to what had happened to the animal. Sven himself sat house-bound till after Yule.

Ranald got back to the village under the first star, in the company of the other men.

News of the victory had gone before, and all the village women were there to welcome him, and he was kissed over and over again by them all, from old Trudda with the whiskered mouth to little Sigrid who was just learning to milk the cows.

Hoof-flinger was the most famous horse in Greenland from that day on.

He did not get on with the other horses on the farm. In the end they let him graze on the foothills.

Whenever Hoof-flinger saw Leif or Ranald standing between the rocks, he would come galloping to meet them with a joyful whinny.

11

As winter approached and the nights lengthened, the villagers stayed beside the fires, and there was much visiting and ale-drinking and telling of stories.

The men who had made the Vinland voyage got much fame. Their stories were told over and over, and men came from the other settlements to hear about the country in the west, and about the skraelings, and about the abundance of fish and deer and birds.

'There is no place on earth so rich,' said Leif Ericson. 'Greenland is like a poor gnawed fish-bone and Vinland is like a huge sturgeon brimming with oil and stuffed with roe.'

The old men looked envious and some of them said that Leif and the sailors must be greatly exaggerating. But the younger men, and some of the young women, listened to the stories with light in their eyes.

There was much talk of making a new expedition to Vinland the following spring.

Ard recited some poems that he had made about Vinland, but the Greenlanders thought poorly of them.

'Ard has left his talent behind in Vinland,' said one old man.

Ard was angry about that. He said his talents were wasted on such clod-hoppers and fire-huggers, and he walked out of Eric the Red's house into the darkness.

Ard did not come back to the village that night and his place was still empty next morning.

The villagers thought that some evil must have befallen Ard the poet. Either he had fallen into a snowdrift on the mountain – because it was a night of blizzard when he had gone sulking out of Eric the Red's house – or a great wave had rolled in from the ocean and washed him away.

But Ard returned after seven days and he was looking very pleased with himself.

Leif Ericson and the villagers asked Ard where he had been.

Ard said he had been bitterly hurt by the scorn they had heaped on his Vinland verses. He had thought he must starve, since no one from then on would feed him or shelter him, now that he had lost his skill at verse-making. He intended to walk north and with luck some other village on the coast would appreciate his work and ask him to stay. But if not, then it would be as well if he got lost in the blizzard.

Such had been Ard's thought after his verses had been mocked in the hut of the ale-drinkers.

Indeed as he left the village the first snowflakes of a new blizzard began to dance and whirl about his head.

'The end is coming quicker than I thought,' Ard said then. 'When they find me, I'll be wearing a snow-coat, my mouth will be locked forever with a key of ice.'

At the thought of that, said Ard, his mouth trembled and he felt a warm teardrop on his face.

Then he saw the light of a lantern, and a woman's voice said, 'Traveller, go no farther on such a night, you're welcome to come and sit at my fire.'

So Ard followed the lantern and the voice, and presently he found himself in a house of children's voices, a horn of hot ale was put into his hands, and he was set in the best fireside chair. When he wiped the snow out of his eyes, he saw that he was a guest in the house of Bula, the widow of Bjorn of the golden hair.

Ard thanked Bula for the ale and the fire.

He would not stay long with Bula and the children, he said. His destiny was to wear the coat of snow and to have his mouth locked with the key of ice somewhere in the wilderness to the north, and so be utterly lost and forgotten.

Bula said he must do as he wished.

But, said Bula, there were better coats than snow-coats, and there were three coats of bearskin hanging on hooks that had belonged to her late husband Bjorn, and Ard was welcome to one of these.

Ard replied that he was grateful to Bula for that offer, but now that his life had no meaning any more it was better that he should walk north into the dark of winter and not be seen again.

Ard said that two or three of the orphans began to weep at his words. At that, Ard thought to himself that perhaps his powers had not entirely deserted him. No poet can ask for greater reward than to make children dance or weep.

Bula said that fate decides the life of every man, and that if Ard must be lost in the dark of night northward, so it must be. But, in her opinion, he had a few winters to look forward to yet.

'I think, on the contrary,' said Ard, 'that now it is time for silence. I have uttered many poems in my time that were thought to be well made. But now the time has come for my mouth to be locked with the key of ice.'

At that, the rest of the orphans began to weep.

Ard began to feel happier, both on account of the mulled ale and of the power of his words.

'Now,' said Bula, 'if it comes to keys, the key to this house is hanging on a nail at that wall, and I think it is a better key than the ice key that locks the mouth of a man forever.'

Ard was silent. The children of Bjorn and Bula looked at him with tearstained faces.

'I am glad', said Bula, 'that the ashes of Bjorn my man are buried in a howe at the end of his glebe. The children are glad because of that too. It is good for the dust of a dead farmer to be mingled with the living dust of his land.'

Ard said that was true.

'Listen to the storm outside,' said Bula.

Indeed the tempest was shaking the shutters.

'You would not have got far on such a night,' said Bula.

'I think not,' said Ard.

'Now,' said the widow Bula, 'I do not know what makes the ghosts of the dead glad or angry. I think they may be in a state beyond anger or joy such as we mortals feel. But I think that the ghost of Bjorn my man, if he feels delight at all, is honoured that a good elegy was made for him after his death.'

Again there was a silence in the house.

The tempest beat more loudly against the shutters.

Then the oldest child, a boy of twelve, recited the elegy that Ard had made for Bjorn of the golden beard.

At the end of the poem, all the six children clapped their hands with joy, because their father Bjorn had been so honoured.

So Ard stayed at the farm that night.

The storm had blown itself out before dawn.

Bula set a breakfast of fish and ale and bread before Ard.

Bula asked if he was thinking of going north that day.

Ard said he would have to think about it. 'It seems to me', he said, 'that my harp may not be broken after all. I think I will still be able to make people weep or dance for a year or two yet. It seems to me too that there is still beauty in the world, and women's hands can still offer kindness and comfort, and the voices of children are like streams unfrozen after winter.'

Bula said she was glad to hear Ard talking that way, rather than about coats of snow and ice-keys locking the mouth.

One by one the children woke in their shut-beds, and bade Ard good morning.

The end of the story is that when Ard came back to the village after a week, he said that he and Bula were to be married.

The whole village was bidden to come to the wedding feast in Bula's house before Yule.

Ard and Bula lived together happily for many years after that.

But it happened that Ard made no more poems after his marriage to Bula.

He turned out not to be a good farmer or fisherman either.

But now the sons of Bjorn and Bula were coming into their strength. After a few years the farm prospered, and they turned out to be lucky fishermen.

Ard was well liked by his stepchildren, and his mouth never lacked for bread and beef, fish and ale.

As for poems, the ice-key might as well have been turned in his mouth.

As to his personal appearance, Bula saw to it that his face was regularly washed, and his somewhat scraggy beard combed, and that he was decently clad.

12

Ranald Sigmundson, the boy from Orkney, was held in honour in the village all that winter, and throughout Greenland he was well spoken

31

of, both on account of the Vinland voyage and his famous victory in the horse race.

All that winter men were planning another expedition to Vinland, and getting supplies together.

It soon became apparent that there would be snags. Leif Ericson said he did not intend to sail west again. 'It seems to me', said Leif, 'that if we succeed in making a settlement in the west, we will not be satisfied, but we will want more and more land for ourselves. I have seen that the Vinlanders have lived for a long time in harmony and peace with the animals and plants, taking only sufficient for their needs, and it seems to me that the trees and fish and birds and bears know that the people honour them and are their friends, and so the whole of creation in Vinland is a kind of dance in which all the creatures participate joyfully.

'I had a dream last night that has disturbed me very much.

'The skraelings and the animals and trees were dancing together, in this dream. A man with fair hair and blue eyes came and stood at the edge of the dance, watching. The leader of the dance invited this stranger to become a part of the dance. In response, the man from the ship put a gold mask on his face. At once the dance began to fail. The dancers – deer and cormorant, salmon and tree and man, snake and eagle – left the dance, one by one. It seemed to me in my dream that the gold mask put a sickness over all it looked on. At last only the man in the gold mask was left on that shore.

'Then in the dream I looked out to sea, and the horizon from end to end was covered with ships.

'And the man in the gold mask was beckoning the ships to make haste, the land belonged to them alone.

'And the mask was such a bright dazzlement that the life-giving sun looked wan, up there in the zenith.

'I take this dream to be a warning and a prophecy.

'It may be we should stick to our old ways, trading with Iceland and Norway and Orkney. There, our greed and cunning are held in check, after a fashion, by the laws that the old wise men have devised. But in the western places, our greed would raven on without let or hindrance, and I cannot see an end of the evil.'

The Greenlanders sneered at Leif Ericson and his dream.

But Leif Ericson stuck to his resolution to stay at home in Greenland.

13

That spring a ship called *Laxoy* from Norway came to Greenland with a cargo of timber and wool.

The skipper, a man called Hakon Treeman, had long talks with Leif Ericson. It came out that after Hakon returned to Bergen with a cargo of whalebone and walrus tusks from Greenland, he intended soon afterwards to sail west again, but only as far as Shetland and Orkney with another cargo of timber and goat cheeses. In Orkney the goat cheeses lacked the mountain flavour of the Norwegian goat cheeses.

It happened that when Hakon was unfolding his plan to Leif Ericson, Ranald came and stood in the door.

As soon as the Norwegian skipper mentioned Orkney, a great homesickness came on the boy.

He asked leave to speak.

Leif Ericson said he was always willing to hear anything Ranald had to say.

Ranald turned to Hakon and asked him why he was called Treeman.

Hakon the skipper laughed and said he was called by that name because ever since he had bought the ship twenty years before, most of his cargoes were of timber. He brought cargoes of timber to all the treeless places – Faroe, Iceland, Greenland, Orkney, Shetland – so that the people could live in wooden houses rather than in caves and cold stone, and sail in wooden boats rather than in boats of ox-hide and other animal skins. 'Scandinavia', said Hakon Treeman, 'has an abundance of timber.'

Ranald stood listening with his eyes downcast.

'It seems to me', said Leif Ericson, 'that that is not the important question that you want to put to Hakon.'

'I will answer whatever you ask', said the Norwegian skipper, 'as well as I can.'

Then Ranald asked in a low voice, that hesitated and shook a little, whether Hakon Treeman would be willing to take him to Orkney. 'I have been happy here', he said, 'with Leif and the Greenlanders, but now I'm anxious to see how things fare with my mother and my other kinsfolk back in the Orkneys. They will know for sure that my father Sigmund and his ship have miscarried, and it is likely that my mother thinks I have gone down in *Snowgoose*. That will be a grief to her, for my grandfather in the farm at Breckness is old and hardly able to see to the work of his farm, far less to guard my mother's interests.'

Hakon Treeman asked Leif if Ranald Sigmundson would be worth his keep on the voyage.

Leif said that Ranald was now a good seaman. He would work well and earn his passage.

'But', said Leif to Ranald, 'it has seemed to me that you were the keenest of all to return to Vinland and live the rest of your life there.'

But Ranald said that first he must go to Orkney.

Then Hakon Treeman told Ranald to make ready, for as soon as *Laxoy* had her cargo stowed they would set sail. In three days there would be a new moon, and that was a good time for setting out.

Then Ranald went round all the houses in the village. Most of the villagers were sorry that soon he would be leaving them. They gave him small gifts, bone-carvings and thin silver rings, and the oldest woman gave him a bearskin coat that had belonged to her grandfather. 'For', said she, 'sea spray and cold sea gales have been the death of many a promising young sailor.'

Hakon Treeman told Ranald he must be on board ship in the morning. 'Now the moon has come out of her black cave of death. She is a beautiful maiden. She will pour silver blessings upon our voyage.'

Some of the seamen and some of the Greenlanders on the quayside laughed.

'Hakon Treeman should have been a poet, not a skipper,' said Thorvald Ericson, Leif's brother.

Indeed it seemed to the Greenlanders that the skipper of *Laxoy* loved always to turn the simplest of matters, like the phases of the moon, or women's tears, into images, and that he was both moved and delighted with the phrases that he minted so effortlessly then.

Ard the poet was standing in the crowd. He looked glum, for he wished no one to be thought of as a poet but himself, in spite of the fact that he had made no verses since his marriage to Bula. 'Contented men don't need to write poems . . .' Yet Ard resented it if other men were praised for their word-craft.

Hakon Treeman said he was no poet. It was only that certain images flocked to the tree of his mind, and made a happy disturbance there, and whenever that happened it would be disgraceful to utter his thoughts in gray matter-of-fact words.

'Truly', he said, 'a poet must give his whole life to his art, like you, Ard. I am only a poet by chance. I lack the skill to hammer out intricate

34

verses. My true vocation is ship-craft.'

At these words, Ard the poet looked pleased.

Ranald went up to the high meadow and Hoof-flinger came galloping to meet him. The horse and the boy laid their heads together. When Ranald turned to go, for now the sailors were shouting from the shore, Hoof-flinger gave a great whinny of grief.

Hakon the Norwegian saw that Ranald's eyes were aswim. 'Enough of that,' he said. 'There will be plenty of that kind of salt between here and Bergen. Sailors on a dangerous sea have more urgent things to busy themselves with.'

Then Ranald flung the tears from his eyes with a sweep of his long fingers.

'And yet', said Hakon, 'there is a certain beauty when women and children weep. It touches the heart. The fountain of sorrow is full, it rises up, it overflows, it splashes and makes a brief beautiful music among the stones below.'

The sailors laughed. Their skipper was at his images again.

Hakon Treeman bade them sternly to man the oars.

Then Ranald waded out and was pulled into the ship *Laxoy*; and he sat beside the skipper at the helm, and fixed his eye steadfastly on the east.

The old Norwegian Fiord had asked to be taken on as a seaman on the *Laxoy*, and Hakon had enrolled him gladly.

They had a fair wind all the way to Norway.

North of Faroe they passed two ox-hide boats sailing in the direction of Iceland. All those sailors had gray cowls on their heads.

Some of the sailors suggested to Hakon Treeman that they should attack those ships. 'For', they said, 'those monks are said to carry cargoes of great treasure.'

The skipper said that on the contrary those monks travelled in the greatest poverty. 'If they have treasure at all,' he said, 'it is laid up in their spirits, beyond the reach of our greed. We will sail on east, in peace.'

Then Hakon shouted a greeting across the quiet water to the pilgrim monks.

The oldest monk uttered one word, 'Pax'.

Then they sailed away from each other.

Ranald played his part at the oar-bench, and with the bailing pans whenever sea sifted into the ship, and he helped with the furling and unfurling of the single sail that had a leaping salmon stitched on it.

At night, for twelve nights in all, the moon kept a watch over the ship. Soon she was no longer the slim shy girl child, but she seemed like a bride looking into the trembling mirrors of the sea, and then she was a princess scattering their way with silver coins, and then she was a woman who sets a lantern in the window at a cottage so that the shepherd in a blizzard can find his way home to fire and board.

Such images would not have occurred to Ranald, seated on the stern bench with Hakon Treeman, but they drifted through the mind of the old skipper, and he gave them utterance.

One night there were many clouds, and the moon was mostly hidden. But from time to time there was a brightness at the edge of a cloud, and the moon seemed to hurry through clear patches of sky until another cloud and another and yet another covered it.

'What business are you out on tonight, moon?' said Hakon the skipper. 'What are you troubling yourself about? Is it a cow that's wandered away from the yard? Is it a sick child you have in a crib beside the fire, and you're off to get cures from the herb-wife? Have you heard that the boats are in from the west with a great haul of herring, and you must hurry to get your share? Don't trouble yourself, goodwife . . . There, you shake another cloud from you, and another, in your great haste this windy night to finish your business, whatever it is. Be in no hurry. The time will come soon enough for you, of shrinking and withering. Then you will sit at the threshold of a black cave with a jar of cinders, and as the dead of this world troop to that place, you put ash on each mouth and eyelid. And last – poor moon – you yourself turn and grope your way into the black cave, bearing your jar of cinders.'

Hakon Treeman spoke so low to himself that only Ranald heard his words.

Then Hakon gave a sigh so sorrowful that it seemed to Ranald like a cry of pain.

Soon Ranald covered himself with his bear blanket, and fell asleep.

14

Laxoy dropped anchor in the harbour of Bergen.

At once the skipper Hakon Treeman went ashore. For two days he intended to be in the booths and storehouses of the Bergen merchants, negotiating for the sale of the cargo he had brought from Greenland and also arranging for a cargo of timber and goat cheeses and smoked reindeer meat that he had promised to deliver later that year to the Orkney merchants.

Most of the crew went ashore and drank ale in the taverns along the waterfront.

Ranald Sigmundson was alone on the ship most of the time with the old Norwegian sailor Fiord.

'Why don't you go ashore?' said Ranald to Fiord. 'You must know many folk in this town. They'd be glad to meet you again, after such a long voyage.'

Fiord laughed. He said he dared not set foot on any part of the Norwegian coast. In his youth he had been outlawed for killing a man. This man and Fiord had fallen out about a beautiful girl. One night this rival of Fiord's had struck the ale horn out of Fiord's hand in a Bergen tavern. And Fiord, being young and reckless, had struck out with a knife that he had in his belt, and when he looked again the man was lying on the floor clutching his side, and blood was oozing out between his fingers.

The keeper of the drink-shop had advised Fiord, as a matter of urgency, to go at once to some distant part of Norway: into the mountains among the trees and torrents and snow where he would never be found. Instead, Fiord had gone to the house of his sweetheart, hoping that she would be impressed by this evidence of his love, and offer him shelter until the trouble died down.

But news of the man-slaying had spread quickly through Bergen. Fiord was met at the door of Svena's house by her father and two brothers, and they gave him a greeting colder than ice.

It turned out that the men of the house had been negotiating with the dead man about a marriage with Svena.

Fiord was young and handsome, but poor, a journeyman carpenter, and the man he had killed was a merchant with first gray hairs in his beard, but the owner of two ships and a fine house behind Bergen.

Not a word was spoken at the door. Fiord could read in their faces that they would be glad to see the back of him forever. More, they would be glad to see the black cloth over his face.

Fiord hoped that he might get a glimpse of Svena, but she must have been told to keep to her room. He heard the clack of her shuttle, and she was singing at her loom.

'Svena!' he cried in the doorway. 'For your sake I have killed the fat old pig of a merchant, Jom Orre.'

For a moment the song faltered, then Svena began to sing again and drive the shuttle.

Then Fiord turned away from that house.

He went into an ale-shop at the far end of the town. He drank deeply. He wished it was he, Fiord, that was lying dead with the old merchant's dagger in his heart.

The law officers came into the tavern and arrested Fiord for man-slaying.

He lay that night in the dungeon of the castle.

In the morning he was brought before the court.

Fiord readily admitted killing Jom Orre the merchant. 'But I did it', he said to the lawmen, 'because Jom dashed a brimming ale horn out of my hand, out of rage and jealousy. I am not a coward, intimidated by wealth and overbearance.'

The six assembled lawmen, said Fiord, looked like wealthy elders themselves and he had no sooner spoken than he thought that things would go badly for him.

Svena's father and two brothers were called as witnesses. They swore that Svena had been deeply in love with the merchant Jom, and since the murder she did nothing but sit about the house in a cold vacant melancholy. Only if the name Fiord was mentioned, the girl would rouse herself and shriek that Fiord must be put to death. 'Were you cowards', she kept asking her brothers, 'that you did not kill the murderer when he came and stood on our threshold?'

Then Fiord called to mind the song of Svena at her weaving, and he knew that lies and false testimony were being uttered in the court.

When he realized that, Fiord laughed out loud in the courtroom, and then the six lawmen turned grave disapproving faces on him. And the case against Fiord looked blacker than ever.

The keeper of the tavern where the killing had occurred gave testimony on Fiord's behalf and also three young men from the carpenter's workshop who had been drinking there that day.

But they looked such cowed wretches in the solemn courtroom that it was obvious their testimony carried little weight.

Fiord began to think then of the death sentence. At that time a condemned man was taken out to a little skerry off shore and bound to a rock, and the rising tide covered his mouth and so he drowned.

'It is not the way I would have chosen,' said Fiord to himself.

The six lawmen began to consult together.

The longer they laid their heads together, the deeper and darker became the furrows between their eyes.

Fiord hoped that they would take him out to the tidal skerry before sunset, for now he wished his life to finish soon.

Suddenly the court door was thrown open, and a young woman thrust the guard aside and went up to the lawmen.

'My name is Svena,' she said quickly. 'That young man is the woodworker called Fiord Elkson. He is a good man and I had hoped that soon he would take me away and we would live in a forester's hut in the mountains. But my father, a month ago, unknown to me, more or less sold me to the merchant Jom Orre, a man I had small liking for. In four days' time we were to be married. *See to it*, my father said. *There will be no forester's hut for you. No, you are to be mistress of a fine house at the edge of the town. Go now, Svena, get your bridal clothes together. Jom Orre doesn't expect a dowry. He is even willing to provide the wedding feast. You are a fortunate girl. That tree-cutter, Fiord Elkson, he would have kept you in misery and poverty all your days. Make ready a bridal gown, quickly.*

'So my father said, and I sat down at the loom, and my heart was like ice.

'But I sat at the loom, and I wove and wove to forget my pain, and when I looked at the cloth in the loom, I saw that what I was weaving was a shroud, not a bridal gown.

'And that seemed to me like a sign from fate, that this matter would end in the death of someone.

'It seemed to me, justices, that I would rather die and wear the shroud than be the wife of that old skinflint Jom Orre.

'Then, yesterday at noon, my brother Erling came home with the news that there had been a man-slaying in an ale-house called *The Mermaid*.

'No one paid much attention to that. There are always brawls and woundings in the drink-shops along the wharfs.

'Then my younger brother Bald came in, breathless, and cried, *The dead man is Jom Orre, and Jom died among the spittle and the sawdust*.

'At that news, I went to my loom and I drove the shuttle very fast. The shroud, I thought, must be ready for Jom Orre's funeral. I wove for an hour with great fluency.

'I heard, next door, the low bleak voices of my father and my two brothers, discussing what should happen next.

'Then there was a knock at the door. When a loved one comes to the door and knocks, there is no need for words. For a moment my foot faltered on the treadle, but it was for joy. And then I drove the shuttle again, and I heard a song, and I realized it was myself singing because Fiord Elkson had come to see me.

'But, justices, I neither saw nor heard Fiord. I heard them close the door against him, wordlessly, and again I heard the black whisperings of the men of the house.

'Still I worked at the shroud, making it broad and long for Jom Orre.

'Then, at lamp-lighting time, the door opened again and I heard a shout. *They've arrested him*, cried Bald my younger brother. *The constables took the murderer Fiord in the Falcon tavern. He is to stand trial for his life in the morning*.

'At that outcry, justices, I rose up from the loom and I went to my bed, but for sorrow I did not sleep. For sorrow, and also because next door the black whispers of the father and brothers grew ever more intense and wicked. I rose out of bed and put my ear to the door. And I heard the lies they were concocting to lay before this court, a tissue of falsehoods to bring about the shameful execution of Fiord Elkson.'

Then Svena fell silent, and looked at the floor of the courtroom.

And the lawmen laid their heads together once more, nodding and considering and examining the ends of their fingers. But one old silver-haired lawman argued eagerly and urgently, looking from time to time at Fiord and Svena, and one after the other the lawmen seemed to acquiesce and to come to some measure of agreement.

Then Svena spoke again in a low sweet voice, 'I pray, justices, that the shroud I have just finished will not cover this man, Fiord. So much evil has been spun about him this day. He is young and brave. Let him not die.'

The lawmen consulted again.

Then the lawman with the silver beard said, 'Fiord Elkson, forester, we find you guilty of man-slaying. All things considered, you should be rowed out to the skerry and bound to a rock there and left until the tide rises and covers your mouth. But in view of what this woman has just said, the sentence is reduced to outlawry. You must leave Norway and never set foot on this land again. If you are found within the king's realm, whosoever wishes may kill you, and you will have no protection from the law.

'Now we give you one day's leave to make ready and leave this shore.'

What was Fiord to do then? No man in Norway could shelter him or protect him. No doubt about it, the father and the brothers would hire a man to kill him sooner or later.

Fiord the outlaw, thinking such bleak thoughts, found himself in the harbour district among the masts and cordage and tar-smells.

An old sailor was standing at a wharf. This man spoke to Fiord. 'You look miserable, shipmate,' said he. 'A month ashore is too much. It's time you had the sea-spray in your beard again. Cheer up, we're sailing with the first of the flood. England – a town called Grimsby – cargo of walrus tusks and salted reindeer. Good, shipmate, you look better already. Come and have a word with the skipper.'

Fiord the forester had never set foot on a ship before, but the skipper said he would do. Before they sighted the Northumbrian coast, however, the skipper regretted signing this new hand on his ship, because Fiord made every mistake it was possible for a novice to make – he was seasick, he swung his oar out of rhythm, he said the words that should never be said at sea, he got in the way of the other sailors, he didn't know larboard from starboard, he got the rope in a frightful tangle more than once.

Still, the skipper was patient with him, and when Fiord told him, one night-watch, the story of his outlawing, the skipper was delighted. 'For', said he, 'wild free men like you make the best vikings...' Gradually Fiord learned the sea skills, and at the end of two voyages the skipper assured him that he was a passable sailor.

That first voyage, off Scarborough, sailing south, the skipper sighted a merchant ship. 'And by the look of her,' said he, 'she's heavily freighted. I think now we'll have a look at her cargo.'

The merchant ship saw the Norse vessel bearing down on her and the helmsman swung the hull about till the wind filled her sail, but still she was too slow for the Norse ship. When the first Norse arrow fell into the ship, the English skipper said, making a trumpet of his hands, 'I hope you are not the kind of vikings who kill for the joy of it. This is a new ship, and this is our first voyage, and all the sailors are young, and either new-married or in hope to be married when they return from Lübeck with silver in their purses.'

41

'Still,' said the Norwegian skipper, 'I would be glad to have a look at your cargo, out of curiosity.'

So the two ships rode alongside, roped together, and the skipper and four of the seamen, including Fiord, crossed into the English ship and undid one or two of the hundred bales in her hold, and they saw that the ship had a cargo of the best wool.

'Well,' said the Norwegian skipper, 'we're not so badly off for coats that we need all this wool. Out of friendship we will take two bales, thank you for offering them to us so freely. In exchange we'll give you a barrel of reindeer meat – there's nothing so delicious as stewed reindeer, after a hard day's work at sea.'

The English skipper, a tall grave gray-bearded man, saw that no blood was to be spilt that day. After that, he exchanged friendly words with the Norwegian skipper. They parted on the best of terms, and the Norwegian ship sailed on south and had no more adventures till they reached Grimsby . . .

'Now,' said Fiord to Ranald as they sat together on the ship *Laxoy*, just the two of them, because the crew were ashore spending their wages, and Hakon Treeman the skipper was busy with important business somewhere, 'I will not weary you, boy, with any more of my sea-exploits. I have told you what I have told you in order to make it plain why I dare not set foot in this seaport of Bergen or in any other part of Norway. I am still an outlaw and will be till the day of my death. My killing of Jom, and my trial – all that is forty years in the past, and ever since I have sailed back and fore on the ocean, to Grimsby and Dublin, Orkney and Faroe, Spain and Sicily, Iceland and Greenland and Vinland, and never once set foot on my native land.'

Ranald said, 'They would not know you in Bergen if you were to go ashore. It's likely that your enemies are dead. You are still a strong man, Fiord, and few would dare to do you a mischief.'

Fiord said, 'What you say is true, Ranald. It is more than likely that death has closed their eyes. It is not fear that prevents me from walking the streets of Bergen. It is the dread that someone may say in passing, "Svena, she lives, an old crazy hag now, in a house in such-and-such a lane . . ." Or worse, "Svena died, long long ago, a young woman still, soon after Fiord Elkson was driven out of Norway for man-slaying".'

That night the crew of *Laxoy* returned to the ship, some of them very drunk, from the taverns of Bergen. Some had been fighting, and had bruises about the eyes or the mouth. Most of them had spent all their wages.

The seamen turned in at once, and the ship was a scattered cacophony of snores soon.

'Now,' said Fiord, 'I hope it is not too long till Hakon our skipper comes back. He has been in the counting-houses and the merchants' booths for three days now. I have not known him to negotiate about a cargo for so long. It is a simple cargo after all, timber and goat cheeses and smoked reindeer meat for Orkney.'

The sailors woke next morning, gray in the face.

Two more days passed, and still there was no sign of Hakon Treeman the skipper.

The sailors began to grumble then, wishing to be seaborne again, for now their purses were empty and it was unlikely that the Bergen taverners would give them credit.

In Orkney, there would be a little shower of silver for every one of them, once the cargo was sold.

Another day passed, and still Hakon Treeman did not come to the wharfside and the ships.

Instead, a messenger arrived on the wharfside riding a horse. This man was wearing a leather hat with an eagle feather in it, and his coat was embroidered with coloured wools, and a silver trumpet hung at his belt.

The messenger made his horse rear, and he called out in a very refined authoritative accent, 'Is this the vessel *Laxoy* recently returned from Greenland?'

The sailors sniggered behind their hands and mocked his accent, and made their eyelids droop in a superior way, and laughed out loud. It has always been that way – sailors make fun of the affectations of landlubbers, however high and mighty.

At last Fiord said gravely that this ship was undoubtedly the *Laxoy* recently arrived from Greenland.

'Do I address the skipper of the *Laxoy*?' said the messenger, and made his horse prance on the cobbles till sparks flew.

The slight wind blew scents from the messenger's hair into the ship. One or two of the sailors held their noses. Others hawked into the sea.

'The skipper of the *Laxoy* is ashore, doing business,' said Fiord. 'We expect him back very soon.'

'It is no matter about the skipper,' said the messenger. 'It is not with the skipper that His Majesty the King would speak.'

A messenger from the king! The sailors set aside their mockery and accorded a certain degree of respect to the scented splendour prancing his horse around in a semicircle on the cobbles. It could be that his majesty wanted them to crew the new ship of state he was having built in Trondheim – though this was unlikely.

'Is there a sailor among you of the name of Fiord Elkson, and also a very young sailor, from Orkney, of the name of Ranald Sigmundson?'

Fiord Elkson stepped forward. 'I am called Fiord Elkson,' he said.

'Then you are to put aside all other commitments and come to the King's palace at once,' said the royal messenger.

'Thank the King for his invitation,' said Fiord, 'but tell him that Fiord Elkson has been an outlaw in the kingdom for forty years and has vowed to live out the rest of his days on the oceans of the world.'

Now the sailors pushed Ranald forward. 'Here, your high-and-mightiness, is the Orkney boy Ranald Sigmundson.'

The messenger looked at Ranald like the far end of a fiddle.

'You are to accompany me to the royal palace at once, boy,' he intoned. 'His Majesty the King commands it.'

Four of the sailors pushed Ranald from the ship's side on to the quay. The messenger with a grand gesture signified that Ranald should get up into the saddle behind him.

And the chestnut horse went in a full circle round the cobbles, in a scatter of hooves, neighing magnificently.

'As for you, Fiord Elkson,' said the messenger, 'His Majesty the King will take it ill that you have disobeyed his summons. You are in the King's realm now, even though you are on a ship. It may be that you will have to answer for it.'

And with that the messenger turned the horse about and dug his spurs in and the horse went in a headlong gallop up the long wharf, and Ranald's hair streamed out behind him.

After a brief thunder of hooves, the horse slowed to a canter and Ranald saw that they were passing under an arched heraldic gate.

In the courtyard, a trumpet sounded.

44

II
Norway

1

King Olaf of Norway sat on the high chair and summoned Ranald Sigmundson to sit in front of him on a stool.

A scribe sat at the nearby table and wrote down much of what the king said.

A chamberlain with a white beard stood behind the throne. That old man looked tired and Ranald was sorry for him. But still the chamberlain stood, steadying himself from time to time with his hand on the high gilded corner of the throne. The hand was frail as a leaf in late autumn.

King Olaf looked curiously at the boy and waited.

'Your Majesty,' the chamberlain whispered in the king's ear, 'the boy who has been to Vinland.'

King Olaf sat up at once. 'A Vinland-farer,' he said, 'and so young! This gives us pleasure.'

Ranald inclined his head. He did not know if he should kneel at King Olaf's feet and kiss the gold ring on his finger. He had however been brought up among independent people. He managed to say 'Sire' as gravely and courteously as he could, before sitting down once more on the low stool before the king.

'Now,' said King Olaf, 'we are most interested to know everything about this Vinland. We have heard that the land is possessed by savages, and they have only one foot and when they want to get from place to place they must hop along on this one immense foot.'

'I did not see such people, sire,' said Ranald.

'We have heard also,' said the king, 'that they eat a disgusting mixture of marrow and blood, and this makes them savage and murderous.'

'No, sire,' said Ranald, 'they eat salmon and geese and venison. They are a beautiful people to look at, though their hair is straight and black-glossy, and they have eyes dark as night.'

The scribe's quill stumbled and spluttered across the parchment, trying to get as much of this information down as he could.

The chamberlain pressed his fingers to his old weary eyes, briefly.

Ranald, urged by King Olaf, described as best he could the forests, shores, rivers, and plains of Vinland. He did not forget to mention the clusters of small sweet berries that grew everywhere in profusion, and the wild corn on the prairies that surged this way and that in the wind, also the salmon and the lithe deer in the woodlands and the eagle that stood up near the sun, turning. 'It is a sign of honour among the skraelings, sire, that the chief men wear the eagle feathers in their hair.'

'Savages, heathens indeed,' whispered the chamberlain, and tottered slightly with weariness.

'We are informed furthermore', said the king, 'that those skraelings take their enemies' hair as a sign of conquest. Not just a few locks cut off either, but the entire scalp severed clean from the skull with a knife and hung on poles in the middle of their villages. Their houses are made of skins and branches.'

Ranald said nothing in answer to that.

The scribe's eyes grew big with astonishment, and his pen fairly scurried across the skin, scattering small blobs of ink.

Ranald was aware of singing in a distant part of the palace, boys' voices in a slow solemn chant.

'Furthermore,' said the king, 'it has been told us that further north, among the ice, there are skraelings who live – if you can call such an existence "life" – in another way. Those northern skraelings – so we are informed – are small people and very fat, and necessarily so because they eat nothing but the blubber of whales and seals. It has been suggested that those ice-folk are not true men at all but half-human and half-walrus. And they live in snow houses.'

Ranald said, 'Sire, those are rather northern Greenlanders than Vinlanders. The Inuit people they call themselves. Not long ago they thought themselves to be the only men on earth. Three of them came once to the village in Greenland where I stayed with Leif Ericson. They offered us wolf-pelts and walrus ivory in exchange for timber and beer. It is true that those skraelings are round and fat as barrels, but they have happy smiling faces, and it was a joy to have dealings with them.'

'Savages, ice-men,' whispered the old chamberlain, and half yawned, half sighed.

The scribe dipped his quill deep into the stone ink pot.

'Well,' said King Olaf, 'we will keep ourselves informed about this Vinland and its people. It seems to us a pity that the oil and fruit and mines of such a land should be wasted on the greedy Greenland and Iceland merchants. It may be that in the yards of Norway we could build a fleet of merchant ships and so trade westward. But from Norway to Vinland is a long hazardous voyage, and we fear that in the end our account books may show a debit rather than a profit, what with whirlpools, shipwrecks, icebergs and sea monsters ... In the meantime, alas, we have troubles enough nearer home, and all our energies must be given to the mountain bandits and the vikings.'

The scribe paused. There was no need to record what had been recorded many a time in the past year or two: the king's troubles with the mountain-men, the Laplanders and the pirates.

'Vanity, all is vanity,' said the chamberlain, his voice as dry as the cinders in a sinking fire. 'What profit hath a man of all his labours?'

Now the choir of boys began again, a sound of such purity that the three voices in the throne-room seemed tawdry and meaningless.

After a time the king said, 'How comes it that a boy like you has sailed so far and seen such marvellous things?'

Then Ranald told the king of his leaving Orkney in the merchant vessel *Snowgoose*, and how his father's rages had driven him to stowaway in Leif Ericson's ship *West Seeker* in Iceland, and how in their journey to the world's edge they saw after a storm the broken timbers of his father's ship, and how the starved raven let out of its cage had directed them the way to Vinland. And he told the king in detail all that had happened there.

The scribe wrote only a word or two now and then, for it was the rich wisdom that fell from King Olaf's lips that he was supposed to record, not the imaginings of a half-licked boy.

The choir sang, in the king's chapel far away.

> Though I take the wings of the morning
> And flee to the uttermost places of the sea
> Still shall thy mercy seek me
> And thy right hand shall hold me ...

Ranald had learned enough Latin from the monks at Warbeth in Orkney to follow the meaning. But truly, he thought, the music is the meaning and the meaning is the music, so seamlessly were the Latin words and the plainchant woven in one. The beauty of the psalm made him pause in the middle of his narrative.

'Your story is of the greatest interest to us,' said the king. 'We visited Orkney not long since and converted it to Christianity. Sailing from the Scillies to Norway, our ships ran for shelter into Osmundvoe in the island of Hoy. Through the curtains of rain we saw three ships of Sigurd, Earl of Orkney. Sigurd seemed none too pleased to see his liege-lord. He thought, no doubt, that Norway might require some share of his viking-venture. "Have no fear, Sigurd," said I, "you can keep your silver cups and tapestries – we want none of them – we are going, on the contrary, to bestow a great treasure on you, namely Christianity."

'"I am well enough content with Thor and Odin, the Norse gods," said Earl Sigurd.

'"But I am your king," said I, "and I have lately decreed that Christianity is the religion of Norway and the earldoms of the west. You must now become a Christian. Your king commands this."

'"No," said the Orkney earl, "for I and my ancestors have sailed on Odin's ocean, and Odin has prospered us well. I have no wish to hazard myself on this unknown ocean of Christianity."

'"There will be no difficulty about that, Earl Sigurd," I said. "It happens that I have on board my ship two priests, and they have the waters of baptism in a jar. A few drops from the jar on your forehead, Sigurd, and you are launched on the ocean of Christ."

'"I do not desire to be a traitor to the gods of my ancestors," said Sigurd stubbornly.

'"Now, Sigurd," said I. "Now, my good friend, you would not wish me to execute you as a rebel against your king. Tell your men to kneel along the thwarts and tilt their faces up at the sun. My two priests will go from man to man and pour the baptismal waters on their foreheads. You, Sigurd, will take the water drops first, here at the high bench of the royal ship. By such simple means you and all Orkney with you are launched upon the magnificent ocean of Christ, where there are treasures beyond price to be discovered . . ."

'So there, in Osmundvoe in Orkney, Earl Sigurd and all his court became Christians.

'Still, it seemed to us that Sigurd was none too pleased about this change in his religion. It seemed to us that once we had sailed on east to Norway, Sigurd would be quick to return to worshipping the old gods. I know Sigurd well. He is a good and a brave man in many ways, but he is stubborn as an ox.

'There, on his ship, Earl Sigurd had his son with him, a good-looking gentle lad called Hund. It seemed to us that the earl was devoted to his son. Often he put his arm round the boy's shoulder, as much as to say, *Look, King Olaf, for all the wealth in your treasury you do not have a jewel like Hund, my son . . .* But also he seemed to be protective of the boy, as if he feared that some great danger might befall him. We could not help, when looking at the boy Hund Sigurdson, to observe the delicacy of his mould and features. He was by no means cut out for viking assaults and sieges, this Hund. But his father was taking him on this first voyage, no doubt, to have stitched into him a red strand of toughness and heroism. He might have to rule in Orkney one day, this Hund, and that is no job for a weakling.

'So Earl Sigurd, that day in Osmundvoe on his ship, with the waters on his brow, gathered his boy Hund to him, in great affection and pride and anxiety. And he said, *Hund, what Fate decrees, it is that that must happen. We will set out together on the voyage.*

'At this point I said to Earl Sigurd, "My friend, that's a fine son you have with you on the ship. We, King Olaf, are greatly taken with his looks and his bearing. It seems to us that such a son should not be hazarded in viking raids. Even in Orkney his winsomeness will be seen by only a few islanders. I think you should give this boy Hund to us, to be fostered in Norway. There he will be well looked after, and instructed by the best men in all the arts and accomplishments necessary for a young man of noble stock. Besides, he would be nurtured carefully in the Christian faith."

'Earl Sigmund gave a great shout of pain. "Hund is my son and he will never be parted from me. Better tear my heart out! You have done enough to me today, King Olaf. Now sail on to Norway and leave me in peace with my son, my ships, and my men."

'And that strong ox of a man, Earl Sigurd Hlodverson, gathered his son to him and his eyes were bright with tears. His great body shook with grief.

'I gave commands. The boy Hund was taken from his father's embrace, and led into the royal ship. And he seemed much taken with the gilded prow, the beaten bronze bosses on the shields along the hull, and the well carved dragon on the prow.

'Indeed, Hund scarcely looked back to wave to his father the earl after the ropes were loosed, and the Orkney fleet lingered on in Osmundvoe and the royal Norwegian ships, five in all – a magnificent array – turned one by one into the Pentland Firth, and so on east and north towards Bergen.

'The boy Hund is still here, in the palace. Listen, perhaps you can hear his voice now in the chapel choir. Hund has a voice of the greatest sweetness . . .'

They listened.

Then King Olaf said, doubtfully, that Hund Sigurdson's voice did not seem to be there in the choir that morning, interweaving sweet and grave through the voices of the courtiers' and merchants' sons. 'He is rather delicate, our Hund,' said the king. 'He is often troubled with sore throats and coughs. Those are troubles of boyhood, we are sure he will grow into a strong capable man. That will be necessary if he is to rule over the turbulent Orkneys. But we spoil the plainchant with our doubts and speculations. Listen.'

From a distant part of the palace, through labyrinthine arched corridors, came the choristers' plainchant.

The heavens declare the glory of God
And the firmament proclaims his handiwork
Day pours out the word to day
And night to night imparts knowledge . . .

'So', said King Olaf, 'we will make this Hund Sigurdson a great Christian knight, before we return him to be earl over the heathen Orkneys, after his father Earl Sigurd is dust. For we doubt if that same Sigurd will remain a good Christian to the end of the story.

'Still, it gladdens our heart, the knowledge that we, Olaf the King, first took the light of Christianity to Orkney.'

The old chamberlain was almost asleep on his feet. Indeed, a thin buzzing came from his nostrils as he drooped on his feet beside the high seat.

The clerk had long ceased his writing. He had written out several times in the course of the last year the account of King Olaf's ship-meeting in Osmundvoe with Earl Sigurd.

'Sire, pardon me,' said Ranald, 'the candles of Christ were lit on the altars of Orkney long before the event you describe. There have been Irish monks in Paplay and Papay and Eynhallow and Birsay and Warbeth for a very long time. The monks at Warbeth taught me to read and write, and also Latin grammar and ciphering and scripture.'

The scribe's eyes grew large at the impudence of this boy, contradicting the king's majesty!

'That may be,' said King Olaf, smiling. 'I am sure it must have been so. But those holy men were always at the whim of your pagan earls. One word from Sigurd and they would have been scattered to the uttermost places of the sea, their parchments burned and their silver melted down. The seal of a king secures all. We have spoken. It will be so.'

Ranald bowed gravely.

'Now,' said the king, 'we invite you to have supper with us before you return to your ship. At supper, you will meet Hund Sigurdson the future Earl of Orkney. You are about the same age, you two. We are sure of this, that you will agree together well. We have looked deep into your minds, you are greatly gifted and intelligent youths.'

King Olaf rose to his feet and clapped his hands thrice.

The old chamberlain was so startled that he cried, 'Yes, yes, the horses are saddled, the falcons are hooded and out of the barn. All's ready for the hunt . . .' Then he saw that he was not in the courtyard getting the falconry organized, as he must have done many a time in the days of his vigour . . . 'Oh, dear me,' he said, 'there I go, falling asleep on my feet again. This will never do, this will never do.'

Three footmen came and stood in the doorway of the throne-room, their heads inclined towards the king.

'We have a young guest from Orkney,' said Olaf. 'He will be staying to supper. Ranald Sigmundson will need to wash the salt and the sea-grime from him. He will be the better of a clean linen suit and coat. See to it.'

The scrivener was busy tying his roll of parchment with a ribbon and gathering up his quills and corking his ink bottle. No more golden words of wisdom would be spoken in the throne-room that day.

The scrivener bowed to the king, and still bowing, walked diagonally towards the door like a retreating crab.

The three footmen, once they had Ranald to themselves and away from the throne-room, shed all their obsequiousness and reverence at once.

'Pooh!' said one, 'you stink like a water rat. Disgusting. Come along with you. This way.'

They led Ranald down two corridors and round three corners and into a kind of closet with an oak water-cask and oak basin and a linen towel.

'When did you last see fresh water, boy?' said another footman. 'Were you reared in a pigsty? Ugh!'

The third footman drew water from the cask into the basin. 'I wonder his majesty could suffer such a filthy young beast in his chamber! I'd hate to be down-wind of you. See you scrub yourself thoroughly, scarecrow.'

Ranald washed himself well in the clean cold water (though there was a dead spider in it, and a snail), and by the time he was red and ruddy from the towelling, the three footmen came to summon him to the wardrobe.

'He doesn't exactly smell like a rose still,' said the first footman.

'Still, he won't make the ladies shudder too much now,' said the second footman.

'He might just pass for a merchant's son on a feast day,' said the third footman.

Ranald, in a new linen suit with a blue silk neckband and shoes of Spanish leather over his woollen hose, was escorted now to the great royal dining-hall.

The guests entered, one by one, lords and ladies alternately, and stood beside their chairs at the long table, waiting.

A silver trumpet thrilled.

King Olaf entered. The lords and ladies bowed to the king as he took his place at the high bench. There were two empty seats, one on each side of the king.

The king gestured. The court sat down, with rustlings of clean crisp linen and waftings of scent as if the dining-hall was a garden in high summer. 'Indeed,' thought Ranald, 'the women look like gorgeous butterflies . . .' Ranald recognized the old chamberlain and an old lady seated opposite each other at the board. They nodded to each other, gently and kindly.

Then Ranald heard, startled, his own name being uttered ceremonially. 'His Majesty is pleased to entertain at his royal table tonight a young far-travelled guest from his Orkney dominion, Ranald Sigmund-son of Hamnavoe.'

'Step forward, cabbage-head,' whispered the first footman, and pushed Ranald into the light of a score of candelabra.

'Bow till your head hits the ground, you yokel,' whispered the second footman.

'Be as silent as a fish in the sea,' whispered the third footman. 'You'll show your ignorance if you speak one word.'

King Olaf gestured for Ranald to sit beside him at the high bench.

There was a sudden sound like a water-torrent. The ladies and gentlemen of the court were clapping their hands.

King Olaf spoke only to Ranald through that long meal.

All around them the talk rippled like the sea along a wide shore.

There were half a dozen musicians in the gallery above, playing on pipes and harps. From time to time a hidden skald recited episodes of a long poem, and the music stopped while the intricate word-patterns were uttered.

The diners ate, first, lobster-claws and oysters from the shell, and afterwards thin slices of venison and ham, with oatcakes. There were no plates. The guests reached with their hands to the great heaped platters set here and there on the bare scrubbed oak, and ate from their fingers. They spread the butter over the oatcakes with their thumbs. Soon their knuckles and jowls were dripping with fat. Several of the guests belched, and if one of them gave vent to a particularly loud eructation, there was laughter and words of appreciation all about him. Ranald was astonished to see that the gentry rubbed their greasy fingers on their fine linen sleeves, and sometimes on their neighbours' sleeves, and none of the guests seemed to take offence at that.

Only King Olaf had a servant who stood beside him with a large napkin, and the king wiped his fingers and his mouth from time to time on that linen.

'The ruffians at sea eat more cleanly than the lords and ladies,' thought Ranald to himself.

He took care to lick the fat from his own fingers, and from the corners of his mouth too, with his long fluent tongue.

Meantime three or four attendants were going up and down the table, pouring wine and mead from silver jars into the silver goblets that stood in front of each guest. The honied ale was poured into Ranald's cup too. He sipped from it, increasingly, as the meal went on.

The mead tasted delicious to him, after his months at sea.

'We promised', King Olaf was saying to him, 'that Hund Sigurdson would be here tonight, sitting on the other side of our high chair. Unfortunately, Hund has been unwell since morning, and is confined to his bed, and my physicians are seeing to him . . . I am greatly concerned about Hund. This is the third time that he has been sick this winter . . . He has, this time, a high fever. Once after a bout of coughing today – so the physicians told me – there was a thread of blood at his lip . . . We will have special prayers in the chapel tomorrow for the restoration of health to Hund, that good and pleasant hostage.'

Ranald, seeing how truly grieved the king was at Hund's sickness, took a deep gulp from his mead-cup, and almost at once the conversation along the table seemed like voices out of a dream.

The harps and pipes interwove their music from the gallery above, and Ranald thought he had never heard such a ravishing sound. When the skald uttered his verses, it seemed like a voice from the turrets of Valhalla, heroic and immortal. But the language of the poem was so ancient and ornate that Ranald could barely follow it.

His cup was empty. At once a flunkey came with a jar and filled it almost to brimming with mead. Ranald tilted his goblet again, and the sweet liquor ran from the corner of his mouth and dripped from his chin.

The platters of meat had been removed from the table, and the attendants now brought in platters of cheese, some new and soft, others blue and well wormed, others as hard almost as board, others as light as butter with herbs worked into them. Beside each cheese platter was set a new warm loaf smelling of honey.

Ranald found himself holding a hunk of blue-veined cheese in one hand and a hunk of bread in the other. But he could not remember having stretched out to the cheese platter.

The voice of the king went on and on, gravely questioning. The mouth of the king was only a handslength from Ranald's ear, but it seemed to Ranald to come from far away and to be laden with questions and comments of the utmost sweetness and gravity. And when Ranald replied to the king, his tongue in his head was as loose and carefree as a thrush in April.

Yes, *Laxoy*, that was the name of the ship he had sailed in, the shipmaster Hakon Treeman . . . Ah, the king had heard good reports of Hakon Treeman, an honest mariner who paid his taxes annually and

54

had kept his hands clean of piracy. That was good. Ranald said he was pleased to hear such a favourable opinion, especially from the mouth of the king ... 'And', Ranald went on, the mead fumes making now a glad summertime of his brain, 'Hakon Treeman the skipper utters his thoughts so movingly, it is almost like listening to poetry. But, to tell the truth, sire, we sailors on *Laxoy* are concerned a little about Hakon Treeman, for he went ashore to do business with the merchants and money-lenders as soon as *Laxoy* arrived in Bergen, and we have not seen him since ... Yes, sire, we carried a cargo of wolf-pelts and walrus tusks from Greenland, and at the next new moon we are set to sail west and south to Orkney with a cargo mainly of timber. There is a great dearth of timber for house-building and ship-building in Orkney, there being only a few wind-stunted trees in those islands ... Yes, indeed, sire, I love the sea now, and voyaging, though at first I was very much afraid of ships ... Sire, what you say is true, Norway is a good and a pleasant land, and the mountains and the fjords, the people and the city of Bergen, are delightful to me ... Stay here always, sire? In the royal palace, as a young courtier, and learn such skills as falconry, boar-hunting, verse-making, travelling as an envoy to such lands as Latvia, Holland, Scotland, Iceland? You do me the greatest honour, sire, my spirit dazzles at the prospects you hold out before me ... But at the moment it is impossible. I am most anxious to get home to Orkney as soon as possible. My mother is now a widow, it is hard to know how things are faring with her, now that my father is drowned in the Greenland Sea. Besides, my grandfather, if he is still alive, is very old, and he looks to me to carry on the farm of Breckness in Stromness of which my remote ancestor laid the first stone and staked out the bounds two centuries ago ... Sire, believe me, the spirits of my forebears would have no peace if that fertile spacious farm sank into ruin because I was not there to save it from bandit, rat, and thistle ... Sire, this mead is a magical drink, and my thoughts are singing like an orchard of birds at sunrise. I think I should not drink any more, but now that the flunkey is here at my shoulder once more with the jar, I will have him pour me half a goblet ... Sire, I look at all the mouths opening and shutting here at your long table, speaking for the most part triviality and nonsense, and I wonder that you have the patience to endure their chatter night after night! To me that would be insufferable. Two people alone in this company of diners please me, and that is your old chamberlain and his wife. This morning, in the throne-room, I thought him a silly bumbling old man, but here he sits and his silver-haired lady opposite him, and they say nothing but they look at each other like blessed spirits waiting for death to free them . . . Sire, you must forgive me, I have not spoken such a torrent of words in all my life, you must put it down to your hospitality, your offer of friendship and preferment, and most of all to that wonderful mead-jar . . .'

Ranald paused for breath. His face was flushed, he could feel his pulses beating merrily in his wrists. Still his thoughts thronged and jostled for utterance.

He was aware, through the golden mists of candlelight, that many of the guests were casting angry offended looks in his direction. That a young upstart like this, from an island province in the southwest, should monopolize the king's ear in this way – it was intolerable! Why, this very morning had he not been swilling water from a bucket across the deck of some cargo-ship, and knotting a rope? And here he was, chattering so hard that even the king's majesty could hardly get a word in edgewise.

The old chamberlain and his wife turned their faces to Ranald, and there was such kindness in their eyes and dimpling mouths as if Ranald was a well loved grandson.

King Olaf said gravely, 'I think at last that you would become a great man here in Norway, Ranald Sigmundson.'

Ranald took another sip of mead. 'Sire,' he said, 'it may be that once the affairs of my family west in Orkney are settled, I will return to Norway and labour here in your service and enjoy the fruits of this fair land.'

'What you say pleases us greatly,' said King Olaf.

The pipes, horns, and harps in the gallery were making music now of the greatest yearning, the mood was of some state beyond human attainment, a vision of peace and world-wide brotherhood (or so it seemed to the mead-enchanted heart of Ranald. He was aware that his eyes were brimming with tears.)

'And yet, sire,' he said, 'what I long for most is to return to that land in the far west, Vinland. Before I die I would like to make my peace with that skraeling boy. In the end there was trouble between him and me, but at the first we greeted each other well across the water.'

'It may be so, if God wills it,' said King Olaf. 'And now, first, we give you fair leave to sail to Orkney.'

There had fallen a silence on the dinner table, and only the voices of the king and the ship-boy could be heard.

As soon as the king had given his blessing to the imminent forth-faring of *Laxoy*, the guests clapped their hands, and turned smiling faces to the king and his guest. And Ranald saw, in the clarity that mead bestows before inebriation sets in, that the smiles of the courtiers were obsequious and false, but the faces of the old chamberlain and his wife were full of goodness and blessing.

'And now, lastly,' said King Olaf, 'if you are to sail to Orkney at the time of the new moon, you should be on shipboard, helping to make all ready. The old moon is a cinder in the sky now. It is a long dark walk from here to the wharfside, Ranald, and there are dangers at the street-corners between. Besides, you have drunk rather too much of that mead for a boy. So you will sit on a litter, and four soldiers will carry you, and there will be a soldier going before with a torch and another behind with a torch and a sword.'

Then Ranald knelt, and kissed the gold on King Olaf's finger, and said 'Thank you, Your Majesty,' for the one and only time.

And after that he remembered little till he woke on board ship next morning, feeling as if his head was stuffed with ashes . . .

'Well,' said Fiord, 'you got a supper out of that royal summons, and a bit too much to drink, it seems. And a fine suit of clothes, and a purse in the pocket with a gold sovereign in it.'

Ranald said not a word. If he had opened his mouth he would have groaned.

'The ship's ready for sea,' said Fiord. 'The timber and the whale bone are in the hold, lashed down. But still there is no word from our skipper. We can't sail without him. What can be keeping Hakon Treeman? He has finished his business with the merchants, the cargo's stowed, he's always eager to sail with the new moon, and in two nights from now we'll have sight of her. Hakon Treeman has never been so long ashore, in my minding.'

The moon had gone into her cave with her pot of ashes and her quenched candle-stump.

That night, when the sailors were throwing dice on a thwart amidships, a very old shawled woman stood on the wharf where the *Laxoy* was tied up.

The sailors looked up at her from their dice.

'Hakon Treeman is dead,' she said in a voice like a crepitation of cinders. 'You will have to get a new skipper.'

Then the old woman turned and shuffled off along the cobbles, and soon she was lost among the piles of ship-gear and the watchmen with torches and fires and the cargoes waiting to be shipped.

2

The sailors of *Laxoy* considered that Fiord should now be skipper, since he was the man with greatest sea-knowledge among them.

'But I know nothing about trading and merchandise and markets,' said Fiord. 'What good is a ship without cargoes? Are we to sail an empty ship from port to port? Besides, who owns the ship, now that Hakon Treeman is dead? We will deliver this cargo of timber in Orkney, and after that both we and the ship *Laxoy* are in the hands of fate.'

A few of the seamen were of the opinion that they should from now on be vikings.

'There is a great wealth on the high seas,' they urged. 'English ships, Danish ships, French ships freighted to the gunwales. The sea gets richer summer by summer.'

'Yes,' said another, 'in a few years we would be wealthy men and we'd build fine houses in Orkney or in Iceland and have many beautiful girls, and so end our days in ease and honour.'

'Yes,' said the ship's cook, 'and I'll have six or seven horses in a meadow.'

They were off Fair Isle, sailing south, and the waves in torn sheets were falling into the *Laxoy*, and everyone was wet and cold.

'Yes,' said the ship's carpenter, 'and when our viking days are over we will sit at big fires and we will eat hares and capons stewed in ale, and afterwards sleep in warm beds.'

'If you take to viking ways,' said Fiord, 'your days will not be long. I'll tell you one picture that I see in my mind – law-breakers taken to a skerry at low tide, and bound to a rock there, and left for the tide to rise and cover their mouths. That's what happens to murderers.'

Another great wave broke over the ship. The sailors were gray and wet and shivering.

'Besides,' said Fiord, 'viking ships are long and lithe, like sea-wolves, and they are very fast either for pursuit or flight. But look at our ship.

She is built for carrying cargoes, she is deep and onerous and broad-beamed. She is no sea-wolf, the *Laxoy*, she is a sea-ox and is meant to carry burdens . . .'

Then the sailors spoke no more about piracy and a wild free lawless life on the ocean streams.

It happened then that the weather got worse, so that the men had to take to the bailing pans, and one huge wave, off the northernmost island of Orkney, called Rinansey, broke over the ship and ruined what was left of the foodstore.

'We won't be needing salt in our stew-pot tonight,' said the cook. 'Nor will there be ale to quench our thirst . . .' For the big wave had wrenched out a stave of the ale barrel.

Fiord, going forward to see to the sail, was struck on the shoulder by the swing of the sail-beam, so that for a while he had no strength in his arm and could not hold the steering-oar. The ship was now turned broadside on to the waves and began to lurch dangerously.

Then Ranald Sigmundson took over the helm and shouted an order into the wind as to how the sail was now to be set. 'And be quick!' Then the *Laxoy* turned head into weather, and stood against the wave onset like a strong ox. Presently the wind swung about and blew more from the north, and Ranald steered the ship well through the northern Orkneys, till they came to the small sea village of Kirkvoe (which men afterwards called Kirkwall), and there they dropped anchor.

Fiord praised Ranald for his ship-handling. 'I could not have done better,' he said. 'I think you will be a good merchant-skipper, and Sigmund Firemouth your father would be proud of you.'

But Ranald said he had had enough of the sea for a while. 'Now I think', said he, 'I will turn my strength to the land.'

'But first', said Fiord, 'you must see to the sale of our cargo. I myself have no skill in dealing with merchants.'

Already Fiord and Ranald could see a small crowd standing on the shore. The arrival of a merchant ship always excites interest in a seaport. Mostly it is idle curiosity. But no sooner had Fiord and Ranald waded ashore than three important-looking men stepped forward to greet them. These men gave their names separately, and added that they were merchants. It was soon clear to Ranald that there was no love lost between the three, for they kept watching each other out of the corners of their eyes.

'This is no bad thing for us,' Ranald whispered to Fiord.

Ranald answered the questions that the three merchants asked, simply and clearly. The name of their ship was *Laxoy*, and they had left Bergen on the morning of the new moon. They had a cargo of the very best timber, and bundles of walrus tusks taken from those islands of Norway where the walrus flourish mightily, and their ivory is weighty and flawless in texture and each piece has a fine curl to it. 'And', said Ranald, 'a good craftsman could make rare and lovely things out of that walrus ivory, and you would have ivory hilts on your daggers, and ivory buttons on your coats, and the women of Orkney would have ivory combs to comb out their long bright hair.'

The merchants eyed each other shiftily. One said they had heard tales like that before, a many a time . . . Another said the last cargo of Norwegian timber had been so rotten that it could only be used for firewood. The third said one cargo of so-called walrus ivory – it had been landed ten years ago – had turned out to be whale bone, and it took a yellowish tinge before the end of winter.

The three merchants of Kirkvoe rowed out to the *Laxoy*. They turned over a log here and there, and dug deep into the piles of walrus ivory to make quite sure that the best pieces were not on the outside.

Then one of the merchants, a man with a face like a fox, said it was a passable cargo, no more. He took Ranald aside and made him an offer in a low voice.

The second merchant seemed to be always merry, as if trade and merchandise were the greatest enjoyment imaginable. This man, while his rivals were still poking about among the timber and ivory, took Ranald aside and whispered a sum of money in his ear.

Ranald looked grave, and pursed his mouth. 'We shall see,' he said.

The third merchant was an old man who gave occasional snorts and, whenever he spoke, wasted no words. He threw down a log he was examining – he gave a fierce look at the two other merchants, who were examining a walrus tusk and disagreeing as to its merits, then he took Ranald by the sleeve and led him to the ship's stern, and he snorted like a bad-tempered boar and roared out a figure, 'Ten marks, take it or leave it!' All on the *Laxoy* looked startled. The old merchant looked triumphantly at his rivals, as if he knew well that they could not match his offer. And indeed they were both disconcerted – one frowned and looked towards the shore and the other gave a laugh that had little merriment in it.

'Ten marks!' shouted the old man.

Ranald had been in his father's office often enough to know that a mark is a considerable sum of money. A mark might keep a fair-sized household in food and fire and lamps for a whole winter.

'I will think about it,' said Ranald, 'I will have to consult with my men.'

'Now or never!' roared the old merchant. He opened his purse, and poured a small torrent of gold pieces into his free hand. 'I can't wait. Your answer, now. Ten gold marks. Yes or no.'

The crew of the *Laxoy* gaped. They had not seen so much gold in all their lives.

Ranald looked at Fiord. Fiord nodded.

'We accept your offer,' said Ranald to the choleric old man.

Just then there was a clatter of hooves along the shore. One of four horsemen blew a horn. The crowd of idlers on the shore scattered like chaff.

The four horsemen dismounted and their leader began to wade out to the ship. He leaned into the water and swam the last few strokes. He pulled himself up into the ship, and stood there in the well with sea splurging and oozing out of him.

Ranald saw that the three merchants were lowering themselves into the small boat as quickly and unobtrusively as possible. Their boatman sculled them towards the small jetty. The merchants did not look at each other once. The old merchant was red in the face as a turkey-cock, and his frail fingers were webbed tight about his purse of gold pieces.

The stranger said, 'I am Earl Sigurd's treasurer. Earl Sigurd heard in Birsay this morning that a Norwegian cargo-ship had anchored in Kirkvoe. What is the cargo? Ah, timber and walrus tusks. And the very best quality. None of your firewood this, none of your buttons for fishermen's coats. Ah, Earl Sigurd will be pleased with this lot. Where is your skipper? I do not see Hakon Treeman. Where is the old rogue? I always like to have dealings with Hakon Treeman, though fate meant him for a poet rather than a merchant-skipper.'

Then Fiord told him that Hakon had died in Bergen a fortnight before.

Sigurd's man said he was sorry to hear that news.

'Now,' he said, 'whom am I to do business with, now that Hakon Treeman is a long cold earth-shelterer?'

Ranald said that the sale of the cargo was in his hands.

'Well,' said the earl's treasurer, 'I have not done business with such a young merchant before. How long have you been in the trading-booths and in the counting-houses, eh?'

Ranald said that his father Sigmund, whom men called 'Firemouth' on account of his rather hasty temper, had instructed him in trading and bookkeeping. So he knew more or less what he was talking about.

'Well then,' said the man from the palace, 'I estimate the value of this cargo at two marks. I will arrange to have it carried ashore at once.'

'The cargo is worth much more than two marks,' said Ranald. 'If we do not get eighteen marks for it, we will sail on to Aberdeen or Grimsby or London, and sell it there.'

Earl Sigurd's treasurer looked hard at Ranald, then he smiled. 'I was testing you,' he said. 'You are a true son of Sigmund Firemouth, that scoundrel. Now then, we will stop jesting and talk sense for a change. Seven marks – I think that is a fair offer.'

All the crew of the *Laxoy* nodded. With seven gold marks divided among them, they could be drunk for a whole winter in the ale-houses of Bergen; or better still in the taverns of Dublin, where the ale was dark as midnight and richly frothed and yet had a star or two hidden in the depths of it.

'Seven marks is not a fair sum,' said Ranald. 'Men died of cold cutting down those trees. Men drowned among ice-floes, battling with walrus for this ivory. We ourselves had a difficult voyage between Norway and Orkney. I will accept nothing less than fifteen marks.'

The earl's man looked at the ends of his fingers for a long time.

When he looked at Ranald again, his voice was cold.

'You are a clever youth,' he said, 'but arrogant. Take care that your cleverness is not your undoing. I ask you to consider this, Ranald Sigmundson. I have only to say a word, and this entire cargo, and the ship too, will be impounded. It so happens that Earl Sigurd of Orkney does not think highly of King Olaf of Norway. Earl Sigurd has an old score to settle with King Olaf. It could be that this ship and its cargo would go some way to settle the score.

'However, you are men and you have four sea-craft to work at for a living. Earl Sigurd would not wish to harm honest sailors merely for the sake of tweaking the King of Norway's nose. What sum did I mention? Seven marks was it? I will make you a most generous offer. Earl Sigurd, I think, will not be pleased with me for the extravagance. Ten marks.'

The crew of the *Laxoy* gaped with joy.

Fiord, for all that he was in pain from the heavy blow he had got from the sail-beam, nodded vehemently.

But Ranald said, 'Your offer seems to be on the low side still. I think some sum between fifteen and ten might satisfy us both. Think what bosses Earl Sigurd would have on his shields from ivory of such quality. Think of the harp-frames. Think of the scalloped axe handles when he rides into battle . . . Twelve marks. I think twelve marks is a fair sum.'

For a while the earl's treasurer said nothing.

Fiord and the sailors looked anxious, as if this youngster (whom they all liked nevertheless) might have got them into deep trouble.

The treasurer glared full in the face of Ranald. Then he threw back his head and vented a full-throated shout of laughter.

'Oh boy,' he said at last, 'you'll go far! I'd best be careful of my job. I see that you're a better bargainer than me. I hope Earl Sigurd doesn't get to hear about this, or he'll have you for his treasurer, and I'll have to sing about the roads for my keep . . . Twelve marks let it be. I don't know what the earl will say to me. Never has he bought such an expensive cargo. And yet it is the best of timber, just what he wants for his new Hall in Birsay. And as for the walrus tusks – Sigurd's eyes will widen with pleasure when he sees the bales.'

Then the treasurer opened his purse and he dropped twelve gold coins, piece after ringing piece, into Ranald's hand.

Then he turned and signalled to the retainers on the shore that the cargo must be unloaded at once.

Soon a dozen labourers from the village of Kirkvoe had been recruited to bring the cargo from ship to shore. The men of Kirkvoe had a barge for this purpose, with ropes attached, and after standing throat-deep in the water beside the *Laxoy*, some hauled themselves on board and manhandled the timber and tusks on to the barge, spreading the load evenly so that the barge was not upset, and then they dragged the barge to the shore, straining at the ropes. Nine times the operation had to be repeated, before the cargo was stacked above the high-water mark and all the time the labourers were goaded and insulted by the earl's horsemen. 'Lazy dogs!' they were called. 'Stupid oxen!'

Once an immense fardel of timber toppled into the sea, and then the horsemen raged, 'You'll hang for this, you oafs!' But their rage was tempered with a coarse joviality, so that the workers knew that their necks were not in danger. The spilled logs were quickly dragged ashore. At the end of the morning the cargo stood in piles, beside the wooden carts that had been hired from the shore-porters.

'Rough roads between here and Birsay,' said Fiord. 'It seems to me that it would have been easier to sail round to Birsay in the ship and unload there.'

The sailors made no reply to this. They were passing the twelve marks from hand to hand, gloating. They were rich men forever! They were misers! They were prodigals! Prem the cook cupped the coins in both his hands and raised the hoard over his head and rang the coins together three or four times like a bell.

The sailors grinned with greed. Their eyes glittered.

Fiord said, 'Gold brings its own troubles. Soon enough we'll be poor again, and go in patches, and have the old salt in our beards in winter.'

Meantime the earl's treasurer had taken Ranald aside.

'When you were in Norway, did you hear any word of Earl Sigurd's son, the boy Hund who is a hostage in the court of King Olaf?' he said. 'Hund was always his father's favourite, and he grieves much for the boy, especially as Hund's health has been uncertain since infancy. It isn't likely, I know, that sailors would know anything about the King of Norway and his affairs and the people in his court. But it may be that you heard this rumour or that along the waterfront of Bergen.'

Ranald said that in fact he had had dinner with the king and his court in Bergen, and he had kept his ears open.

The treasurer said, 'I know well that boys tell lies in order to impress, and normally I would not believe this that you have told me. But you have managed the disposal of the cargo so skilfully that I believe nothing is impossible to you, you impudent young rogue. Even the worming of your way into the king's court, I think you may well have achieved even that.'

'I dined with king Olaf and his court,' said Ranald solemnly, 'and I heard this and that about Hund the earl's son.'

'You sound so grave,' said the treasurer, 'that I fear the news is not good.'

'Tell Earl Sigurd', said Ranald, 'that his son is in high favour with King Olaf, and well loved by all the Norwegian court. He has a good voice and sings in the chapel choir. The women spoil him. When the snow is on the ground, they knit him bonnets and gloves and scarves. Hund is skilful at the chessboard and other fireside activities. The women bring him hot drinks when he coughs and drinks with ice in it when he has a fever. Hund Sigurd is well looked after, and he is happy as a bird.'

'Earl Sigurd will be glad to know this,' said the treasurer.

'Also the priests instruct him in the catechism,' said Ranald. 'He is an apt pupil.'

The treasurer said he did not know what Earl Sigurd would have to say about that particular matter.

'Hund does not ride out with the falcon on his fist,' said Ranald. 'Nor does he climb the streams and fish for salmon with the other young men. Nor does he go out with the hounds when a stag is sighted at the edge of the forest. The truth is, Hund Sigurd is easily tired, and if he over-exerts himself the fevers come on, and then he has to lie in bed for some days until the doctors say his heart-beat is steady again. So now this boy – who has put a kind of enchantment on the king and the whole court – spends most of the time indoors, at the chessboard, or spelling his way through the manuscript of some ancient Norse poem, or having his hair combed and trimmed by the ladies. On a fine morning, they allow him to sit under the apple tree in a sheltered corner of the garden, and then the birds sing about him in the branches. Then the ladies come out to him, one with a honeycomb on a dish, it may be, another with a little ivory flute to make songs for him, another with a little lap-dog that runs barking about his feet. The boy loves dogs – it is not for nothing that he is called Hund . . . Hund passes his days in a web of love and comfort.'

'Earl Sigurd will be glad to hear of this,' said the treasurer. 'But he will be concerned to hear about the fevers and the coughing. There are men who are delicate in their youth, but they grow up to be warriors of note, and they die – if they are lucky – in a battle or a siege or a sea-fight, with only a few gray hairs in the beard.'

'It may be that way with Hund,' said Ranald. 'I only tell you what was told me.'

'But you saw him at King Olaf's table the time you dined at the palace?' said the treasurer. 'You spoke with him, did you not?'

'No,' said Ranald. 'There was a chair set for him beside the king's chair. But word was brought, at the last minute, that Hund had a sudden fever, and the physicians were of the opinion he should keep to his bed. And so, though I was eagerly looking forward to see the young Orkneyman that night, he was confined to his room in the palace, and one lady was putting slivers of ice in his mouth, and another lady was crushing those herbs and roots that cool the blood. I did not see Hund. I thought I heard from time to time, distantly, a distress of coughing.'

'I think I will not say anything to Earl Sigurd about this latest fever,' said the treasurer. 'Only that Hund is the centre of a web of care and love.'

'It would be best to say that in Birsay,' said Ranald, 'no more.'

Then the earl's treasurer left the ship and was rowed ashore.

The laden carts had left for Birsay an hour before. The labourers had been paid their penny each and gone home.

The sailors sat down at the fire amidships to eat their supper. The dream of gold lingered still in their eyes.

'Now that Hakon Treeman is dead without heirs,' they said, 'what is to happen?'

'The *Laxoy* belongs to us now,' they said. 'She is ours by right, this ship,' they said. 'We have worked long and hard on her, for small wages. Now she is ours.'

They began to broach the subject of freebooting again, and piracy, and plunder on the high seas.

But Fiord rebuked them sternly.

'I remember what Leif Ericson dreamed a while ago in Vinland,' said Fiord, 'that gold is a poison that rots the hearts and minds of men. I tell you what will happen if we hold this ship in common. Disputes will blow up on this matter and on that, there will be wranglings and unbridled rages, it will end with throat-cuttings and dumpings in the sea. The profit on this voyage – the twelve marks – will be shared out evenly, but from now on there must be one skipper who will also order the shipments of cargoes here and there, wherever may be most profitable.'

The sailors considered individually for a while what Fiord had said. Then they discussed the matter for a while, their heads wagging close together, and at last Trygg the ship's carpenter got to his feet and said, 'I'm speaking for all. There is wisdom in what Fiord has said. It seems to us that the man with most experience of sea routes among us, and of the behaviour of winds and tides and weathers, is Fiord himself. In spite of him being an outlaw in Norway, we know him for a true and honest man. And so we ask Fiord Elkson to be the skipper and sole master of this vessel *Laxoy*!'

The seamen rose to their feet and cheered.

But Fiord said, 'I am a good enough sailor, and I know my way around all the islands of the northern ocean. But I am not a merchant. I have no skill for trading in the markets, and haggling for a shilling this way and that. You have seen the way that young Ranald Sigmundson conducted business with the earl's man this morning – how he out-manoeuvred him with the greatest skill, so that instead of two marks to share among us we have twelve. I tell you this too, this same Ranald is a most promising navigator, and when he comes into his strength there will not be a more famous captain between Vinland and the Volga. My proposal is this, that we put Ranald in full command of this ship. I myself will be only too glad to serve under him.'

But Ranald said that that was impossible. He had many matters to see to in Orkney, such as the settlement of his father's affairs, now that his mother was a widow, and also he was anxious about his grandfather and the farm at Breckness. 'The last time I saw my grandfather,' said Ranald, 'he sat all day beside the fire, and he could see no further than a vole, and a ploughman had to hold the cup up to his mouth.'

Ranald went on to say that all those matters would take up his full attention for a winter at least. 'But if things have gone badly with my mother and with the farm at Breckness, so that I am a landless man, it may be that when you sail back to Orkney in the way of business, and still need a skipper with knowledge of the market-places, I will be glad to be your comrade once more. Till then, let Fiord be your master and guide.'

Fiord said he would do his best, but he greatly feared what fate might have in store for the *Laxoy* and her crew.

That same day the three Kirkvoe merchants had themselves rowed out to the *Laxoy* once more – the cunning one, the laughing one, and the old ill-tempered one. Now they no longer looked at each other furtively, as before. They seemed to have entered into some kind of pact.

The sailors helped them into the *Laxoy*.

'Ah,' said the crafty one, 'your cargo hold is empty again. That is good.'

Fiord said that, owing to the merchants' hasty departure earlier, just as they were beginning to bargain amicably, they had had to sell their timber and walrus tusks to the earl's man. A fortunate business for the *Laxoy* in a way – they had got a very good price for their merchandise.

The cheerful merchant smiled, and congratulated them. Then he asked Fiord and Ranald where their next landfall would be. 'May it be another most fortunate voyage for you,' said he, 'but it would be good for us if you were to sail back to Norway seeing that we have a business matter in hand there, in Norway.'

Fiord said that he did not know where fate would take them next. 'As for me,' he said, 'the less I see of Norway, the better. If I so much as set foot in Trondheim or Bergen, I run the risk of being arrested for a rash thing that I did in my youth. I want to end my days in peace, not tied to a rock on a skerry till the sea rises and covers my mouth. So I would rather sail to Iceland or Sweden or Greenland or Vinland or Ireland or Spain or Sicily than to Norway.'

The old merchant snorted impatiently. 'It must be Norway or nowhere,' he said. 'We have this order from certain master masons in Norway. They have heard of the high quality of red sandstone blocks taken from the quarries in the island of Eday. I think it is a church they want to build, for the bishop has put his seal on the letter also. So they want a quantity of this Eday sandstone, and urgently. Likewise they make mention of the Stromness granite, which is as hard as a lawman's heart and glitters like stars. So they ask for five hundred blocks of granite in addition to the thousand blocks of red sandstone. Once the cargo of building stone is landed in Trondheim, you will be well rewarded. We have had dealings with those master masons before. They are honest men.'

Fiord said he doubted whether the *Laxoy* was sufficiently strong and deep draughted for such a cargo.

'Well,' said the old curt merchant, 'we offer the freightage to you. Take it or leave it.'

Fiord looked at Ranald. Ranald said he would leave this matter entirely in Fiord's hands, since he was now the master of the ship. 'I think it is better to sail full freighted than to leave port with an empty hold.'

Then Fiord told the three merchants that he would carry the building-blocks to Trondheim.

'Good, good,' cried the crinkle-eyed merchant. 'The carts will start rolling from Tingvoe and Stromness tomorrow.' And he laughed, as though they were all sharing a great joke together.

The foxy-faced merchant said, 'Seeing you have been so well paid for your last cargo by Earl Sigurd's men, you will not be needing a deposit from us, as is sometimes demanded by skippers. The full fee for freightage will be settled in Trondheim.'

Fiord said he agreed with that.

Ranald said, 'The skipper ought to be given a small token fee – one mark, say. I think that would be fair to all concerned.'

The merry dealer laughed aloud. At every pause in his speech he had to pause to wipe mirthful tears from his eyes. 'And how do we know that you sailors will not carry the sandstone and granite to some other port, say Grimsby or Reykjavik or Gothenburg, and sell the valuable building-stones there? Eh? Just tell us that . . .' And he laughed again, as if such roguery was really the greatest of fun, if you stopped to think about it . . .

The merchant with the thin white beard said, 'No, that is unlikely. It is impossible. Who in England or Sweden or Iceland wants a mountain of stone dumped on their waterfronts, if they haven't specifically ordered it?'

Fiord looked gravely offended. 'We are all honourable sailors,' he said. 'If we undertake carriage of a cargo, that cargo is delivered at the place specified, sooner or later according to wind and time and weather. But we have not failed in an assignment yet – I tell you this solemnly – and I have sailed on the north ocean for forty years.'

The merchant with the perpetual dimples in his cheek laughed again. 'Well and gravely spoken, old outlaw,' he said. He made a sign to the foxy-faced merchant, who opened his purse and took out a gold mark and parted with it as if his heart was being torn out by the roots.

III

Orkney

1

Next morning Ranald Sigmundson said farewell to Fiord Elkson and the crew of the *Laxoy*.

He bought a horse from a dealer in Kirkvoe. He rode across the flank of the hill of Wideford and through that gap in the hills of Orphir called Skorradale, and he forded the shallow water at Waithe where the sea mingles its waters with the loch water, and so on over the Cairston brae to the house in Hamnavoe where he had been born and reared.

As he expected, his mother was not living there. A man opened the door, and Ranald recognized him as one of Earl Sigurd's tax-men, who had ridden round twice a year to collect the dues in this parish, and in the parish to the north called Sandwick, and in the islands to the south, Hoy and Graemsay. This tax-man was called Amund.

Amund did not recognize Ranald, he had grown so tall and broad since he left home.

'No,' said Amund. 'Thora, Sigmund Firemouth's wife, no longer lives here. Sigmund was drowned when his ship *Snowgoose* was broken by a great wave between Iceland and Greenland. His son Ranald is lost, too. When news reached Orkney of Sigmund's death, the earl foreclosed on the house and land, for Sigmund left many debts, including unpaid taxes. And Thora his widow was set outside with her few chattels, and the door barred against her.'

Ranald said, 'Can you tell me where the woman has gone?'

The tax-man shrugged his shoulders. 'How would I know?' he said. 'I do not chart the movements of penniless people. She may have gone to her father's farm west at Breckness. But I think that fortune does not stand smiling in the threshold of Breckness either. That old farmer died last winter and there is much trouble there.'

Ranald did not thank the tax-man for the information he had got.

He mounted his horse and rode on the track along the far side of the hill that guards the fishermen's harbour of Hamnavoe, and the hooves splashed through a wet marshland called the Loons till horse and horseman halted on a ridge above a region of fertile farms and crofts. There, down at the sea, lay the large farm of Breckness that belonged to his grandfather. The farm had been in possession of Ranald's ancestors since it had first been settled two hundred years before.

Ranald spurred his horse, and rode down to the field where the barley and oats were growing tall and green now in high summer.

Forty cows moved here and there across the high meadow, and more than a hundred full-fleeced sheep were strewn about the hill called the Black Crag. The hill sloped steeply from its heather summit seawards and ended in a high abrupt dangerous cliff-face.

Three men were working in the Breckness smithy, amid a glare and a clangour, fixing a shoe to the horse called Flame. They stopped work and came to the door when the strange horseman passed. Ranald looked back at them. He had known them well, but now the three farm workers did not recognize him.

'Have a care,' said old Sverr who had been shoeing the horse. 'Whoever you are, don't go near the farm. There are three dogs here that would tear the throat out of a stranger.'

Ranald had been hearing, all the way down from the ridge, the howling and snarling of dogs. Now he saw them straining at the ropes that secured them to the wall of the farmhouse. They curled their lips. They howled. They slavered.

'I have come to visit the good old farmer who lives here,' said Ranald.

'Do you mean Thorkeld?' said Sverr.

'Yes,' said Ranald.

'You must be a great stranger in Orkney', said Sverr, 'not to know what happened to Thorkeld and his farm.'

Ranald said he had been out of Orkney for a year or two. Now that he was back, he wished to pay his respects to the good and wise old farmer Thorkeld of Breckness.

The old blacksmith Sverr began to weep. 'Alas,' he said, 'our good master is dead. Thorkeld is dead. The farm has passed into other hands.'

The other two farm workers shook their heads sadly.

A man came out to the door of the farm and bade the three dogs stop their howling. The man glared at Ranald, and then went inside again.

'It is a bitter story,' said Sverr. 'Truly Thorkeld and his folk have fallen on evil times. For, first, Thorkeld's son-in-law, Sigmund the merchant, was drowned in the ship *Snowgoose*, between Iceland and Greenland, and the boy Ranald too. Ranald was Thorkeld's only grandson, and this farm was to be his when old good Thorkeld went down to mix his dust with the dust of his forebears. So, that news was a hard thing for Thorkeld to bear. Then Thorkeld's daughter Thora, the widow of Sigmund Firemouth, came over the ridge from Cairston carrying only her spinning-wheel and lamp and cheese mould. The door of her Hamnavoe house had been locked against her by the earl's tax-man. "Sigmund has left too many debts," Thora was told. "He borrowed heavily to have the ship *Snowgoose* built. The house and furnishings are no longer yours. Go where you will." So Thora came to stay here with her father. And her father gave her a fair welcome, and said that now she would be mistress of the house, and the farm and the animals and the gear and the fishing boats would be hers after his death. "And if it so happens", said old Thorkeld, "that some good man wants to marry you, I will not stand in your way, for I know that you will never sully this farm of Breckness with any evil or worthless husband . . ." Thora said she had not liked Sigmund her man over-much, but that other men might turn out to be worse, and so she would be content to remain a widow. "Yet it is right", said the old man, "that one of our own blood and lineage should work this farm after we are dust. The dust of a farm is richer for the dust of those who have watched over the plough-times and the harvests . . ." Thora said she would think about it. A week later old Thorkeld went out in the snow to see to a sick calf in the byre, and he stayed there overlong with his lantern and his healing hands – for, sir, he was ever a kind man, even to his beasts – and that same night he sat shivering and sweating before the fire. It seemed that shadow after shadow entered into him. But he would not go to bed. "For", said Thorkeld, "I think it is a poor kind of a death, to die in bed. I would rather die when my hands and my head are busy . . ." Towards morning the old man said, "Light the lantern for me once more. I want to go out to the byre to see how things are now with Buttercup the calf . . ." They urged him to stay near the fire, and to drink the bowl of hot ale they had prepared for him. But

73

Thorkeld took the lantern and walked slowly out through the door towards the byre. Then soon afterwards, Thora and the house women heard a cry, and when they ran outside the farmer had fallen in the stall beside Buttercup. He was dead. Thora was quick to blow out the lantern, lest the byre and the whole steading go up in flames . . .'

Here old Sverr the blacksmith could not contain himself any longer, but he broke out into another fit of weeping.

The man who owned the three savage dogs now approached Ranald. The farmworkers went here and there about the outhouses; the old man went, still weeping softly, into the smithy.

The man said to Ranald, 'Who gave you permission to trespass here? This is a private farm. If you have any business, say it now.'

At that, the three dogs set up an insane howling and yelping.

'I was hoping', said Ranald, 'to have some friendly words with the farmer who used to live here, Thorkeld.'

'Thorkeld was an old man and he is dead. He died in that byre over there. He fell among the beasts and died. The old and feeble must make way for the strong. And that's the way it was with old Thorkeld.'

'But Thorkeld had a daughter called Thora,' said Ranald. 'It seems to me that Thora would have inherited Breckness.'

'I do not see what business this is of yours, stranger,' said the man. 'Thora Thorkeld's daughter owns the farm, but she is a weak woman, unused to the management of a big farm, and so I am overseeing it for her until such time as we both come to a better understanding. I am hoping that the widow will marry me soon. After that, the farm will be ten times more abundant than it was in the last days of old Thorkeld, who was lazy and stupid in addition to being old.'

And the three dogs stretched their throats and began howling again.

'Yet Thora had a son, and by rights he should be managing this farm on behalf of his mother,' said Ranald.

'Dead,' said the man. 'Drowned among the ice-floes off Greenland, himself and that bully and scoundrel of a father of his, Sigmund who owned the ship *Snowgoose*. So he is out of the story, that boy. Even if he had been alive, he would still be incapable of managing a big farm like this.'

'Things often turn out otherwise than we expect,' said Ranald.

'I don't see why I should be telling all these things to you, a stranger,' said the man. 'I have told you what I know. Now I have work to do. It is no easy thing, keeping the farmworkers of Breckness at their tasks. I wouldn't linger round here, stranger, if I was you. My three dogs have small liking for snoopers and vagabonds.'

The dogs growled deep in their throats. Hot saliva dripped from their jaws.

'Tell me one thing more,' said Ranald. 'The woman Thora, who rightfully owns this farm, where is she now?'

'She lives in that hut on the side of Black Crag,' said the man. 'She keeps a few goats and a pig. It is a rather poor life for her, especially as she is used to more refined ways. Twice I have asked the woman to marry me, and twice she has refused. I think, once the winter winds begin to howl through the cracks in her door, she will change her mind and say "Yes". Then she will be installed in Breckness, as keeper of the hearth and baker of bread and mistress of the six girl-servants, besides being my wife. Things will go well here in Breckness after the marriage.'

Ranald looked towards the hut on Black Crag, and there was a woman in a dark shawl filling a straw basket with peats from the peat-stack at the end of the hut. And the dog Glen, that had belonged to his grandfather, was running here and there in the heather. The sheep had grown used to Glen, and were not afraid.

'That is how matters stand,' said the man. 'It must be obvious that a strong man is needed to farm Breckness. As soon as I heard that old Thorkeld was dead, I rowed over from Hoy with my dogs, and I spoke for a long time at the shore with the woman Thora, urging her to take me as her farm manager. She was very high-handed with me. It was too late then to row back to Hoy, so I walked up to the house and sat at the fire and told the six girls to bring me fish and ale. And here I have been ever since. And here I hope to be for the rest of my days after Thora has agreed to the marriage.'

'It is a good story, if somewhat unpleasant,' said Ranald. 'You have not done me the honour of telling me your name.'

'I don't see', said the man, 'why I should give my name to any tramp who happens to be passing through this farm. But I'll tell you, and then let you go. My name is Harald Thorn – it is a name not unknown in northern seas.'

Ranald knew well the reputation of the man Harald Thorn, it was spoken about in hushed voices in all the farms and fishing-bothies of Orkney and Shetland and Caithness. Harald Thorn had been a forecastleman on the viking ship *Sea Wolf* that had prowled round the coasts of England and Ireland and Brittany for seven years, and done much damage in the delicate golden web of lawful sea trafficking. They were outlaws of the sea, these sailors, in every kingdom in Europe. But nothing, it seemed, could stop their summertime depredations – for always they fared out when the days brimmed with light, and lawful cargoes were being shipped here and there in the calm seas of summer. In winter, the vikings would hole out in some hidden bay or creek in the broken west coast of Scotland, and there they stayed ashore and hauled *Sea Wolf* into some cave, and careened her and got her ready for more piracy in late spring.

The story went that the skipper of *Sea Wolf*, a Swede called Berg, had fallen out over some division of spoils with his forecastleman Harald Thorn, and had set him ashore on the island of Hoy. There Harald had been a nuisance to the farmers for some months. They were glad when one morning he had taken one of their small boats and rowed out into the Sound with his three dogs, and then he had steered round the small island of Graemsay and they had lost sight of him – for good, the Hoy men hoped.

Now here he stood before Ranald, transformed from a sea-pirate into a land-pirate.

It happened then that the dog Glen came bounding down the steep hill and leapt the dyke and ran towards Ranald. The dog barked joyfully and ran about Ranald in circles, then it stopped and licked Ranald's fingers. They had once known each other well, the young man and the dog.

Harald's hounds raged and frothed at the sight of the farm-dog Glen. They strained at their ropes.

Thora, Ranald's mother, stood with her peat basket on her shoulder and looked at what was passing below. She did not know, either, who the young stranger was with the faint gold moustache on his lip.

'Now that you have told me your name,' said Ranald, 'it is only courtesy to tell you who I am. My name is Ranald Sigmundson, and my mother is Thora, Thorkeld's daughter, who owns this farm, though she seems to be little better than a goatherd here.'

Harald Thorn said, 'I have heard of ghosts, but I don't think I am talking to a ghost this day.'

Ranald said he hoped not to be a handful of dust and a ghost for another fifty years.

'Now,' said Harald, 'it seems to me that there's no room here at

Breckness for two men like us. Would you like to put it to the test of fighting – axe and dagger? It would be fair enough. You are a young man coming into your full strength, and I have been sorely battered and scarred by twenty years at sea. The best of my strength has run out. It would make a good contest. We will name a day. The people of the seven parishes would flock to see that fight.'

Ranald said that he did not see why he should fight for his own farm. 'I advise you', he said to Harald, 'to put your three monstrous hounds in the rowing boat you stole from a Hoy fisherman and go somewhere else. No, now that I think of it, you would be a nuisance wherever you sailed, and a disturber of the peace. The best thing that could happen is this, Harald, that you rowed out west to where the tide and ocean meet, with a great noise of waters. There a wave will rise higher than your mast, and you'll make a passable meal for crabs and mackerel.'

Harald laughed, and said it was a great pity. He had been looking forward to end his days on land, a prosperous farmer here in Breckness. 'That, it seems, is not to be,' he said. 'In my experience, what one plans for carefully and with forethought turns out to be sand or smoke. When a man's luck begins to wane, it must run out to the last grain. So, Ranald Sigmundson, I will be a trouble to you and your mother and this farm of Breckness no longer. I will leave the place before sunset.'

'I wish you well then,' said Ranald.

'Still,' said Harald Thorn, 'I do not think I will take your advice about rowing into a wave of drowning. The waves have had poor success for twenty years, trying to drown me. The ocean doesn't want me, nor does the land, it seems. A plan has occurred to me, I think I may act on it. There are caves not far from here. It will be no hardship for a man like me to live in a cave, and be a beachcomber. So, I will be a man bound both to the sea and to the shore, and I will eke out a living somehow, with driftwood and mussels and seaweed on the fringes of land and sea.'

By this time, all the farmworkers and the house-girls were standing in groups nearby, listening eagerly to the talk between the usurper and the stranger, for still none of them recognized Ranald, so great was the sea-change in him.

They saw Harald and Ranald clasping each other by the hand, and laughing together.

Then Harald Thorn unloosed his three dogs from the wall, and led them down to the beach where his boat was drawn up, and he rowed round the cliff-face where the caves were.

Then the farm folk saw Thora running through the barley-field – a thoughtless thing to do now that the barley stood so high and green towards ripening – and she came running towards Ranald and threw her arms about him.

Now she knew her son.

Now she knew that Breckness would be farmed by the true inheritor, and the dust of the forebears would not be troubled.

2

Ranald Sigmundson of Breckness soon became known as one of the ablest farmers in Orkney.

It was considered to be a good omen that soon after his return he and his men reaped the heaviest and best crop in the west of Orkney.

He was accepted at once by the other men who had large farms in the western parishes and shares in merchant vessels, both on account of his grandfather Thorkeld and for his own sake. He was thought to be open and straightforward in his dealings, and the women considered him to be very handsome.

Earl Sigurd in his palace in Birsay knew about Ranald and the astuteness of his business dealings in regard to the *Laxoy*'s cargo, and how he had got twelve marks from the earl's treasurer instead of two – a feat no merchant had ever managed before.

Earl Sigurd invited Ranald to visit him in Birsay at Yule. 'We should get to know each other better,' he wrote in a letter to Ranald.

And the earl suggested that Ranald take part in the assembly of the farmers and merchants of Orkney, where many knotty lawsuits were unravelled and judgments made. This 'ting', or parliament, took place every year at a place called Tingvoe, in the northeast corner of the biggest of the Orkneys, called Hrossey or 'the horse island'.

Ranald was asked to take a share in a trading vessel called *Otter*, along with some of the other farmers in the parish. That he did willingly. He offered good advice about what cargoes they should trade in, and the best routes to take, and how best to negotiate with foreign merchants.

Ranald was invited to take command of *Otter* on several trips, but he declined to do this. He said that he wanted now to put the farm Breckness in good shape, and make a few improvements. 'Besides,' he said, 'I have had my fill of seafaring. Also, all that handling of gold and silver coins has left a bad aftertaste in my mind. Maybe, when I'm an old man, I'll build a ship and launch out and sail westward. There is a country there still I would like to return to, and it isn't Greenland.'

He was often asked, round the fires at Breckness that winter, about Vinland. But as soon as Vinland was brought up, Ranald would call for more ale to be brought, and then go on to talk about the cod-fishing, or whether the stony hill ground on the slope above Breckness should be ploughed out.

His mother Thora was now the mistress of the household. She was renowned in the countryside for her hospitality. Even when an old beachcomber came up from the caves below with an empty bowl in winter, Thora would seat him at the fire and fill his bowl with broth, and afterwards with fish and bread, and lastly with ale. 'Now, Harald,' she would say, 'don't go searching in the seaweed in a northwest gale, or you'll get your death.'

Harald told how his three wolfhounds had died, one after the other. They had got thin on a diet of fish and dulse and had barked their last barks before midwinter.

3

Just before Yule Ranald Sigmundson rode north to Birsay at the invitation of Earl Sigurd of Orkney.

Earl Sigurd had a fine Hall on the shore of Birsay, and he gave Ranald a hearty welcome.

'It is always good for the earldom', he said, 'to have young eager forward-looking men tilling the soil and improving it, and sending out ships in the way of trade. So all the Orkneys grow prosperous and not so beholden to the king in the east, Norway.'

Sigurd the earl was a small fat man, but he was strong and energetic. He would allow no one to contradict him once he had made up his mind on a certain course of action. Two young men and a child sat at his table for meals. Sigurd introduced them to Ranald as Sumarlid, Brus, and Thorfinn, his sons.

'I have another son, Einar, but he is not here – he is away at sea on some wild business of his own,' said Earl Sigurd. 'We are better without Einar. And I have a fifth son who is a prisoner of the Norse king.'

Sumarlid and Brus were mild courteous young men, and Ranald took to them at once.

Sumarlid loved fine coats and shoes, and his beard was scented and combed. Brus had a sleepy tranquil look on his face, as if all he wanted was to be on the best of terms with all men.

The youngest, Thorfinn, was a dark scowling child. Ranald thought, 'It will be a bad day for Orkney if this blackavized ruffian ever sits in the high seat of the islands . . .' Yet Ranald soon saw that the ugly child Thorfinn listened eagerly to all that was being said, concerning Norway and Orkney and Scotland, and the tensions and treaties and compromises that were continually having to be adjusted between those powers. And sometimes the boy would make some remark in passing, about (for example) the web of little princedoms in Ireland, and how the fertile north coast of France might be settled by Norsemen, and then it seemed to Ranald that the boy Thorfinn showed astonishing sagacity for a child.

Sigurd the earl listened gravely to his youngest son whenever he spoke. The two eldest brothers, Sumarlid and Brus, would chaff Thorfinn gently. 'Nestlings should lie quiet in the nest until they learn to fly,' said Sumarlid.

Then Thorfinn would scowl into his bowl and say nothing for a while.

The earl and the two young men and Ranald talked for a while about horses and verse-making and the coursing of hares.

Once, in the middle of the meal, a servant came in and whispered in the earl's ear. The earl got up at once and went out.

'It is the old Irish mother,' said Brus. 'She has lost a needle, or her pillow is too hard, and so our father has to put things to rights for her. A servant won't do. It must be Sigurd. Sigurd is her lapdog.'

'Either that,' said Sumarlid, 'or Eithne our grandmother has been dropping white-of-egg into a cup, and reading prognostications in the shapes she sees. Warnings, dooms, promises.'

'Our grandmother is a witch,' said Thorfinn, and tore a piece of bread from a loaf and dipped the bread in the honey bowl.

A thin man in a black coat walked the length of the Hall and sat down at the far end of the table and untied a scroll and began to read from it.

'Good morning, Father Giles,' said Sumarlid and Brus.

Thorfinn whispered darkly to Ranald, 'The priest only dares come to table when our father is not here. Our father can't abide priests.'

Sumarlid passed the board of bread and cheese and honey to the priest. The priest crossed himself, muttered a few words and began to eat rapidly, not pausing to speak to or even look at his board-companions. He stuffed bread and cheese into his mouth and chomped his jaws.

Earl Sigurd came in and sat down at the table. He said gloomily, 'Your grandmother has a pain in her head, right here, between the eyes. It is a sign always, with her, of bad news.'

'It is a sign that she should walk out a bit more in the sun and wind,' said Sumarlid. 'She keeps too much in that dark closet.'

Earl Sigurd looked up and saw the priest at the far end of the table. He scowled but said nothing.

The three young men conversed well with one another. Sumarlid and Brus promised to visit Ranald at Breckness.

'I will come too,' said the boy Thorfinn.

'We will be hunting otters and flying falcons,' said Sumarlid. 'Little boys should stay at home and play with shells.'

Thorfinn gave the ale jar a push, so that it fell on the table and the ale ran in a torrent on to the floor.

'Leave the room, sir,' cried Earl Sigurd. 'You are nothing but a trouble in this house. Go!'

The boy Thorfinn rose from his stool and he kicked the table until the bowls and platters rattled.

He turned and gave Ranald a dark smile. Then he ran through the door, in what was more of a dance than a run.

The brothers shook their heads.

'Now', said Earl Sigurd, 'you see the kind of sons I have – a peacock, a pigeon, and a young fierce hawk. There is another, Einar, a stupid greedy raven – I'm always glad when Einar isn't at home. What's to become of Orkney, after I'm dead? Misrule, anarchy, tyranny. Take your choice. Fortunately, I have another son, who is at present detained as a guest at the court of King Olaf in Norway. Hlodver his name is, but I call him Hund, because he is like a coursing dog, faithful and swift and true. In my son Hund I have placed all my hopes. Hund will rule here in Orkney after me. In a way, his courtly imprisonment in Norway will have done him good, in that he will have learned chivalries and accomplishments he could never have achieved here in the bleak

81

Orkneys. The thing I mistrust is this, that he – my dear Hund – has been lured away from the old gods who have been so good and so bounteous to us from the very beginning.'

Here Earl Sigurd gave a sour look along the table at the priest, who was now at the honey and oatcakes, eating as quickly as possible.

Sumarlid and Brus seemed not at all put out by the slurs their father had cast on them.

'The lost coin has always the purest gold in it,' said Sumarlid.

'Might-have-been is a beautiful maiden compared to Has-been the Scold,' said Brus.

The brothers laughed.

'It is a great pity', said Earl Sigurd to Ranald, 'that you did not see my boy Hund in Norway. He was a little indisposed, I hear, when you were there. It often comes about that the most talented men are delicate in their health. But in the end they are the ones who make the oceans and the shores resound. The sagas and the poems are starred with the names of such as Hund Sigurdson. May he return to us soon . . .'

The priest whispered to Brus to pass the ale pot to him. 'I have bits of sticky bread in my teeth,' he said.

The earl glared at his chaplain.

Then, towards the end of the meal, Earl Sigurd began to unfold an intricate political situation in Ireland. Ireland, it seemed, was a patchwork of little Norse kingdoms and Celtic kingdoms, with shifting alliances and wars breaking out here and there. 'Now,' said Earl Sigurd, 'it seems the Irish have reached some kind of a settlement. They have appointed a high king, a very able and just man called Brian Boru. Most of the small princelings have sworn allegiance to King Brian. But, naturally, not all of them. The Irish are famous for factions and fratricidal feuds. So there is a loose alliance of princes and chiefs opposed to Brian Boru. The time is coming on fast to an outbreak of war in Ireland. Already the opposite factions are gathering in as many allies as they can, by persuasion and bribery. Oh, I have been approached, no doubt about that – Orkney is a powerful weight to throw into the balance. As far north as Iceland the rival envoys have gone, and young promising men have had torrents of silver poured over their hands. The envoys have come here to the palace too, separately: they have spread out maps on this table and promised the Earl of Orkney this rich piece of Ireland and that. I am greatly tempted to rouse the levies here in Orkney. There is the promise of great fame and enrichment. I will be honest with you, Ranald Sigmundson: I think that in the end war brings more evil than good in its train. So I am half resolved to stay at home and rule my earldom in peace. How could I leave Orkney in the hands of these three sons – the peacock, the pigeon, and the young fierce hawk? Worse still would be Einar the raven. But if I stay at home and keep out of this Irish war, I will be held in contempt by every Norseman of note between Iceland and the Scillies. Every petty chieftain and lordling will give me the cold shoulder . . .'

The earl looked troubled.

Sumarlid and Brus had pushed their plates and goblets away and were setting out ivory chessmen on the table, into which a lacquered chessboard had been inlaid by the carpenter.

The priest had dared to carve himself a slice of smoked mutton, and he dragged another chunk of bread out of the long crusted loaf.

The priest knew that once the earl was launched into politics, he could eat in peace.

'The priest has a large appetite for such a thin man,' thought Ranald.

'Something stronger urges me into Ireland,' said Earl Sigurd. He dropped his voice. 'It is the mockery of my mother,' he said. 'I dread it worse than dragons,' he said, 'the bitter scorn of Eithne my mother.'

The round red face of the earl looked drained all of a sudden.

A man smelling of the sea came in and whispered into the ear of Earl Sigurd.

The earl got to his feet. 'No,' he shouted. 'It can't be! There must be some mistake.'

He banged his fist on the table.

The two sons paused in their game of chess.

The priest took the mead cup from his mouth.

The sailor took a scroll from inside his coat and handed it to Earl Sigurd. Ranald recognized the royal seal of Norway.

'I can't read,' said Earl Sigurd. 'I've always been too busy.'

He called to the priest at the far end of the table, 'Make yourself useful for once. Read what the King of Norway writes. Have a care for what you say.'

The priest wiped the crumbs from the corner of his mouth with his sleeve, and he leaned forward and took the scroll from the earl.

The priest sat and scrutinized the message, from beginning to end, his lips moving silently.

'Is it good news, or bad?' said Earl Sigurd.

'It is good news, in a way,' said the priest. 'It can be said to be very good news, what the King of Norway has written here.'

'It is about my son Hund, is it not?' said the earl.

'Yes, my lord, it is about Hund.'

'This Norwegian skipper says Hund has been gravely ill. So what is the good news? That Hund is now recovered?'

'My lord, it is good news, in the spiritual sense, when a soul has quit this vale of tears.'

'Be plain with me. Is Hund my son living or dead?'

'The king's secretary writes here that the young man Hlodver Sigurdson of Orkney, called Hund, died on the third evening of the new moon. He is buried in the new church at Bergen. He was given full honours and a requiem Mass. The royal court was in mourning for a week.'

The two young men, having heard that their brother was dead, went on with considered movements of the chesspieces.

'Requiescat,' said the priest gravely.

Earl Sigurd stood silently at the end of the table. His face, that had been gray as ash to begin with, now began to flame like a forge.

He pointed to the priest. 'You!' he shouted. 'Get out. Shut up your chapel. If you are not up and gone from this palace, sir, it will go badly with you. See to it. I don't care where you go. You can sail back with this envoy to the tyrant Olaf in Norway. I see now that I did a foolish thing, renouncing the gods of my people – the one-eyed Thunderer with the owl of wisdom on his shoulder. I did wrong, and so I am punished. My dear son, my Hund, is taken from me. Forever and forever.'

Earl Sigurd, his eyes brimming, his beard a galaxy of tears, went blundering out of the hall into the dark corridor outside.

'The names of the newly dead have always a dark music woven into them,' said Sumarlid. 'The names of the living are uttered mostly with malice and spite.'

'Requiescat,' said the priest. 'The earl your father will get over this. As for me, I was never welcome here. I think I ought to ask the Birsay fishermen to row me over to Scotland later today. I have few possessions, it will not take long for me to get ready. I will leave the key of the chapel here with you, Sumarlid. I hope at least that the prior in Moray will be pleased to see me.'

The priest bowed briefly to Sumarlid and Brus and went out. The brothers paid no attention to him.

The scroll announcing Hund's death lay on the table. Ranald glanced at it. 'We have to tell you, Sigurd, Earl of Orkney, that your son, Hund, or Hlodver, is dead. We wish that you had seen the solemn throngs that passed, one by one, up the steps to the catafalque, and crossed themselves, and so came down again, each face made pure by grief. Also, about the catafalque, were seven candles that cast a heavenly radiance. Boys with smoking censers came and went for three days. The requiem bell did not cease its tolling from sunrise to sunset, in the steeple. Prayers for the soul of Hund were murmured, in our new church, in a continuous stream. On the third day the interment took place in great splendour, inside the church. Then a marble stone closed his face from the light forever. He lies with the great ones of Norway, who, had he lived, would have been a great one either in battle or in council. Hereunto we set our seal . . .'

Ranald got to his feet.

The brothers Sumarlid and Brus turned tranquil faces to him.

'I think it is time', said Ranald, 'for me to ride back to Breckness.'

'It will come to war rather than farming soon,' said Sumarlid. 'Our father will sail his warship to join the Norse fleet that will flock into Ireland. The mouth of the Liffey will be black with ships.'

'It is not that our father is a war-loving man,' said Brus. 'He would rather fish in the burn for trout or shoot grouse on Greenay hill. But he is afraid of his mother. She has only to look at him, he is a grovelling dog eager to go here or there, do this or that. The worst death a man can have, in her opinion, is a straw-death. No, he should go among the heroes with a shout of defiance in his mouth. Then the gates of Valhalla will be flung open to receive him.'

Both the brothers laughed.

'Long ago,' said Sumarlid, 'Eithne our grandmother wove a magic banner for him, with a raven embroidered on it. The raven banner would bring certain victory to the army that carried it into battle. But the standard bearer, he was sure to be hewn down in the onset.'

'So, Ranald Sigmundson,' said Brus, 'when you sail to the Liffey, and ride from there into the battle against King Brian Boru, I advise you to decline when our father the earl appoints you at last to be his standard bearer.'

'Unless', said Sumarlid, 'you are particularly eager to go to Valhalla.'

'We will not be sailing to Ireland ourselves,' said Brus. 'We must govern Orkney. We must keep our grandmother company. We must put a hood and a bell on that wild hawk of a brother of ours, young Thorfinn.'

Sumarlid and Brus resumed their warfare at the chessboard.

While Ranald was saddling his horse in the courtyard, a boy came from the Palace and said that the lady Eithne, Earl Sigurd's mother, would be pleased to speak to him.

Ranald followed the boy along a corridor to the women's part of the Palace. Here, in a wide airy chamber, women were sitting at looms or at embroidery frames. But one of the girls was sewing a blue patch on a fisherman's coat. The earl had a dozen fishing boats at Birsay – but surely this was too coarse a task for a young lady of the court . . .

Some of the girls looked at him, others bent demurely over their tasks. Ranald paused to look at the patcher of coats. She seemed to him to be a plain-looking girl. The long fingers drew the needle through the patch, then her hand drooped at the wrist, and the needle fell and made tiny music on the stone floor.

The girl raised her head. She did not look at him. Ranald saw her profile against the window. What was there about a girl sewing workaday patches that gave him a catch in the breath? He longed to say a few jesting words to her – such as 'Why don't you give me a smile or a greeting, like the other women . . .?' But he found that he could not speak a word.

The boy guiding him said, 'Hurry up. It doesn't do to keep the lady Eithne waiting. Do you want to get me into trouble?'

The boy parted a curtain and whispered, 'Ranald Sigmundson is here, my lady.'

The boy drew the curtain wider and ushered Ranald into the lady Eithne's chamber.

The earl's mother was old, but she had a handsome face much given to laughter and good-nature, judging by the fine-etched wrinkles about her mouth and eyes. Her voice too was young and vibrant.

'Ranald Sigmundson,' she said. 'Come and sit in this chair beside me. So, you are the young man who has packed so much experience into his life! You have been to Iceland, Greenland, Vinland, Norway. Well done. If you were to die tomorrow, it would be a good thing, you have done more things than many a greedy snuffling old man.'

Ranald said that he hoped to live for a good while yet.

'And so you will, I know it,' said Eithne. 'You have a rich cluster of years in front of you. I see that you will have great honour in the land, and that you will marry a well handed woman, and be blessed with five children, and you will reap forty harvests mostly good (though there are years when the worm gets in the root and easterly storms blast the green corn). Men will be glad to see you riding to the assembly at Tingvoe, and they will weigh your words more carefully than the words of most speakers. (These parliaments are full of windbags.)'

Ranald thanked her for wishing him well.

'It is by no means a matter of wishing you well,' said Eithne. 'I am telling you for a fact what is going to happen to you, whether you want it that way or not.'

Ranald thought of asking the lady Eithne how she could read the runes of fate. But he thought a question like that might be an impertinence, and he said nothing.

'The worst thing that can happen to a man,' said the old woman, 'is to grow old in stupidity and complacency. The silver hairs come into his beard. He gets aches in his joints, his breath comes short, his children pay no attention to his advice and go here and there about their own affairs. His heart flutters now and then like a bird. He thinks people are mocking him behind his back – and so they are, most like, and little wonder. "Oh dear," says he, some morning, happening to glance at a stone that a shower of rain has made a brief mirror of, "how wrinkled and old I have become all of a sudden. Death can't be that far away. And I have this piece of business to do, and that land deal to settle, and that hawk to buy . . ." So off he goes, our hero, to the niche sealed with a stone where he keeps his hoard of silver. He counts it anxiously, he rings the silver pieces into his open palm, piece after piece till his withered hand is like to snap off at the wrist, it is so heavy. And then his eyes gloat, his face actually shines, he thinks himself to be a fine successful man – this old done creature, who is going to be a ghost the day after next! . . . But he stows his treasure back into the niche, looking over his shoulder from time to time in case one of his greedy ungrateful sons is spying on him. And then, his hoard secure, he shuffles over to the fire, and says he's cold, why don't they pile on more peats, will somebody put a shawl over his shoulders – oh, what a raw cold day it is! But in fact it's a fine bright day in high summer. Then the old wretch gives a cough or two and a groan, and two servants come and heave him into bed and cover him up. And before sunset they're putting the pennies on his eyes ... That, Ranald Sigmundson, is the kind of death that men seem to want nowadays. But it won't happen to you, I'm glad to say.'

The lady Eithne laughed.

Ranald laughed too. He said the lady Eithne had a wonderful picturesque turn of phrase – in fact it was almost like a chant, a poem.

It got darker in the countess's chamber. She struck a small bronze gong. The boy came at once, carrying two lighted candles that he set on the small round table. Then he went out again.

A harp melody drifted into the lady Eithne's chamber. It lingered, then drifted into silence.

'I am glad for the sake of Hund, my grandson who is dead in Norway. It is well for Hund. Hund will never know what it is to die in the sourness and ugliness of age. What is next best, after such a good death? It is for a man to go into the darkness in the full beauty of his strength. He jests, he sings. He doesn't ask death for leave to let him creep through the gate. No, he knocks boldly on the door. He calls, "Here I am, you invited me to call a long long time ago, in fact the very day I was born. It's been a hard way – I'm tired – I'm longing to sit down and rest." Death opens the door to him – no skull wrapped in a shawl either – a woman more lovely than he had ever seen. "Welcome, traveller," she says, "I have a place for you tonight in my Hall. You are young forever."'

There was silence for a while in the room. The candle flames fluttered.

Then Ranald said that what the lady Eithne had said was like the high chanting of a skald.

'I am sending out my son Sigurd to the war in Ireland,' said the old woman, 'before he gets too fat and too old and too stupid. I think he may atone for everything on an Irish battlefield. Here, now, in Orkney he is beginning to make a muddle of everything. There is one grandson of the five who will become a great ruler in the islands. I don't mean the peacock or the dove. I don't mean the half-starved raven in the west either. The young fierce hawk. Watch him.'

Ranald said it had given him much food for thought, sitting there in the light of two candles listening to the wisdom of the countess.

'Go out and get ready to sail with Sigurd to the war in Ireland now,' said the old woman. 'You will acquit yourself well – I can see that – but it will not be given to you to come face to face with Death at the dark door. You are to return to the forty golden harvests.'

Ranald thanked Eithne for her fair promise. He stood up. He drew the curtain aside. A draught came and fluttered the candle flames and one candle went out. The reflection of the new moon trembled on the loch.

'The name of the girl with the needle and the blue patches', said Eithne, 'is Ragna. You will be seeing her again.'

IV

Ireland

1

The Orkneymen who had volunteered to sail with Earl Sigurd to the war in Ireland joined his ship at Scapa.

Ranald Sigmundson put his farm Breckness in the keeping of Stedd, a grieve he trusted, and rode to Scapa.

There was great bustle on the beach there, as the young men gathered with their war gear, and provisions were ferried out to the earl's ship.

There, in the booths above the shore, Ranald made friends with a troop of young Icelanders, lately exiled from Iceland for their part in the burning of the good and wise man Njal in his farm, and all his household with him.

The burning of Njal had been a bitter and a cruel necessity. Now the young Icelanders hoped to make amends in battle.

There was a noise of many hooves on the road above. Earl Sigurd and his men had arrived.

Ranald noticed that Sumarlid and Brus were not in the earl's company.

The earl, among all the young Orkneymen and Shetlanders and Icelanders, seemed a little self-important tub of a man. He went here, there, everywhere, giving orders and countermanding them, his face often russet-red with rage or impatience.

All the preparations for the embarkation seemed to creak and slow down after Earl Sigurd's arrival on the scene.

Over one piece of baggage the earl hovered anxiously as it was being transported from shore to ship. It was enclosed in a long wooden case, fastened with bronze clasps and an iron lock.

'The raven banner,' said Thorstein the Icelander. 'The mother's token of victory and death.'

A silence fell on the boisterous company, as the raven banner woven by Sigurd's mother was rowed out to the ship *Odin*.

In two days all the gear, provender, and weapons were stowed into the *Odin*'s hold. The last horseman had ridden from Deerness to offer himself as a soldier.

The ship *Odin* was a magnificent vessel. Shipwrights in Denmark had been working for more than a year on her. There was even an inlay of gold in the oaken prow. A sculptor in wood had carved a fine figurehead, a Valkyrie. It was a terrifying face, set between laughter and rage and cruelty.

'The farmers of Orkney', thought Ranald, 'will be well taxed for a year or two to pay for this ship.'

The skipper sat in his cabin now with his chart, marking a route through the labyrinthine islands and tides of the west of Scotland.

The skipper told Earl Sigurd that now the *Odin* could sail at any time. There was a new moon. On a brimming tide the ship could sail south between Hoy and Ronaldsay into the Pentland Firth, then hold west through the Pentland Firth until they reached the open Atlantic, and then rounding Cape Wrath turn south among the Hebrides.

Earl Sigurd was scarlet in the face with excitement. He gave orders to weigh anchor.

The hundred young men on board raised a cheer.

In the Minch, Earl Sigurd called a meeting of the men he thought most important in this venture. Ranald was invited into the earl's cabin too.

'Now', said Earl Sigurd, 'I have pledged my support to the King of Dublin, Sigtrygg, in his quarrel with Brian who calls himself the high King of Ireland. This Brian Boru is a Christian, and by all accounts a good and a fair-minded man. But that has nothing to do with it. Sigtrygg, when we spoke together in my Hall in Birsay two years ago, did me a very great honour, and the honour involves all Orkney as well as myself, Sigurd. In exchange for my ship of soldiers, Sigtrygg offered me his mother Kormlada in marriage. Well, a man seasoned in years doesn't place much importance on an offer like that, especially as the lady is a virago of the worst kind who won't be happy knitting stockings for me in winter. I am all for peace in my old age. But not to insult Sigtrygg, I said I would marry his old wildcat of a mother. But now I must let you into a secret. It is this. After we have crushed Brian Boru, Sigurd Earl of Orkney is to be crowned high King of Ireland. All the little kings and princelings from Ulster to Kerry will kneel before me on the golden throne! Imagine that.'

The little fat earl swelled with pride as he uttered those words. It looked so strange that an Icelander standing at the cabin door laughed, and soon they were all laughing.

But Ranald felt ashamed for Sigurd.

The earl flushed as the waves of mockery rippled about him.

He held up his hand.

'I must admit', he said, 'that I do not take seriously the offers of Sigtrygg, either the marriage to his terrible mother or the supreme kingship of Ireland. I will tell you in all seriousness why I am sailing now into Ireland. It is to make some amends to the god Odin to whom I was faithless for a year or two. I trust the ancestral god will not take it amiss that I call this ship by his name. There is a more particular matter. I had a son that I loved well, his name was Hund. Hund was reft from me by the Christianized King Olaf of Norway, and I must think the lad died of grief among the fjords and mountains. Hund was ever a gentle boy, and the low green fertile hills of Orkney were a joy to him. I go now to avenge Hund, and to flesh my sword on Brian Boru, the so-called high king and the Christian.'

Again there was a ripple of mockery in the cabin, to think of this little fat man flashing a sword like lightning, then breaking like thunder through the shield wall that guarded King Brian Boru, the mighty warrior. A young Shetlander threw back his head and laughed loudly.

Earl Sigurd stammered with rage and embarrassment.

Once more he took a grip of himself.

'I don't say', said he, 'that I will do much fighting myself – my fighting days are over. But fighting men, such as yourselves, need a commander, and I will see to the tactics and the overall strategy, once the great battle begins. Let me tell you, I am no novice when it comes to the ordering of a battle array.'

Ranald nodded. Sigurd had been a good soldier in his youth.

'So', said Sigurd, 'I would keep my laughter until such time as you bestride your fallen enemies . . . What I am telling you now is that, as we sail south, powerful allies will flock to join us. I am thinking of the viking brothers, Brodir and Ospak, who will meet up with us in the Isle of Man with thirty ships. I tell you, it will be a mighty invincible fleet that anchors off Dublin. No army will be able to stand against us.'

A young Icelander said, 'Brian Boru is a great soldier. He has a very formidable army, commanded by such men as Kerth the king's foster-son and Ulf the king's brother and the other sons of the king whose names I forget. It will be no easy task, breaking such an army.'

'It will not be easy,' said Earl Sigurd. 'But we are not going to Ireland to visit a fairground and throw pennies to maskers. It will not be a meeting for horse-racing or falconry. It will be a terrible and a cruel battle, make no mistake. We will be victorious – I have an infallible token, the raven banner my mother wove me long ago. The army that carries that standard into a battle is always victorious. That banner is here on the ship – it is safely stowed under lock and key.'

'And who is to carry the banner?' said a man from Caithness. 'The banner will go from corpse to corpse. How many? It's well known, whoever carries the magic flag is cut down even as it flutters over his head. An arrow goes twanging into his throat, or an axe bites into his skull. Who is to be your standard-bearer, Earl Sigurd?'

At this, Earl Sigurd flushed again. He rose to his feet and clapped his hands. 'The meeting is over,' he said. 'We will stop in Barra for a day or two. I think some recruits may join us there.'

Here and there down the long broken west of Scotland a few men joined them, mostly malcontents and outlaws and men anxious to get away from nagging wives and from fathers who drove them too hard in the fishing boats and on stony acres.

They sailed on. Merchant ships turned from the bristling armoured *Odin* and sailed west. Ranald could see, on the Scottish shores and hillsides, men putting shutters on the big houses and herdsmen driving cattle and sheep inland.

A ship like *Odin* had never been on that sea before.

Off the Isle of Man, instead of the promised fleet of thirty, only the fifteen ships of Brodir awaited their coming.

Brodir said that he and his brother Ospak had quarreled.

Brodir said to Earl Sigurd, 'Ospak, like you, earl, is an Odin-worshipper. But he has been impressed by what he has heard of Brian Boru, in the way of sanctity and good governance. A week ago he told me he could take no part in this rebellion. Instead, he sailed off with his fifteen ships to offer his services to Brian.'

Sigurd said he was sorry to hear that. The battle when it took place would be a harder thing than they expected.

'Still,' said Brodir, 'it is worth the cast. Sigtrygg of Dublin has made me a generous offer, after the victory. I am to be high king of all Ireland, and also I will be given his mother, Kormlada, as my wife and queen.'

Sigurd laughed. 'He's a slippery customer, this Sigtrygg. He promised me, last winter in Birsay, the same rewards – the Irish throne and Kormlada.'

Brodir said, 'We will untie that knot when we come to it. Do you not think, Sigurd, that this is a strange business? I am an ordained deacon in the Church, and you have also been baptized. And here we stand, ready to move against the great Christian King, Brian Boru. Yet Ospak, my brother, the pagan – he is flocking with his fifteen ships and his hundreds of men to fight for Brian the Christian.'

Sigurd said that the battle would be very hard now.

He said later to Ranald and the other northerners, as they sailed on south between Ireland and England, that he had not liked the look of Brodir's men. 'They looked to me like the worst kind of vikings,' he said, 'very brave and reckless when the opposition is weak, but they'll run for cover as soon as the dogs start barking.'

Then Sigurd said at the supper board, almost as if he was thinking aloud to himself, that they might have to brace themselves for a repulse, once they landed in Ireland.

The young northerners put down their cups and turned to face him. Sigurd, gray in the face that night, said that many of them would not see Orkney, Iceland, Caithness, or the Hebrides again.

Thorstein the Icelander said that he expected to get a good wife in Ireland, and a fine farm once the victory was theirs and Sigurd was the high king.

The young men laughed and raised their cups.

'What I mean is', said Sigurd, 'that a few of us – maybe many of us – will leave our bodies on the shores of Ireland.'

Ranald Sigmundson thought of his farm at Breckness: it had never seemed more dear and pleasant to him.

It is a bad thing, before a battle, for the commander to contemplate defeat.

Then Ranald thought of a young girl sewing a workaday patch on a coat. A longing for something impossible to conceive took hold of him – and it lingered, a yearning, a tenderness, an image (as the plough breaks the glebe among bitter hail-showers) of the ripening cornstalk.

There was something beyond that, even: a hunger to be in complete harmony with all nature – the plants and fish and animals and stars. The skraelings in Vinland had seemed, of all men, to be a part of that most intricate delicate web that 'the great spirit' had made, in the beginning, for the delight of all his creatures.

'And yet,' thought Ranald, 'it is possible to be made one with nature now, in the time of youth, on an Irish hillside, with battle horns blorting around, and the clash of swords and the shouts of victory and the groans of dying men . . .' Again it came to him, the image of the plough and the cornstalk at Breckness in Orkney, and a girl sewing a patch on a homespun coat.

The image was like the point of a sword touching his spirit.

Ranald found that he was alone at the table on shipboard. All the young men had left and were crowding the side of *Odin*.

On the shore, near Dublin, were line upon line of torches. Shouts, made thin and pure by the sea, drifted from the shore.

The host of Sigtrygg, King of Dublin, had come down to greet the ships.

It was night.

From a church on the shore, faintly illumined with candles, came one fragment of plainchant between two outcries – greeting and vaunt from the soldiers on land and the warriors on shipboard.

Ranald was not entirely alone at the supper board, after all.

There, at the head of the table, sat Earl Sigurd, his face flushed with wine.

'And yet it is impossible that we will be defeated,' Earl Sigurd was saying to himself. 'The raven banner is in the hold. A doomed man will carry it to the threshold of victory, and fall there. But we will all go on to triumph and victory through the broken gate.'

2

There was a brisk market for horses in Dublin.

Ranald managed to buy a young chestnut, and the colt took to him at once, and they became great friends.

And Ranald longed to ride this horse, which he called Liffea, across the hills. (Liffea is the name of a hill-croft at Breckness.)

But he was caught up in a great surge of horses and horsemen that began now to move out of the town towards a headland beyond called Howth.

For there, it was said, Brian Boru had taken a stand with his army.

Again, at intervals of shouting and snorting and stomping of horses, Ranald heard the fragments of plainchant from a church here and there, and the music, though beautiful, seemed to him dark and desolate.

'It is Holy Week,' said one of the Barra men, 'the saddest time in the church year.'

The surge of horsemen gathered to a great wave that broke and scattered on a plain between the River Liffey and Howth.

There was great confusion before the host was sorted into ordered ranks, with yells and blowing of horns.

Then Ranald had his first sight of the Irish army of King Brian Boru.

A great curving shield-wall protected the king. The king was not only unarmed but he had no helmet or shield to protect himself. 'A score of archers could turn this king into a hedgehog in a short time,' said Thorstein the Icelander. 'But I like the look of him. Men would die willingly for a king like that.'

Dag from Caithness who stood at the other side of Ranald said that it was Good Friday, a very holy day in the Christian calendar, and King Brian Boru had vowed not to take part in the battle on that day, 'for Christ had stood defenceless in the face of his enemies'.

Now Ranald was able to see the dispositions of the two armies.

A great honour had been paid to the Earl of Orkney: Sigurd and his host occupied the centre of the 'pagan' host, with Brodir and his vikings on one flank and Sigtrygg, the double-tongued King of Dublin, on the other flank.

Immediately opposing Sigurd were Kerth, foster-son of King Brian, and his army. They seemed well disciplined and eager for what was to come.

There wasn't much discipline in Brodir's viking columns. They were uneasy on land, they would much rather be attacking well laden merchantmen, they jostled each other and shouted as if a sea-gale was blowing through them.

Immediately opposite Brodir stood a commander more like a savage wolf, and his soldiers melled behind him like a wolf-pack hard to restrain. 'You wouldn't think so,' said Hrafn the Icelander to Ranald, 'but that fierce brute of a captain is Brian Boru's brother, and his name is Wolf the Quarrelsome.'

Now the horns were sounding everywhere across the battlefield.

Earl Sigurd was riding here and there in front of his men, his round face aflame with excitement. He twirled his axe in his hand. The blade glittered whenever it caught the sun.

Sigtrygg and his Dubliners, a tangled forest of pikes and swiltering ale horns – for they were tapping a great tun of black beer when they were meant to be forming ranks – eddied back and fore, this way and that, opposite the quiet vigilant columns of Ospak the disaffected viking and the sons of King Brian.

On the outskirts of the battlefield cooks were busy with pots and hunks of meat and fires, and blacksmiths' hammers rang and stammered, and a few hucksters had even set up their booths to sell fish and cheese and religious trinkets. King Brian's cooks had only fish to grill that day, Good Friday.

Crowds had come in from the city and the countryside to see the battle, and in hopes to pick up scraps of booty here and there, after the last horns of retreat had sounded out under the first stars, and before the blood-smelling wolves began to stir in the forest.

A harper went here and there with his songs, among the spectators.

Clontarf was a noisy place that morning. Ranald had never known such babble and outcry and clangings, not along the waterfront of Bergen or at the horse-racing in Greenland.

Brodir's vikings were taunting Wolf's army opposite them, a violent barrage of insults and mockery. 'Be patient,' said Wolf to his men. 'Have great patience. We will have something to say to those sea gentlemen in a short time.'

Brian Boru had gone into a tent to hear Mass, with his sons and the boy Takt who was his cup-bearer.

The noise of Clontarf was increasing by the minute, as latecomers arrived to join this army or that, and more villagers and country folk came from the hinterland to view the spectacle.

Then an extraordinary thing happened. The tangled webs of noise – the horns, the hammers, the taunts and insults, the twanging of bows and hoof-stampings, the hucksters' cajolings and the harp-strokes of the balladmen, the shouts of the captains and the screechings of women on the hillside – all fell silent and one sound only was heard, the small ringing of the sanctus bell in the tent of the priests . . . And then once more the dense web of discordancy covered the morning.

King Brian came from the service and took up his place behind the shield-wall. The boy Takt stood at his side.

The sons of the king went to take up their post beside Ospak, the viking 'renegade', the man who had been entranced by the goodness and majesty of Brian Boru when those things had been told to him off the Isle of Man. Had some Irish laureate enchanted Ospak's ear, on shipboard? Or does the cloud of goodness let its rain fall gently on any heart, as it moves here and there about the world, who knows how?

The heralds had not yet raised their trumpets to announce formally the opening of the battle, when Brodir's men, restless and half-mutinous so far from their ships, moved forward like a ragged wave, howling, against the shields of Wolf (or Ulf), King Brian's brother. And broke there. And half of them were cut down coldly and methodically by the swords and axes of Wolf's men.

The sea-plunderers were unused to such treatment. They wavered. They half turned. Wolf gave an order, his army advanced three paces with the swords raised. The swords flashed and fell. Brodir's vikings turned and ran in confusion and were lost in the small greening wood that formed one edge of the battlefield. Brodir stumbled after them, shouting with anger.

Then Wolf and his men thought of rushing into the wood after Brodir. But not for long. They turned their cold faces and blood-splashed edges and faced Earl Sigurd and his Orkneymen and Icelanders in the centre of the array.

Meantime the heralds were blowing their trumpets. All preparations having been now accomplished, let the arbitrament of battle decide the issue.

The crowds of spectators on the hillside cheered.

Fishermen drying their nets on the shore below came up to see what the noise was all about. They stayed to watch, forgetting the shoals of fish in Dublin Bay. They edged around and sold some baskets of herring to King Brian's cooks.

Now one flank of Earl Sigurd's army was completely exposed, after the defeat and flight of Brodir's men.

The Orkneymen waited for Ulf Hreda (Wolf the Quarrelsome) to attack them, or for Kerth to attack them frontally. The odds had shifted against Earl Sigurd.

But it seemed that Wolf and Kerth, King Brian's foster-son, were in no hurry. Ranald saw them consulting with each other, pointing here and there, turning their faces to look up at the sun, wetting fingers to test the wind, often sending a horseman to the shield-wall where King Brian sat.

The centre of the battle was otherwhere now. Sigtrygg, King of Dublin, was embroiled with Ospak and the two sons of Brian Boru.

The battle on this front was much harder than the opening affray. The columns mingled and locked and swayed this way and that, with screams and yells and the clash and clang of armour.

Things were going ill with the royal Irish army. Word was brought by a horseman that both of King Brian's sons had been hewn down, fighting side by side. The horseman rode by a roundabout way to bring the news to King Brian himself. The king covered his face with his hands. The boy Takt brought a napkin to the king.

Still Earl Sigurd and his northerners in the centre of the battle stood and made no movement. Had they stirred to help Sigtrygg, so sorely beset now, both Wolf and Kerth would have fallen on them and drowned them under waves of fire and steel.

Sigtrygg of Dublin, in spite of killing the two sons of Brian Boru, was more and more beleaguered. His men were being pushed back, step by step, towards the sea. Ospak moved forward to lead his men in a last thrust. Those viking soldiers of Ospak were the same sea-tramps as those of Brodir, but they were held together by a more resolute will. Besides, they could smell the sea now, through the reek of scorchings and blood, and that seemed to put an eagerness into them. They surged after Ospak with a great shout, like the clash of Atlantic waves, and Sigtrygg's men scattered suddenly – those of them who survived the axe-storm – and ran this way and that about the sea-banks and the shore.

Sigtrygg, King of Dublin, was himself lost under the ordered tramp of the sea-boots.

And where was Ospak? Leading the onset, his arm had been half-severed by a random sword.

He laughed with joy at the victory, as the blood welled out of his arm. King Brian's physicians led him out of the fighting to a tent with fires and a cauterizing iron. Ospak laughed still, as the doctors tried to heal the wound with the hot irons.

Ospak's men reformed and clasped hands with the Irish soldiers who had followed the two sons of King Brian – now both dead – and this flank, victorious too, turned cold faces towards the cold untried army of Sigurd, Earl of Orkney.

And they sent a horseman to King Brian, to tell him about this great victory on the far side of the field.

And they sent a second horseman to Wolf, King Brian's brother, saying that they had men and swords enough to move strongly against Sigurd of Orkney.

And Wolf the Quarrelsome sent the horseman back with word that they should co-ordinate the attack on Earl Sigurd on three fronts, as soon as the sun had touched its high meridian at noon.

And Ospak, gray faced from the healing fires, and with a great bandage about his arm, agreed to that strategy.

And Ospak sent a horseman under a flag of truce to Earl Sigurd, suggesting that the earl surrender to avoid the frightful butchery that his men would have to endure if they were attacked on three sides.

Earl Sigurd said to the messenger, 'Tell Wolf and Ospak and Kerth that the Orkneymen are not in the habit of running away from bogmen and sea-scavengers.' They did not know such a word as 'retreat', said the earl. Their mothers had not brought them up in wool-baskets. They were here at Clontarf to achieve a victory. If there was to be butchery, let King Brian Boru look to the shambles that would soon take place in his own columns. They were here fighting for Odin and the gods of the north. Odin would lead them on to certain victory.

Then the envoy furled his white flag and spurred his horse back to Ospak.

And Kerth, whose soldiers, like Sigurd's, had done no fighting that day, took three paces forward at the blowing of a horn, and those in the first three ranks fitted their arrows into their bows.

And a breeze of excitement blew through the young Orkneymen and Icelanders in Sigurd's army. This army was now beleaguered on three sides.

'We are like fish in a net,' said Thorstein the Icelander to Ranald. And he laughed.

Earl Sigurd ordered his trumpeter to blow the horn.

He had the long box with the iron lock brought to him. He ordered the steward to unlock it.

Then Sigurd lifted the raven banner out of the box and he said to his standard-bearer, 'The army that marches under this banner can't be defeated.'

Storr the standard-bearer raised the raven aloft. It shook out, blotting out the sun, and the linen fluttered in the wind as if the raven were stretching its black wings.

Immediately a shower of arrows fell into Sigurd's army, and Storr the standard-bearer fell with an arrow in his chest and the banner fell with a crash on to the ground.

The earl turned to a young Lewis-man and said, 'Colm, I am bestowing this honour on you, to carry the raven banner.'

Colm the Lewis-man picked the banner out of the dust and held it high so that the whole army could see it.

At that moment Kerth's vanguard moved against the army of northerners, and broke the first line. But the men gave as good as they got, and quickly closed ranks. But when they looked for the raven banner of victory, it was nowhere to be seen.

Then they saw Colm lying dead on the ground with a wound in his head. The raven banner lay beside him.

'Well done,' said Earl Sigurd. 'You have not retreated by as much as a foot. It seems the raven is down again, though. You, Veig – do us all the honour of restoring our raven to the wind and the sun.'

Veig had some difficulty in prising the raven banner out of the cold fist of Colm. But soon he gave it back to the wind and the sun.

Now Ranald could see that Wolf's army on one side and Ospak's army on the other side were getting ready to attack them. And Kerth's army immediately in front was regrouping.

'This is to be between hammer and anvil,' said Asmund the Icelander to Ranald. 'And also, the forge is blazing.'

Kerth had a small troop of horsemen with him. The horses were being kept reined in meantime, until it was time for them to pursue the beaten enemy.

Now one of the Irish horsemen took matters into his own hands and charged at the van of Sigurd's army. He was thrust through with spears and axes, but not before he had killed Veig with his own axe.

Once more the banner clattered into the dust.

Now Wolf and his men moved strongly against the flank of the northern army, and made deep inroads, but Wolf paid with a life for every life he took.

'Well fought,' said Earl Sigurd. 'I'm very proud of you. You were ploughmen and fishermen last month, and today you have proved yourselves to be great soldiers. I wish, though, that the raven wouldn't flap and fall so often. Is that you, Olaf from Shetland? I will have good things to report about you, Olaf. You will be a famous man far beyond the sheep-farm in Shetland, Olaf. Olaf, my friend, lead us to victory under the raven banner.'

Olaf shook the dust off the banner. 'I think I will not be back in Shetland at the next lambing-time,' he said. 'What's a lamb or two to this famous raven?'

Now Ospak's archers let fly a shower of arrows into the Orcadian army, and many soldiers were killed and wounded.

The ranks were thinning by the minute, as Kerth's swordsmen hewed at them in front and Wolf's axemen hewed at them from one side, and from the other side flight upon flight of arrows fell among them.

Still the swords of the Orkneymen and the Icelanders rose and fell, in what seemed to Ranald to be a steady regular rhythm, like shining ebb waves against three rocks. It seemed to Ranald that he was a spectator, observing a ritual, coldly. Then he was aware that his own sword was rising and falling between the swords of Hrafn and Asmund the Icelanders – and that, now and then, here and there, an enemy soldier was crumpling in front of him.

The faces about him were all distorted, like hideous masks. And he knew that his own face was twisted with rage and blood-lust and a kind of terrible joy.

The raven fluttered over the host. Then the raven was down in a flurry, among the scrummage of men.

Olaf the Shetland boy said, 'Ravens and sheep never get on well . . .' Then that shepherd knelt on the ground. Ranald saw blood coming out of his mouth. Then Olaf died.

The raven was lost in the mêlée.

Now Sigurd's army was only half the size it had been when the battle began.

'It seems to me', said Earl Sigurd, 'that now an Icelander should carry the raven.'

Thorstein bent to lift the banner but his friend Asmund held his arm. 'Your time hasn't come yet,' he said. 'Leave it.'

'Icelanders aren't used to obedience,' said Earl Sigurd. 'There's too much equality and democracy in that cold place. But still I'll give you Icelanders another chance. Hrafn, raise the raven over your head. It doesn't look like a victory for us here today, but it will be a victory so long as the raven is flying.'

'Do your own dirty work,' said Hrafn. 'That banner has a devil in it.'

'When a man is having bad luck – even an earl,' said Sigurd, 'the very tramps sneer at him.'

Ranald bent and touched the raven banner with his fingers. At once an arrow came down and grazed his wrist, and a bead of blood issued, and trembled and fell, and then the beads of blood fell faster from his wound and fell and made little dusty blobs until the chaotic dance of the battle beat them into the earth.

Ranald was aware that his sword was still rising and falling. The hideous masks crowded ever thicker about him.

'Certainly,' said Earl Sigurd, 'every beggar should carry his own bag.'

He tore the banner from its pole and wrapped it about him like a cloak.

Ranald admired Earl Sigurd at that moment. He had considered him to be, on the whole, a weak pompous vacillating man. Here, now, beset with terrible danger, Sigurd seemed carefree and content, as though he acquiesced utterly in the decrees of fate. The earl walked into the pounding heart of the battle.

The battle closed about Earl Sigurd of Orkney, and he was not seen again.

'I think', said Asmund, 'it is time for us to go. The feast is over. It is an ill-bred guest who outstays his welcome.'

A small knot of soldiers fought their way clear of the throng.

Ranald saw, as they retreated, many young men lying dead and wounded on the battlefield who had sailed south with them in the *Odin*.

Now they were on the fringe of the battle, and about a dozen of them took refuge behind a small knoll.

From there they looked down on the field. The battle of Clontarf was almost over. There was only a skirmish here and there, a despatching and a red mopping-up of prisoners.

There was so much smoke and dust and dying over the battlefield that now, in the late afternoon, the sun shook like a red gout in the sky.

The army of Earl Sigurd and Sigtrygg was now broken and in full flight.

From the knoll, Ranald saw Thorstein the Icelander running like a young deer before Kerth and his men. Then Thorstein stopped. He bent to tie the thong of his boot. Then Kerth and his men were all about him with hungry swords. Thorstein looked up at them and laughed.

'Why didn't you go on running to your ship?' said Kerth. 'You were going much faster than us.'

'I live out in Iceland,' said Thorstein. 'I won't be able to get home tonight.'

Then Kerth laughed, and all the pursuers threw back their heads and laughed too.

Kerth offered Thorstein his hand. He said he would give Thorstein safe passage to the ship.

Now Ranald and his comrades saw from the knoll that the camp-followers had taken possession of the battlefield. They were taking coats from the bodies of the dead soldiers, and rings from their fingers.

There was one group of twelve women, who seemed to keep in touch with each other. Those women went here and there among the dead soldiers, and they did no pillaging. All they did was to kneel beside a corpse and kiss the cold face as if it was the sleeping face of a lover. And so those twelve picked their way, this way and that among the slain, kissing and smiling as they went.

At last the twelve women left the battlefield. Near the river twelve horses were grazing. The Valkyries mounted those horses and rode on north, their hair streaming out on the wind.

Afterwards it seemed to Ranald that most likely he had fallen asleep and dreamed about the twelve hags. He had heard often enough, in his childhood, about the Valkyries who weave the entrails of dead warriors into the loom of war.

Then Ranald was aware of a stirring in the little wood that Brodir and his men had retreated into early in the battle.

Brodir stood there under a tree, fingering the edge of his axe.

Brodir had hidden himself in the branches while his men were being hunted down like wild pigs by Wolf Hreda.

King Brian Boru was sitting alone, except for the boy Takt, behind the shield-wall. The king seemed to be taking no joy in the victory. He looked sorrowfully down at the hundreds of dead soldiers strewn about the field of Clontarf.

The king did not see the slow circuitous approach of Brodir. Brodir ran behind the shield-wall and came to where King Brian sat and swung his axe high. The boy Takt threw up his arm to protect the king. So powerful was the downswing of Brodir's axe that it cut off Takt's hand and Brian Boru's head at the same time.

Brodir shouted, 'Everyone should know that Brodir killed Brian.'

Then Brodir wandered off slowly, like a man with too much wine in him, back to the greenwood.

In a day that had been a cauldron of horror, this cold act of regicide seemed to be the darkest horror of all.

'I think now', said Asmund, 'we should try to make our way back to Dublin and our ship.'

They saw, close by, a chapel. A threnody, a tissue of sorrow, was being woven inside, men's and boys' voices together.

The young northerners heard the hoof-beats behind them. The pursuit was still on. Kerth and a score of his men rode up the slope.

'I think it is time to pay the priests a visit,' said Asmund. Then Ranald and the fugitives went into the dark church, and stood in a group in the furthest corner.

Popule meus, quid feci tibi?
Aut in quo contristavi te?
Responde mihi . . .

The plainchant went on and on as the light lessened, and never had Ranald heard a sound so sorrowful, and black, and bereft of light. And yet the death-song was being uttered with pure and tranquil voices.

There were shoutings outside . . . 'Enemy soldiers – we're looking for them!' 'We think you have some of them in there . . .' 'Orkneymen were seen going in.'

The pursuers' fists beat on the door panels.

The threnody in the choir went on and on, as if the shouts outside were insect-hummings, or rain-beats on the leaded window.

'We're coming in now to root them out!'

Ranald saw, through the gloom of the chapel, a sword-gleam in the door.

The psalm of the bitterness of death went on and on, dark and tranquil.

An old man left the choir stall and went on silent and sandalled feet to the door.

'This is a church,' he whispered, 'a holy place, a sanctuary. Here all men are welcome. Here there will be no swords or trumpets.'

Harsh whispers answered the old priest, and sword rattlings.

The tranquil voices in the choir went deeper and deeper into the darkness of Good Friday: steps down to a tomb, without tapers, feet on the cold spiral, going down into the first and the last death.

'He's right,' said the voice of Kerth. 'King Brian would not forgive us, violating a sanctuary.'

Then Ranald heard the Irish soldiers moving away and the diminishing hoof-beats.

'Bless you, soldiers,' said the old priest in the doorway after them.

'Bless you too, soldiers from the north,' whispered the priest as he went back to his place in the choir. His hand fluttered about his face like a dove.

Now the plainsong had reached the tomb, in the uttermost darkness. The voices ceased. The silence in the church was as heavy as stone.

One by one, the men and the boys left the choir.

The old priest waited till they had all gone. Then he came to the black corner where the Icelanders and the Orkneymen stood.

'They are ploughmen and fishermen, our choristers,' he said. 'They need their sleep. They must be up early. Their voices will be full of joy tomorrow at midnight – you will be hearing a different music, resurrection, in our poor church.'

Ranald said he did not think they could wait that long. They had horses waiting for them in an inn-yard not far away. They had a ship waiting for them at the mouth of the Liffey. They had a long sea voyage to set out on . . . He thanked the priest, all the same, for allowing them the safety of his church, and also for letting them hear the plainchant, that was so sorrowful and so tranquil and so beautiful at the same time.

The old priest blessed them once more. 'There will be small peace for me this night,' he said, 'praying on my two old bones for the thousand young men lying dead down there at Clontarf. And I must pray, of course, for Brian Boru our King, and for Earl Sigurd of Orkney, and for Brodir the viking who was done to death slowly under a tree by Wolf Hreda. Not that, in the country of the dead, kings and earls and famous vikings count for more than swineherds and milkmaids . . .'

At dawn Ranald and his comrades left the church. The wind blew the reek and mingled putrefactions of slaughter towards them as they walked, with a certain vigilance, to the inn-yard five miles away, where they had left their horses. 'Not that the horses were much good to us after all,' said Asmund.

When they got to the inn, it was a burnt-out shell.

No one tried to prevent them from getting to the shore. All the bells in the town of Dublin were muffled, for the death of Christ the King at

Golgotha even more than for the death of their well loved King Brian Boru at Clontarf (the latter being but a shadow of the former.) The people were going about the streets with covered faces. The merchant booths were shut. Only the children ran here and there, laughing, as though they knew of a great joy that the old people had almost forgotten under the weight of so many winters.

The *Odin* still rode at anchor.

But the fifteen ships of Brodir were lying along the shore like great charred birds, and smoke still rose from some of them, and flames were still breaking out of the longship of Brodir.

A ferryman agreed for a penny to row them out to the *Odin*.

The scroll of sailors and soldiers had many missing names. Only about one tenth of the original complement had so far reported back to the ship. One or two straggled back in the course of the morning.

They waited for another twelve hours. Then the skipper weighed anchor and raised the sail. The wind blew favourably from south and east. It was a long time before they got the stenches of the battlefield out of their nostrils.

3

As they headed north, they were greeted at every promontory and ness by an outcry of bells. The steeples of all the little churches of Ireland were reeling with the joy of the Resurrection.

People in Ulster waved coloured coats at the *Odin* as she sailed past.

The men who had sailed south with Earl Sigurd wanted to be set ashore at the places where they had joined the ship – the Solway, and the Clyde, and Barra and Lewis.

The skipper said however he would drop anchor once, off Galloway. 'You will have to find your ways home from there,' he said.

A score of men were put ashore off Galloway.

The southwest wind sat well in the sail all the way to Scapa.

Ranald Sigmundson hired a horse in Kirkvoe and he didn't stop till he arrived at the farm of Breckness.

All he had brought back from the expedition was a silver scar on his knuckle, where it had been grazed by an arrow on the battlefield at Clontarf just as he had bent down to touch the raven banner.

His mother Thora and all the farm labourers and the servant girls at

Breckness gave Ranald a good welcome; all but one girl, Helga, whose sweetheart, Sven the falconer, had left his body in Ireland, and Helga now stood weeping at the end of the barn.

But presently Helga too came into the house where the farmer-warrior was standing at the fire eating new bread, and she said, 'Welcome home, Ranald Sigmundson.'

And Ranald bent and kissed the bereaved face of the girl.

'You'll have great stories to tell us next winter,' said the old blacksmith.

Ranald said he would leave such contrivings to the sagamen and the skalds.

Then Harald Thorn the beachcomber came up from the shore with a handful of mussels to give him, by way of welcome.

V

Breckness

1

A few years went by at Breckness. It was a prosperous time in all those farms of the west of Orkney, with good harvests and winters full of hearth-fires and music and stories.

The neighbouring crofters and their families would often come to Breckness for those winter feasts, especially for the great Yule feast at midwinter.

A few of the crofters would bring their young daughters with them, in the distant hope of a marriage settlement with Ranald Sigmundson. Many a young unmarried woman thought there would be a worse fate than marriage to a handsome prosperous farmer like Ranald.

Ranald greeted all those girls well, but he appeared not to want to select one from the flock. Furthermore his mother Thora showed some displeasure if she thought that a girl from one of the poorer farms was hanging about Ranald too long and too languorously.

Veila from Creya, a very beautiful girl, on the evening of the Yule feast insinuated herself on the hearth-bench beside Ranald, and asked him many questions about Ireland and Clontarf.

Ranald appeared to be unwilling to talk about the battle. He showed the scar on his knuckle to Veila, and Veila took his scarred hand into both her hands and looked at the knuckle for a long time. Then she raised it to her mouth and kissed the scar-silvered wound.

Just then Thora rose from her place and said sharply to Veila, 'The women are getting the supper ready. Can't you see that? It would be a poor Yule feast if all the young women sat all night looking with dove-eyes at my son's finger.'

Then Veila let go of Ranald. Her eyes blazed at Thora. She went back to help with arranging the baked cod and the smoked lamb on the big feast-board.

Thora said to Ranald secretly, 'Why do you not choose one of the rich farmers' daughters? There are girls here from Cairston and Skaill. It's high time you were married.'

Ranald said he had no thought of marriage for a few years yet. There were still things he wanted to do before he took on himself the yoke of marriage.

'Yet you must be married,' said Thora. 'It is two hundred years since your great-great-great grandfather landed on the shore below, from South Norway, and set boundary-stones here at Breckness, and drained and ploughed. The line of good husbandry should not peter out now.'

'Well,' said Ranald, 'I will speak to Rolf Ivarson of Creya about Veila his daughter. She's a good bonny hard-working girl.'

'Have nothing to do with her,' said Thora. 'Veila of Creya doesn't care about *you* at all. All she wants is to get away from Creya, that poor croft, and rule the roost here at Breckness. She would get rid of *me* soon enough. I would have to go back to keeping a few pigs on the side of the Black Crag.'

Then Ranald said that in the end fate would provide him with a bride – 'If it is so written in the runes of fate.'

Thora said, 'That is another matter I want to raise with you. There is still too much talk of fate and the old gods here in the north. It has made men hard and bitter and cruel. Did you not see, in Ireland, a new beauty and harmony in the dealings of men with men? You have told me yourself, Ranald, about that little church where you and the Icelanders took refuge after the battle. It is there, in those churches, that the looms are set for the weaving of the white seamless garment. Here in Orkney, too, the Irish monks have had their little monasteries for a long time. Did the brothers not teach you Latin at Warbeth, and arithmetic and music-making and the psalms and the parables? Everything they do is a new bright thread woven into the eternal tapestry. Not only the monks, Ranald, work at the making of the web – every man and woman is called to the work. Everything we do well, and with goodwill and charity – even sweeping the hearth-stone or mending a fence or giving a crust to a beggar – that becomes a line of light across the loom, and unites our will with the will of God. I hope I will hear no more talk of the inexorable workings of fate, for only cruelty and rage and ugliness come out of such a belief.'

Ranald had never heard his mother speaking so earnestly and so eloquently.

He said he would think about it. Since the death of Earl Sigurd, he said, the priests were beginning to hold their services openly again. Some Sunday soon, he said, he might go to Mass in the chapel at Warbeth.

'As for a wife,' said Thora, 'it seems to me that any choice you make would be foolish and a great misfortune for the farm here. Young men are easily taken by a pretty face and a flattering mouth. Would you agree to this – that I choose a wife for you, a young woman who will be forthright and well-doing and pleasant? If possible, I would choose a comely lass, but good looks are less important than fruitfulness and efficiency and heredity, when it comes to running a farmer's house.'

Ranald said he would be contented for his mother to choose a wife for him. 'But be in no hurry,' he said, 'I have falcons to fly and a fine new chestnut horse to race, and ale-houses to visit in such places as Westray and Ronaldsay. I made many friends here and there on the expedition to Ireland, and we have promised to meet for coursing and trout-fishing. Sigurd's two sons have agreed to let us stay for a month in summer at the Hall in Birsay. A young wife thinks poorly of such goings-on, after the marriage.'

Soon the women came in carrying food on the trencher boards, and ale in great frothing jugs, and the fifty guests came and sat round the broad table. Ranald sat at the head of the table, and Thora his mother at the far end.

Veila of Creya brought round the ale jar. She lingered long at Ranald's place, pouring ale into his mug. Then Thora called, 'Veila, you are wanted at this end of the table with that ale jar. Or better still, stay beside the barrel and fill the jars from there.'

Half-way through the meal there was a knock on the outer door, and a man carrying a small harp was led in to a seat at the hearth.

The man had snow in his beard, and he seemed to be very hungry and cold. A cup of hot ale was put into his hands, but he said he wanted neither food nor drink. 'Nor', said he, 'does this fire warm me.'

Ranald asked him courteously what his name was.

The poet answered that his name was of no consequence, nor where he came from. 'I don't belong anywhere,' he said. 'I go here and there, and I'm not beholden to anyone for food or drink or shelter. The poem is everything. Without the poem, I am a shadow, a husk, a whisper of wind in dry grass. The poem makes me greater than a king. The poem will be sung when King Olaf's tombstone runs out again into dust.'

Some of the guests began to look fearfully at the man, as though he were really a ghost.

Ranald asked what the subject of the poem was.

The poet said it was about the battle at Clontarf in Ireland. But it had nothing to do with glory or heroism, he said.

Ranald said, 'I will be able to say clearly whether the events of the battle are truly celebrated in the poem. I fought in that battle.'

'I know that you were at Clontarf,' said the poet. 'But for all you knew about it, about the true essential meaning of the event, you might as well have been at the horse-fair in Dounby. You are as ignorant of the meaning of war as old Sverr the smith who stayed at home beside the forge and anvil.'

The flames played about the hollows of the man's face, so that whenever he turned his head there were shifting pools of shadow.

A girl shrieked from the pantry, 'His head is a skull.'

The man looked at the girl, and gave her a wintry smile. And the servant girl, who was called Brunna, said, 'I'm sorry. I see that you must have been a handsome man in your day.'

'What concerns me', said the poet, 'is not only this battle in Ireland that was fought between the river and the headland. It is about every battle that was ever fought or that ever will be fought. It has nothing to do with glory or heroism, my poem. It is a very black ballad.'

The farmer of Garth said they expected more cheerful entertainment at the midwinter feast. A poem like that would go down poorly with their bacon and beer. Perhaps the vagrant poet, having now warmed himself, would like to go out and sleep in the cow-shed.

'Listen,' said the man, and again his cheek-sockets brimmed with shadow.

I saw the death-sisters,
    War-maidens, at their weaving
    Of the war-web

On their shuttles under the hill.
    Thither they rode, urgent
    From Ireland, bearing

Bloodied heroes on horseback,
 Many corpses, a multitude.
 The Valkyries unstrung

Each soldier, laid in their loom
 The guts hot with gore,
 Slimed with death-silver.

The hags howled their hymn.
 Under that howe of history,
 The skullhoard, expect
 No root-stir, water-spring.

Old Sverr said, 'I have never heard a war poem like that – never.
Clontarf was a great battle. We knew all about the heroes who fought
there. Brian Boru and Earl Sigurd and Sigtrygg and Ospak. Tell us,
Ranald, whether there is any shadow of truth in what this vagrant has
been ranting about? Or is it nonsense?'

Ranald made no answer.

Then Ranald invited the wandering poet to sit at table and share the
supper with them.

'No,' said the poet, 'my rags and the various stinks that cling about
me from my travels and rough living would offend the ladies. But if a
hunk of bread were to be flung to me here, in this corner, and a cup of
ale, I would eat and drink.'

'Bring more candles with the meat and the mead,' said Ranald, 'so
that the poet can see to eat.'

A small galaxy of candles was set by the women in the corner where
the poet sat, and then everyone saw that it was no death's head that he
bore above his ragged coat, but on the contrary, with the Yule light
laving him, he seemed to be a cheerful young man, who enjoyed his
food and complimented the brewer – whoever she was – on the high
quality of her ale, and he even blew a kiss from his warm red mouth to
Brunna after she had brought more bacon and bread to his plate. And
Brunna, returning with the ale jug, bent and gave him a kiss full on the
mouth.

The poet smiled, and all the folk in the farmhouse laughed and
clapped their hands.

When the poet had finished his supper and licked the grease from his
fingers and curled his tongue about the last ale drops that hung in his

whiskers, he thanked Ranald and all the household.

Then he said, 'Now I will recite a poem I heard this past summer in the island of Uig in the West. It will in a way be like spring – eternal spring and summer – after the winter of the other poem I inflicted on you.'

Brunna and the girls brought more peat and driftwood to the fire. In the light of the new flames the poet sang of that land in the western ocean where is no winter or sickness, no hunger or withering, no battle or black whispers. There, in the island of the immortals, live the people who have endured their lives worthily on earth, the uncomplaining (however hard their lot in life had been), the open-handed and the open-hearted. There is, there, far in the west under the horizon, no puling infancy or tremors of old age, but all are as they were in the full beauty of their days – young men and women forever. There is no work to be done, for the orchard trees are heavy with fruit always and the fields – innocent of plough or harrows or scarecrow – are forever ripe towards harvest. And then the immortal young in that blessed place move along together in small groups, wisdom and beauty come from their lips, a courteous and most lively exchange of utterance, so that their language is nearer to song than to speech. Then it may be that a young man will see from the hillside a barge approaching the shore, and he will tell his companions, and together they will go down to meet the travellers. Behold, the boat is full of the old and the sick, and death-sighs and death-sorrows shake them still, but as soon as the red-faced boatman casts the rope ashore, and one by one carries the death-shaker on his shoulder to that shore, their years and manifold griefs fall from them, and each one – man and woman – is as lissom and comely as in the flower of his earth-time. And with great astonishment and joy they look about them, and presently the people of the island greet them, and link arms with them, and kiss them, and give them each one the immortal fruit to eat, the apple that Adam has not tasted . . .

There was a long silence after the poet had set his still trembling harp at the wall, then the poet got to his feet and they saw that he was indeed a young man, hardly more than twenty, for the flesh of his hands and neck was firm and fluent (if somewhat dirty). 'Well,' said he, 'I see I haven't moved you to hand-clappings or cries of encore. But I hope this poem has pleased you more than the other. Both poems are but the two sides of a single coin, man's price and man's prize, long sorrow and

116

lasting joy . . . It is a wild night outside, wind and blizzard. I would be glad of some straw in your byre to sleep on. I'll be gone again before the earliest riser is astir. I have to travel the length and breadth of the world with my two songs, and it is a long road.'

Thora said the poet would be more comfortable in a chaff-sack beside the fire all night.

But the poet said that, in a way, he would consider it a great privilege to sleep among the oxen. 'The greatest word-man that ever came on earth slept his first night on earth among straw and innocent beast-breath. And it was this very night, Yule.'

Then he thanked Thora for her hospitality, and wished the whole company a merry feast.

Then Ranald lit a lantern and lighted their guest out, among falling snow, to the byre.

2

The spring sowing was over. The animals were put out on the hill, beyond the fail-dyke that separated the cultivated land from the pasture.

Ranald rode to the assembly at a place in the northeast called Tingvoe, where disputes among the leading men in Orkney were aired and sometimes settled, and land taxes were levied for the year to come, and the earl consulted as to the drift of affairs within the shifting alliances of Norway and Scotland and the earldoms in the west.

The joint earls were then the two sons of Sigurd, Brus and Sumarlid, and they were pleasant and easy men to deal with – weak men, some of the farmers said, who had no appetite for the hard decisions and implementations proper to a good ruler.

With them to the parliament at Tingvoe, Brus and Sumarlid brought their younger brother Thorfinn. The ugly black-headed boy listened eagerly to the debates and the judgments, and he was altogether more eager about the affairs of the earldom than his two easy-going brothers.

There were rumours that the fourth brother, Einar, would soon be in Orkney to stake his claim to a share in the earldom.

This was thought to be bad news; a divided earldom was always a source of trouble. Then, always, the king in Norway sent ships from the east and imposed his will on the earldom.

117

Even without the intervention of Einar, it was thought that trouble enough was in store for Orkney, with two earls that could be swayed by any wind of fancy or flattery, and a young earl growing up who could, men feared, force his will on any faction or situation, and make his own pattern of events, whatever the chief men of Orkney thought.

The councillors and debaters at Tingvoe began to think kindly of their former earl, Sigurd, who had died in the great battle in Ireland, though most of them had laughed behind their hands at the fat man while he ruled over them.

Sumarlid and Brus drew up an easy tax-roll, and everyone in the assembly laughed and clapped their hands. 'We have never had better earls than Sumarlid and Brus,' they said.

Then the scribe of the two earls read out a proclamation to the effect that henceforth there would be no more war expeditions. That last war in Ireland had bled the earldom dry. Now, cried the scribe as he unrolled the scroll, all their energies would be put to the things of peace, such as agriculture and trade, and in that way the Orkneymen would get more wealth than their ancestors had ever known.

The older men at the assembly looked doubtful – when had there ever been peace? And in any case war and the threat and the promise of war had kept always a fine edge on their spirits and enhanced their joy in living . . . But the younger men nodded and smiled and clapped their hands.

The boy Thorfinn curled his lip in a sneer. His milksop brothers were going too far.

The proclamation went on. 'Hitherto the men of Orkney have passed the early summers in viking cruises, and some ships have come home laden with spoils and others have come home like ghost-ships manned by a few skeletons. You are free men, and there is no law as yet to prohibit piracy, but we urge that henceforth no ships be built for viking cruises westward and southward, but only merchant ships for peaceful trade betwixt here and Iceland and Norway, Scotland and Ireland and France. Let the young men spend their summers hunting and hawking and transmuting their energy into the arts of peace.'

Most of the younger men were silent at the end of the proclamation. Some of them had viking ships half-built in the stocks. Idle empty summers lay before them. But a few of the older men applauded; so much of their wealth and of their fathers' wealth had gone to the building of those cruel ships and the planning of those hazardous voyages.

It was not all judgments and edicts and tax-assessments at the parliament in Tingvoe. Every farmer and trader and man of substance in Orkney had set up his tent or booth around the pleasant bay of Tingvoe, and for a few days there was a good deal of entertainment and hospitality and exchange of news.

Ranald Sigmundson of Breckness was invited to most of the booths for food and refreshment. Men were eager to hear about the battle at Clontarf. He was questioned from all sides about Vinland, and about the abundant fertility and wealth there, and about the skraelings who lived in the forest.

'Now that the two earls have abolished viking cruises, I think we should all unite to build a great ship and sail to Vinland,' said one old man, laughing. 'Here in Orkney there are cold winds always, and if there aren't gales there's fog, and if there isn't fog it's perpetual rain. It's a wonder I've lived as long as I have. But over there, in Vinland, the climate is so mild a man might live for ever, and he only has to stretch out his hand and his mouth is full of fruit and fine fat river-fish. Why was I not told about Vinland when I was a boy feeding pigs on my father's farm?'

The guests in the booth laughed. They said that without a doubt the natives of Vinland had to work hard for their food and shelter, like all men everywhere and always. Is it not so? they asked Ranald.

Ranald said gravely that it was so, even in Vinland. Then a look of longing came on his face, and he put down his ale horn and went out and stood awhile in the wind and rain.

Those island assemblies brought together men who hadn't seen each other for a whole year, and a great deal of news was exchanged, in this booth and that, or (when the weather was good) on the hill or along the shore. Ranald met a few young men who had come into their strength and inheritances while he had been away, and with most of them he got on well.

One evening they were invited to the booth of Earl Sumarlid. Earl Brus was there too. The boy Thorfinn, their brother, had been told to go and play outside. Thorfinn put a dark look on them all and went up the hill with his hawk.

'Now that you have prohibited viking cruises,' said Stein of Sandside, a pleasant young man who owned the island of Graemsay, 'how are we going to pass our summers?'

Sumarlid the earl thought for a while. Then he said, 'You will all come to Birsay, of course. I think some of us had a vague agreement about this "summer of the young men", before the Irish expedition. There are many ways to pass the time in Birsay. You will be our guests at the Hall there. I assure you, in Birsay we will have a splendid summer. Isn't that a good idea, brother?'

Brus said he looked forward to having those young men for guests.

'Bring your horses,' said Sumarlid. 'The oats and the barley will grow without you. Your women folk will have the farms to themselves for a while.'

'Also,' said Brus, 'there are beautiful girls in Birsay, such as Ragna and Ingibiorg and Solveig.'

The young men agreed to spend two or three weeks at the earls' estate in Birsay.

'You will have hot ale before you go to bed, to make you sleep,' said Earl Sumarlid.

'If the weather is bad, we will play chess,' said Brus. 'There's an ivory chessboard inlaid in the long table, and a man in the island of Uig in the Hebrides has carved a new set of ivory chessmen for us. It is a joy to look at the pieces, and to feel them between your fingers.'

Hold, who owned Fara in the north islands, said he had had his fill of chess in winter. If the earls couldn't promise them hawking and fishing, he might as well bide the summer out among the gossips and harridans of Fara.

Sumarlid laughed, and promised them all a good time in the month of June.

There was a Norwegian that year in Tingvoe. The Norwegian said he was passing through, on his way to the King of Scotland at Inverness with missives from the Norwegian court. The earls had given the man a courteous welcome. But more than a few of the Orkneymen at Tingvoe said that the man was a spy. The king in the east often got information in this way.

The Norwegian, just as the assembly was making ready to ride home, came to Ranald and said, 'I have news that will interest you.'

'What is that?' said Ranald.

'The ship *Laxoy* commanded by the outlaw Fiord', said the Norwegian, 'sank in a storm off Bergen. The sailors came ashore, drowned, one after the other. Last there was blown ashore the body of an old sailor, and that was thought to be Fiord. As you know, Fiord was forbidden on pain of death to set foot in the the kingdom. When at last he came to a Norwegian shore, it was as a drowned man.'

Ranald said he was sorry to hear that news. 'The ship', he said, 'had a cargo of good stone for the building of a church.'

'Those stones are scattered on the sea bed,' said the Norwegian. 'Fishermen say that sometimes they can hear a church bell ringing under the waves, and a choir singing psalms.'

Ranald said, 'It was their fate to end that way. I am sorry for Fiord – I liked the man very much.'

Then Ranald rode home to Breckness.

3

Near midsummer Ranald put his farm Breckness in charge of Eyvind his steward and rode north to the earls' Hall in Birsay.

Just before he left, his mother Thora said, 'There may be a bride waiting here at Breckness for you when you come back.'

Ranald said, 'Marriage is not in my mind this summer . . .' Then he spurred on his horse.

Some young men – Hold, Keld, Valt, Osmund, Hallvard from Iceland and Thorkel Amundson of Skaill – had arrived before him. Others – Hakon, Amund, Elk, Fors, Tusk – came as he was stabling his favourite horse, Beltane.

They found the two earls, Brus and Sumarlid, in low spirits. Sumarlid had been unwell for a month. He had no relish for his food, or for the work of the earldom, and at last had taken to his bed. But on the day appointed for the coming together of the young men at midsummer, he had got out of bed. When Sumarlid greeted Ranald, he was suddenly overtaken by a storm of coughing, so that he couldn't finish his greeting. Ranald could see at once how thin the earl was, and that he had blue-gray shadows about the eyes. But he rallied himself to welcome the young men as they entered the Hall one after the other.

The guests learned that the youngest brother, Thorfinn, had sailed south to Scotland. The King of Scots, Malcolm, was anxious to foster Thorfinn, who was his grandson. Already he had appointed the boy Earl of Caithness and Sutherland.

As for the other brother, Einar – 'Einar of the Twisted Mouth' he was called – he had sent word that soon he would be sailing from the Hebrides to claim his share of the earldom of Orkney.

'I foresee nothing but trouble once Einar comes,' said Brus. 'There is too much of the ancient viking about our brother Einar. I hoped that Orkney would be a peaceful place with Sumarlid and I sitting here in Birsay, with the cornstalk carved over the lintel of the big house. Einar will drag a harrow over Orkney, year after year. Orkney will be torn with war and dispute, I know it well. We can't see the end of it. It's a great pity Sigurd had so many sons.'

The sun was shining outside, but there was gloom in the Hall for an hour. Sumarlid coughed from time to time, and had to sit down.

Presently a young woman came in: Brus's wife, Hilde. 'Why are you drifting about in here like a company of ghosts?' she said. 'I thought you had all come for the midsummer sports. The boats are waiting down at the shore, the horses are eager to be out and racing on the hill.'

At that the young men stirred themselves, and got ready for the holiday.

But first Hilde led them into the women's quarters. There in a crib slept a baby – the son of Brus and Hilde. 'His name is Rognvald,' she said. 'His great-grandmother, Eithne, came to see the boy soon after he was born. "He will do great things," she said, "then he will have a quick death between the fire and the sea . . ."'

The young men went out to saddle their horses.

The horses were stamping on the cobbles and flinging their heads about like waves of the sea.

Of the days that followed, I think we should let Ranald speak in a poem that he composed the following winter at home in Breckness.

Ranald had no great skill as a poet. He tried first of all to celebrate that time in the strict verse form that he had been instructed in. But he found he couldn't move freely within those narrow confines, and in the end he threw all caution to the winds and the words came as a beachcomber sings along the shore, for the pure joy of living, a careless rapture thrown on the wind.

The Summer of the Young Men

Ranald, leave us, go on now to the simperings and the scents
After the hundred happy days
Coursing hares, wrestling,

Tilting sun-horns in a lanterned bothy,
Word came, a horseman
With runes on a split stick –
A girl has been found, Ranald,
She is sitting now at the loom of the women in Breckness.
She is no patcher of coats, this girl.

At cold dawn, the northeast
A bucket spilling silver at a well-head
Beyond Eynhallow and Westray,
We manhandled, hook to thwart,
King Halibut,
Undersea splendours flowing from his armour.
Thorkel and I brought him
Lordly in death
To a stone at the shore, a knife, fires.

Begotten, my horse Beltane
Of a gray wind
And the roaring burn at Boardhouse.
Beltane bore me
Past Frey the thunderer, in the race
And the whirling hoofs
Of Troll and Asgard and Hjaltland –
Then staggered, knelt, threw the rider
In a nest of thistles.
Urgent nostrils,
Frey and Troll, stretched the wind.
I bear the thunder-mark
Of Beltane's foolishness on my forehead still.

Summer minted, that year, off Marwick and Skibbigeo,
A thousand glittering pieces.
Richer than jarl or prince
We were the young men, unwithering always.
Hallvard returned laughing,
Bright from 'the mermaid lair', with two lobsters.
Fell on my hand, soon,
From the tree in the hall garden
One dry tarnished leaf.

At the farm gate, at Breckness
No lass with Irish eyes.
The girls shook heads at my tinker face.
My mother
Combed grass and salt out of my beard.
A girl sat alone in my chamber,
She was sewing patches on my harvest coat.
A week later she was total whiteness from throat to feet, in the
    chapel.
I could not speak.
If I let my tongue go, now, among wave cries,
It is to sound, beyond skulls,
A song that can never be uttered.

4

After Ranald's marriage to Ragna in the chapel of the little monastery at Warbeth, he settled down to the management of his estate.

One year he would drain an area of marshland. Another year he would break out a piece of hill-land, and put the plough to it. He engaged a good boat-builder in Hamnavoe and in the end he had six fishing-boats on the beach at Breckness.

Servants came and went. The old smith Sverr died one autumn and was buried in the howe not far from the farmhouse. The spirits of good men protect the land and buildings they have loved in their lifetime.

Harald Thorn the beachcomber was found in a cave under the Black Crag. He must have slipped on seaweed, and the high spring tide pouring into the cave drowned him. He was given proper burial above the shoreline.

Every spring Ranald rode to the assembly (or 'thing') at Tingvoe. Some years it was like approaching a wasp's nest. Einar had come home and claimed his third share of the earldom. Einar dominated each assembly for a while. Sumarlid, the gentle eldest brother, had died of 'cough-of-the-lungs', and now Einar proposed to Brus that he (Einar) ought to administer Sumarlid's third of the earldom, as well as his own third. Brus was urged not to give in to his brother, and at one or two of the assemblies he suggested compromises. 'There is our younger brother to think about. Now that Sumarlid is dead, Thorfinn ought to have Sumarlid's third.'

'That brat has a bigger earldom than either of us, south in Scotland,' cried Einar. 'How much land does the whipper-snapper want? Thorfinn has more than enough.'

Whenever Einar was angry or met with opposition his mouth would snag like a key in a rusted lock, and men knew then that there would be trouble.

Brus's advisers, especially Thorkel of Skaill, urged Brus to stand up to Einar. Ranald of Breckness and most of the young landowners supported Brus. But in the end Brus gave way. 'I will not let this earldom of Orkney be destroyed by war,' he said. 'I will rule here in the west of Orkney, including Birsay, Sandwick, Harray, Firth, Orphir, Stenness, Evie. You, Einar, can have the rest. I hope that you will be a good and a just ruler in your scattered islands. We will meet here with the chief Orkneymen each spring as usual, and put our house in order – though it is an unfortunate house, I can't help thinking, that has two keepers. Or maybe three, if young Thorfinn decides that he too wants his name inscribed on the title-deeds.'

Einar had packed the assembly with his men, and they raised a great shout when they knew that Einar had won the day.

Einar sat in his high chair and smiled, and Ranald said to his friend Thorkel Amundson that the earl's teeth that day were like the teeth of a wolf he had seen on the battlefield, after Clontarf.

5

It wasn't long before the Orkneymen saw that Einar's coming had been a misfortune in more ways than one. 'The trouble is', said Thorkel of Skaill, 'that the man is stupid. He fancies himself to be a great viking, so he builds a fine ship and goes a-cruising for loot every summer. A fool can see, surely, that those days of loot and pillage and piracy are over for good. What standing would Orkney have in the kingdoms of Europe if she got the reputation of a nest and breeding-ground of sea robbers? Lawful trade, that's what matters on the world highways now, increasingly. Our Einar is too thick in the head to see that. He must have his magnificent viking ship. Those wolf-ships are expensive to build and equip. So Einar has to screw up his tax demands. Already there are bitter complaints from the farmers and merchants, all the way from Westray to Ronaldsay – the same 'yes-men' who cheered Einar so loudly that day in Tingvoe when Brus yielded him that extra third of the earldom. Still, Einar might get off with it if he makes a success of his maraudings summer after summer – if he comes home with his hold stuffed with ingots and bales of fine English wool. But he is more stupid at sea than he is on land. The merchant ships of Ireland and France have little trouble in out-manoeuvring him. Those he does capture have nothing but a few barrels of salt herring on board, or they are poor pilgrims from Iceland. Or they are going to sell planks of Scotch larch in Ulster. Such are the takings, year after year, of the great viking, Einar. He sails home to poor harvests and dilapidated steadings, because he has taken away all the land-workers and builders to sail on his idiotic voyages. We are lucky, I tell you, Ranald, to be living in this peaceful and plenteous part of the earldom . . . But it can't go on. There will be a queer twist to Einar's mouth the day that he stands face-to-face with ruin and death.'

Thus Thorkel Amundson of Skaill to his friend Ranald Sigmundson.

'And believe me, Ranald,' Thorkel went on, 'the king east in Norway has his spies in Orkney, they keep their eyes open, they know which way the wind is blowing. And young Thorfinn over in Caithness, he is waiting to get a foot in the door . . . I may tell you, Ranald, that a few of Earl Einar's men have been to see me. They have asked me to speak to Earl Einar on their behalf. How does one try to reason with a mad wolf?'

Ranald said that, speaking for himself, he would have nothing to do with those wranglings and follies and ambitions. His only desire was to farm his acres well in Breckness, and to be fair and open with his workers, and to see that his year-old son Sumarlid was left a goodly inheritance, there in the fertile southwest corner of the Island of Horses.

He had called his first-born Sumarlid, after the pleasant young earl who had died.

Ranald rode each spring to the assembly at Tingvoe.

There he could see that now Einar sat alone on the high seat, and he would not brook any opposition; though in the booths, after the lamps were lit, the landowners grumbled (some loudly) about the taxes Einar laid on them.

126

Brus mostly did not attend the parliament. This was thought to be an affront to the authority of the law-makers, and in particular to Einar himself. But Einar said that his brother's absence from the assembly was a matter of small importance. 'Let him play his games of chess,' he said. 'Let him play with his little son Rognvald at the inlaid chessboard in the Hall there over the hill. Brus my brother does not have saga-stuff in the marrow of his bones.'

Einar's bodyguard – a dozen ruffians he had recruited in Lewis and Orkney and Shetland – laughed mightily at Einar's words. But most of the farmers kept silence.

Then Einar went on to put before the assembly a plan he had made for his next viking cruise. There would be six ships in all, and they would reap a mighty sea harvest in the west and in the south. Of course, the building of such fine ships would cost a lot of money, and so the landowners must be prepared to have their taxes substantially increased. 'But', said Einar, 'it will be a wise investment, for you will all be the richer for it in the end.'

A voice in the back of the big tent said, 'We don't want that kind of riches, Einar – a few sacks of smoked puffins in a hold, a few barrels of salt – not to speak of wounds and drowning. That has been the story of your famous viking cruises up to now. We want none of it.'

There was hand-clapping and shouts of agreement from here and there in the company.

It was dark inside the booth. The torches had not yet been lit.

'Who spoke then?' said Einar. 'Maybe I did not hear right. Let the speaker come forward to the high table and repeat what I thought he said.'

Nobody moved forward.

The torches were brought in. Einar's face was as red as blood. His hands lay on the arms of his carved chair and the knuckles were gray as ice.

The bodyguard looked here and there and some of them fingered the hilts of their axes.

It looked as if the assembly that year might end in a pitched battle.

'I did not think', said Einar, 'I would ever preside over an assembly of cowards.'

Discontent moved in the crowd, like waves on stones on a winter shore. The landowners of Orkney had not omitted to sharpen their daggers, though Tingvoe, until Einar's time, had always been looked on as a place of peace, and sacrosanct, where spilling of blood would be a defilement.

Thorkel Amundson of Skaill stepped forward. 'It was not I who spoke those words, earl,' he said, 'and I don't associate myself with the discourtesy, spoken as it was in darkness. But the man, whoever he was, has given utterance to the thoughts of most Orkneymen, that we waste too much money on piracy and war, and so we neglect the things of peace, such as agriculture and fishing and trade.'

Thorkel and Earl Einar stood face to face, and looked into each other's eyes, and in the end it was Einar who looked away.

'Very well,' he said, 'I have thought about it and maybe six viking ships will be too many for me to handle out in the Atlantic. This summer I will have three ships only, built in the yards in Norway. I am glad to have an honest councillor like you occasionally, Thorkel, who can see so clearly into the heart of a problem. An earl like me, who sits at the centre of things, cannot see the whole picture, as they say. Thorkel, I will take your advice on this matter, at this time, but in years to come it must be understood that I am the sole lord here in Orkney, and when I speak, every dog will come to heel. Even you, Thorkel, even you. I will take your advice this once. I will not brook it again. Up to now I admit to a certain degree of inexperience in those broad matters, and to a certain hastiness of judgment. All that is past. Soon I will know all that needs to be known about the governance of a people. At the next parliament, I will open my mouth and that will be the law. Not even you, Thorkel Amundson, will deflect my purpose by the thickness of a blade of grass.'

Thorkel thanked Earl Einar for such a gracious reply. He was glad, he said, that Einar had decided to concentrate more on statecraft than on war and plunder. When that happened, there would be deep golden harvests instead of a few rotten ears, and ships could sail along the horizon, north and south, with peaceful merchandise. 'But ever the wise ruler', said Thorkel, 'goes abroad among the people, and listens gladly to what they have in their minds and hearts.'

Earl Einar struck the board. 'The assembly is over,' he said. 'I will send a messenger over to Norway at once, with an order for three longships to be built and equipped for spring next year. Dig well into your money-bags, Orkneymen, for it is you who will be footing the bill.'

The earl's face was still as red as blood. With his bodyguard on each side of him, he stamped down the steps from the high chair, and passed out of the booth of assembly to his own private booth on the side of the hill.

Thorkel was thanked on all sides for his outspokenness.

'Don't thank me too soon,' he said. 'I think there may be stormier seas ahead.'

He took Ranald to one side. 'The man is mad,' he said. 'What is to be done in the end with a mad dog?'

There was much drinking that night, especially in Thorkel's booth, and laughter and singing till beyond midnight.

Earl Einar did not visit the booths of the farmers and merchants, as was the custom on the last evening of a 'thing'. A single torch burned in his tent, and the revellers could see the shadows of his bodyguard coming and going, but there were no harp-songs or rallies of laughter from the earl's tent.

In the morning the assembly men rode home to their farms, or set sail to this island or that.

Earl Einar walked down to his ship.

He gave farewell to no one. Men on the shore that day said that his mouth had the twist to it, like a key snagged in a lock.

6

The farm at Breckness prospered well.

There was another good harvest. The cradle in the corner brimmed with new cries, for Ragna had given birth to a daughter, Solveig. That cradle had more attention from the women than their spinning wheels and their milk-churns. 'Never', said the women, 'was there a bonnier lass.'

'It's true', said Ranald, 'that the child looks more like her mother than her father. And that's a good thing.'

Ragna was happy with her young children and with the ordering of the household. Sometimes a shadow would come on her face when she had words with her mother-in-law across the table or out in the oat-field. Thora would interfere in this matter and that concerning the household, and offer advice where none was asked or wanted.

'It is not easy', said Skol the new grieve, 'when two women rule the hearth-stone.'

Sometimes Thora, very offended, would leave the house altogether and go to the half-ruined bothy on the side of the Black Crag where once she had lived for a while, in the time of Harald Thorn her wooer. She would go empty-handed, the mother, and she would not lower herself to send down to the farm for bread, eggs, and milk.

In the end, Ranald would have to make peace between the two women.

'To think', said Thora bitterly, 'that I chose for you and for the farm of Breckness a slut like that! What did I do wrong this time? Little Sumarlid fell into the duck-pond, that was it. I happened to say, "A child of that age should not be left to play on his own . . ." Then your wife turns on me. "Mind your own business," says she. "Does the boy ever lack for care and clothes and kisses? A boy is none the worse for getting his boots muddy sometimes. Your own son Ranald, did he never once fall and scrape his knee till the blood came? Where were you then, I'd like to know? And is Ranald any the worse for that, or the hundred other small hurts that happen to a young boy?" So of course I couldn't put up with that, could I? Oh, I'm all right here, I can live here perfectly well on a rabbit or a gull's egg. When you're getting old, you don't need to eat that much . . . Very well, I know the nights are getting colder, and this hut is full of draughts. But here I'll bide till I get an apology from my daughter-in-law.'

Now there was a third child, Ingerth, in the cradle.

Ranald said he brought word from Ragna that she would be glad to see Thora back in the house, baking loaves and knitting little coats for the children – the children seemed to prefer the garments Thora knitted to the scarves and stockings of any other woman.

At that Thora seemed to be pleased. 'Well,' she said at last, 'I'll come back, but she's never to speak to me in that way again. It's true, I miss the grandchildren, and I long to see the new infant, Ingerth. I'll gather my things together and be back in Breckness before sunset.'

Then there would be peace in the farm for two or three months – then a wrong word would be said, or a wrong interpretation put on a word or an action, and once more Thora would put a few things in a bag and walk up to the hovel on the side of the Black Crag.

And Ragna would stand weeping beside the fire, with the children Sumarlid and Solveig clinging to her skirts.

Then Ranald would have to go up to the half-ruined hut and make peace once more between his mother and his wife.

In the end Ranald got two carpenters from Hamnavoe to build a small annex on the west side of the house for Thora, and there she lived by herself with an old woman and a girl to keep her company. They had their own fire and their own spinning wheel, and a goat grazing on the green patch at the gable end.

Then Thora and Ragna met only sometimes at the dinner bench, and they were moderately pleasant and courteous towards one another.

The bothy on the side of the Black Crag fell into ruins, in the course of a winter or two.

One year Ranald couldn't get to the assembly at Tingvoe, because of a sickness that had swept like fire through the parish. One or two of the older country folk died, but Ranald soon recovered, though he was weak in his joints for a time after the fever had guttered out, and whenever he went outside the wind from the sea cut him like a knife.

A horseman rode across the ridge one day when Ranald, too weak still for work, was sitting in the deep chair beside the fire. John Simison the farmer from Cairston came in, bringing news from Tingvoe.

The earl's viking cruise had, once again, been a failure, though Earl Einar had put the blame on the weather and on the cowardice of the French skippers who had turned and fled from his three ships, and most of all on the Norwegian shipwrights who had made the ships too heavy in the water so that they were slow in pursuit. Fate too had turned against him, in that he had given in too easily to bad advice from the Orkneymen (and here, said John, Earl Einar had glowered at Thorkel Amundson). But henceforth he, Einar Sigurdson, sole and true Earl of Orkney, would follow his own inspirations, and then fate would smile on him – fate being always the friend of brave men who venture into the unknown. That being so – Earl Einar informed the assembly from his high seat – after next plough-time he intended to sail out with eight pirate ships. He had had good reports of a company or guild of shipwrights in Denmark whose workmen knew how to build longships as lithe and swift and fierce as lurchers. 'Of course,' Einar said to the Orkneymen, 'the eight ships will be expensive to build, and therefore you will have to pay higher taxes. But it will be worth it, in the end we will reap a mighty sea harvest, and your women will go about in cloth-of-gold, and you will all ride out on the finest horses in the north, and you'll be able to make pilgrimages to Rome and Jerusalem, each man with a half-dozen retainers. That is all the business of the assembly this year. My treasurer will be calling on each of you in the course of next winter, with the revised tax roll. You are all welcome to drink with me in my booth tonight . . .'

And with those final words the earl left the assembly, and his dozen thugs went with him.

There was silence in the great tent for a while. Then the landowners turned to Thorkel for advice. 'I'll speak with him,' said Thorkel, 'but it could well be the last words I ever speak.'

Earl Einar had expected all the farmers and merchants, members of the assembly, to dine in his booth. His cooks were busy over the fires, and the drinking horns had been set out on the long table and the ale barrels had been unbunged, so that delicious fragrances spilled out, and a low, malten murmur. And there sat Einar, ready to receive his fifty grateful guests. He even had a crooked smile on his face.

The one and only guest turned up and he was Thorkel Amundson of Skaill.

'Come in, Thorkel my friend,' said Einar. 'Come and sit here on the bench beside me. You're most welcome. It won't be long till the others turn up.'

Thorkel said that none of the others would be coming. He had come to plead with the earl on their behalf.

'Plead?' said Earl Einar. 'What are the pleas about? I am about to give them what they most desire, wealth and well-being, once our viking fleet comes home laden to the gunwales, the eight magnificent vessels about to be built in Denmark. Now fate has begun to smile on us. I had hoped this would be a great feast in my tent tonight. But it seems only one guest has come.'

Thorkel said, 'The assembly men will endure it no longer, the failures at sea, the neglect in the countryside, the taxes that are making paupers of them all. So they have sent me here, Earl, to plead with you.'

Then the twist came on Einar's mouth, like an ill-made key in a warped lock.

The dozen thugs came and clustered round him, waiting for orders, each man eyeing Thorkel speculatively.

At last Earl Einar spoke. 'I told you last year, at this assembly, Thorkel, not to question any edict of mine again. Now I could have you killed for breaking your word. However, I give you leave to go back and tell those subjects of mine that they have seen nothing of my power yet. But they will, Thorkel, they will. And when they are reduced to

132

rags and begging bowls, that is what they have truly made themselves, being traitors and cowards and skinflints. They ought to be grateful to have a strong far-visioned earl ruling over them. Go and tell the scum that, Thorkel. Tell them to go home and when all their household is asleep to prise open the floorboard where they keep the stocking with the gold and silver coins in it, and to reckon both their hoard and their dues. For they will not know the day or the hour when my treasurer and tax-man come knocking at their door. And as for you, Thorkel Amundson, let me not see your face again. For if we chance to meet, only one of us will walk away from the meeting.'

Then Thorkel walked from the earl's booth and went down to the booth where the assembly men were waiting, and he told them the words that had passed between him and Einar.

It was night, but there was a half-moon. Some men went down to their boats and sailed for home at once, for none of them knew what might be done to them that night if they stayed in their tents. And some took to their horses and rode home.

Thorkel rode home to Skaill in Sandwick. But he knew that he was not safe even there, and next morning he sailed over the Pentland Firth to Caithness.

The young Earl Thorfinn gave Thorkel a great welcome. He listened eagerly to the news of Orkney. 'I didn't think my brother Einar was quite so mad,' he said. 'If he had been a reasonable man, I don't know if I'd ever see Orkney again. And I want very much to have my third of the islands, it is my due. With a mad dog like him, my claim will be easier. A mad dog must be hunted down in the end. Who will put the knife into him? Someone must put the knife in him, and soon.'

Thorkel said that often a mad dog died simply of its own frenzy. 'It is a good thing that the mad dog has no son to succeed him. Once dead, he is out of the story for ever.'

'But Brus my brother has a son in Birsay, a very promising lad, I've heard: Rognvald. I could wish this Rognvald had never come into the story in the first place, because the truth is that in the end I want to be sole ruler in Orkney. There will be no peace in the isles till there is one earl and one earldom.'

The young earl and Thorkel had always been the best of friends. Thorfinn was an astute lad, but still green in matters of statecraft and governance. He listened eagerly to Thorkel's advice, and fell in with nearly all of what Thorkel planned. 'You are my foster-father,' said the

Earl of Caithness and Sutherland. So always after that, Thorkel went by the name of Thorkel Fosterer.

But, of course, it was only news of the direful assembly at Tingvoe that John of Cairston brought to Ranald.

Ranald thanked him, and invited him to stay to dinner. 'I think', said Ranald, 'there are exciting times ahead of us.'

That same night Ragna gave birth to their fourth child, a boy. So the infant Einhof Ranaldson was brought to the font at Warbeth, and christened.

7

Often some rich merchant-farmer or other would ride out to Breckness and say that he was having a keel laid in Norway or Denmark, and he would be glad if Ranald Sigmundson would enter into partnership with him. Ranald's youthful fame as a seafarer had spread far and wide, and it was reckoned that any ship commanded by Ranald would have successful voyages.

Ranald always answered that he had had his fill of seafaring in his youth. He would never put to sea again, he said, other than to visit a friend in this island or that, or to set a few lobster creels under the Yesnaby crags.

Ranald would always invite the merchant-landowner in to his fire and table, and show him with pride his four children and his wife Ragna, who was by no means beautiful but was a most kind and efficient mistress of an important farm.

Then, after dinner, when they were alone, Ranald would say to his guest over the fire, 'The truth is, I'm afraid to put to sea again. It isn't fear of storm and danger and drowning, the sea has put a spell on me that I thought time would weaken. But the fact is, that spell is stronger then ever. Whenever I hear the breakers on the shore down there, a great longing comes on me. When I'm out on the hill at lambing time, and see the migrant ships on the horizon, after the long winter, I have to turn my head away, a yearning like madness stirs in me. Believe me, the craving is worse, much worse, than a drunkard who has broken his leg and so can't get to the ale-houses, and the drunkard's wife and children conspire to keep the ale jug well out of his reach . . . Perhaps I should take an inland farm, in Harray say, where I can't set eyes on the sea. But even in Harray, that inland parish, the sounds of the sea are forever spilling through gaps in the hills, from the Sandwick and Birsay shores, and I would have little rest. I give all my strength to my farm here, and to my family and shepherds and horsemen, and so it must be till I'm an old gray man, dim-sighted and crippled with rheumatism and maybe so dull of hearing I can no longer hear the sea-spells. And then, when I know that seafaring is impossible for me, I will get peace.'

Such words the farmer at Breckness said often to the merchants who came to offer him command of a ship.

Sometimes Ranald would be quite curt with them, and not even invite them over his threshold – an insult almost unheard of. 'Go away,' he would shout. 'I'm a busy man. Can't you see, there are two horses to break up there in the meadow . . . I have to cut the hay-field today and it looks like rain. Why don't you go away and mind your own business? There are plenty of good skippers looking for work. Go and visit them.'

Then a look of pain and longing would come on his face, and he would take his affronted visitor by the arm and say, 'You must pardon me, I am not in the best of spirits today. I get hay-fever from the cut grass and clover. Come inside, I'm pleased to see you, you're very welcome. You'll stay to dinner. No, my good friend, if you're here to make me a skipper of your ship, it's out of the question. The barley harvest will be ready in three weeks or a month. Yes, shut the door behind you, the wind's in the west and that wind fills the house with the sounds and the smells that give me the worst kind of unrest.'

Later, over the ale cups, he would say to his visitor, 'The truth is, if ever I went to sea again, I would never want to come home, even to Ragna and the children, nor to the farm of Breckness, though I am made of its dust and must give my dust back to it in the end.'

But Ranald did agree on three or four occasions to take a share in a merchant ship trading to Sweden or Germany. In such cases he discussed earnestly the cargoes and studied bills of lading and reckoned what the expenses might be, and what fair wages ought to be paid, and what foreign exchange would be acceptable. Nearly always Ranald's advice was accepted by the merchants and invariably the ships returned with a handsome profit for Orkney.

Then for a while Ranald and his occasional guests would talk about the politics of the earldom. Slowly a pattern was unfolding. Earl Thorfinn had, the previous winter, arrived at the shore of Orphir in Orkney with a hand-picked, well armed troop of men, and at once he had sent a man to his brother Einar in Rousay requesting the third share of the earldom that was his by right. Thorfinn's messenger did not return from Einar's hall in Rousay. Instead, ships were seen sailing from Rousay with armed men on board. Earl Thorfinn had said, 'We will ride now to the coast, and see why Einar is keeping my messenger so long.' At once Brus's watchmen on the northern shore reported to Earl Brus that there were armed ships in the Sound of Eynhallow, and also that a troop of armed men were riding between the hills to the shore of Evie. At once Brus summoned his guard and rode to the shore, and he was just in time to occupy the headland before the sailors of Einar and the horsemen of Thorfinn met.

'Welcome, brothers,' said Brus to Einar and Thorfinn. 'What a pleasure for us three brothers to come together by chance on a fine day like this. It is so rarely that we see each other and have a talk. I think, now that we've met, we *should* have a talk, because here in Orkney there are confusions that must be sorted out.'

Earl Brus had by far the largest company of men with him that day on the shore of Evie, and so the younger brothers were forced to hear what he had to say, though Einar was gnawing his lip in a rage and Thorfinn, after the first greeting, gave his chess-playing brother mostly contemptuous looks.

Thorfinn had now the first black hairs on his upper lip, and his voice wavered between treble and bass.

'It seems to me', said Brus, 'that our young brother Thorfinn is entitled to his share of the Orkneys and the revenues accruing from it. Only a fool would disagree with that.'

Earl Einar drove his foot with rage into the shore stones, and then cried out with the pain of it. And Earl Thorfinn laughed, both at Brus's easy acknowledgment of his claim and at Einar's rage and discomfiture. 'A fool doesn't need to make a fool of himself,' he said behind his hand to his men. And his men all laughed loudly.

Then Brus said an unexpected thing. 'I tell you, brothers, I'm tired of the wrangles and intrigues and endless bickerings of this earldom. It seems to me that the king over in Norway, our liege-lord, is forever stirring up trouble here in Orkney, the better to keep us under his thumb. Well he knows that a united earldom here in Orkney would be rich and quite independent of Norway. But he is afraid, at the same time, that the King of Scotland, being closer in terms of space, might have designs on Orkney himself. Already you, Thorfinn, hold lands from the King of Scotland, your grandfather, and owe him allegiance because of Caithness and Sutherland. Well, then, I'm heartily sick of being in the middle of this tug-of-war, pulled this way and that. All I want to do is fish in the burn and take my hawk to the hill, and in the evening play chess with the abbot, or listen to that talented poet from Iceland who called in last October and is still sleeping in a sack in the corner and getting as much as he can in the way of food and drink from the kitchen women. He makes silly songs for them that make them weep into their aprons. Still, he's a good storyteller too, and I like his sagas, and I'll be sorry the day he decides to leave, if he ever does decide to leave . . . Enough of that. Listen well to me, Einar. You and I will unite our separate thirds of the earldom. We will each stay in our own houses, you in Rousay and I in Birsay. A brave chap like you can do any fighting that's required in our joint defence. I think I'd better see to the ingathering of the revenues – though you'll get your share, never fear. (I think, in any case, your tax-men are swindling you right and left. You lack the gift of prudence, brother.) I think you should go on as many viking cruises and war cruises as you can manage, Einar. Orkney never seems to miss you all that much when you're away. I will see to it that your farmers pay fair taxes and have good governance. Did I say a while back that all I want to do from now on is fish and course hares and sit at the chessboard? Well, of course I will do those inoffensive things too, after I've seen to the affairs of our joint estate. Especially I'll preside at the assembly in Tingvoe every year. I've heard word that you, Einar, have not been very good at handling the assemblies. Well, then, just you concentrate on your bits of piracy and your little raids here and there in Ireland and Scotland. Leave the rest to me.'

Einar's mouth was as crooked as a flail on a barn wall.

'One last thing, Einar,' said Brus. 'One of us two will die before the other. In that case, the survivor will inherit. I have a son, Rognvald. You have no children, Einar. Keep on fighting, you brave warrior–earl. Keep on attacking ships and castles. Death comes soon to a warrior, it's true, but don't think of that, Einar, think of the glory. Think of the saga that will be written about you . . .' And Brus smiled with great pleasantness at Einar. And Einar didn't know what to make of his brother's words. His face glowed, half-way between rage at Brus's contempt, and joy at the thought of his name written in gules-and-gold in some saga that might be chanted in the future.

Thorfinn said, 'There are as many clowns and fools in a saga as heroes. I would not like to be Einar's ghost when our own particular saga is recited on a winter night, for they say the ghosts of men attend wherever their names are uttered in time to come, and the fool comes to the storytelling to be tormented time and again, even as the hero comes to rejoice in the spilled treasures of his life.'

At that, Einar cried out in rage and walked up the shore to strike at his brother Thorfinn, but Brus came between them and urged them to make peace with one another.

They did make peace after a fashion, and men say the hand-clasp of Einar and Thorfinn was like two fish laid one against the other.

Then Brus rode home to Birsay, and Thorfinn returned to Caithness, and Einar and his thugs caught the tide to Rousay; but Einar was not a good sailor and he misjudged the current and his ship was carried back towards Egilsay and Wyre. It was late in the evening before Einar got home, and he was in a foul temper. No one should drink in an ill temper, it is like pouring oil on fire. All night he walked in his hall, so that there was little sleep that night in Westness house. 'Ho,' the earl would shout from time to time, 'they will see who the hero is and who are the fools . . . All men will hear the truth of it . . . They will, they will . . . And that in no long time.' Towards morning he shouted, 'Ireland. First of all Ireland. Make the ships ready for Ireland. I, Einar of Orkney, will shake Ireland to the roots!'

These matters Ranald of Breckness learned from the men who came to visit him, on business or in simple friendship, from time to time. He thought it prudent to bide at home and await developments.

One day the farmer of Cairston rode over to see Ranald. John Simison told Ranald that Earl Einar's expedition to Ireland had taken place and had been a total failure. His raiding party had been cut off by one of the Irish princes called Konofogor at Loch Larne, and it had been terribly mauled, with many dead and wounded Orkney-men left on the field.

Einar had returned to Orkney much poorer than he had left it.

Far from chastening him, this humiliation had woven into him a new red strand of bitterness and anger and revenge. 'The mad dog is beginning to froth at the mouth now,' said Ranald.

Earl Thorfinn had sent Thorkel, his friend and fosterer, over to Orkney to collect his rents for the third of the earldom that belonged to him. Thorkel was met on the shore at Scapa by a troop of Einar's thugs on horseback, and if Thorkel hadn't turned round at once and sailed back to Caithness, he would have left his body on the shore.

Then Einar himself appeared on the sea banks. 'I know you, Thorkel Amundson,' he shouted. 'It is you that have caused all this trouble in Orkney. You'll pay for it with your life. I'll seek you out, wherever you are, and the boy Thorfinn my brother won't be able to help you that day . . .'

His mouth after he had said that was like a line of barbed wire.

When Thorkel reported all this to Earl Thorfinn, Thorfinn advised him to sail east to Norway and get the friendship of King Olaf.

King Olaf received Thorkel gladly at the beginning of winter. He was a man of few words, King Olaf, but the Norwegian courtiers could see by the expression on his face and the firmness of his embrace how much he valued this ambassador from the west.

Indeed, Thorkel had such charm and openness of manner that nearly everyone he met took to him at once.

King Olaf was concerned by another piece of bad news that had reached him out of Orkney. One of his merchants, a personal friend of his, had sailed to Ireland on business. This merchant-skipper was called Eyvind Horn. On his way back to Norway with a cargo of Irish linen and malt, a strong northeasterly had forced him to take refuge in Osmundwall in Hoy. (Osmundwall was the sheltered bay where a former King Olaf of Norway had forced Christianity on Earl Sigurd, the father of Brus and Einar and Thorfinn, he who had died in battle at Clontarf in Ireland.) Word of this storm and havening was brought to Earl Einar. 'I think', said he, 'I may be able to do something to make the ghost of my father Earl Sigurd happy . . .' The storm continued unabated. Einar crossed over to Hoy and got horses there and rode with a troop of heavily armed men to Osmundwall. Eyvind Horn and his sailors were being entertained at a farm there. Earl Einar surrounded the house. He sent word that he wanted to do business with the Norwegian skipper. Eyvind came out into the yard and was at once set upon by 'the thugs', and he died almost at once under the slash and trench and criss-cross of their daggers. Then Einar went up and stood in the door of the farm. 'Take the body of your skipper back to King Olaf', he said, 'with my compliments.'

King Olaf said nothing when the news of Eyvind's murder was brought to him. At last he spoke. 'I would be glad if your Earl Thorfinn would visit me here in Norway. I have a few important things to discuss with him.'

Thorfinn set sail from Caithness at the beginning of summer. He had a joyful reunion at the wharfside in Bergen with Thorkel his friend.

When Thorfinn came to the king's palace, he could see at once that every courtesy and honour had been prepared for him: trumpeters on the steps, the hall hung with new tapestries, courtiers bowing as low and perfumed as to a papal envoy or the King of Poland, a tangle of rich odours from the kitchen below to delight the stomach of a young man who had been eating hard biscuits for a week on the sea.

A curtain parted, King Olaf rose from his throne, and took Earl Thorfinn to himself as though he was his own far-travelled son.

Earl Thorfinn was the king's guest all that summer.

They fished in the fjords together, they hunted deer in the forests, they took their falcons up into the mountains, they described intricate ski-patterns on the higher snow. They listened, after dinner, to the court poets and musicians. Men rode and sailed from all over Scandinavia to have words with the young Orkney earl who was earning a great reputation for sagacity and hardihood. 'But', said a few of the women about the court, 'he could do with being more handsome. The young Orkney earl – he's as black and ugly as a crow.'

Other ladies in the court thought his ugliness an asset.

An old deacon said, 'There's one kind of vanity Thorfinn won't be troubled with.'

At night, after the music and the saga reading, King Olaf would take Thorfinn and Thorkel into his private study, and there they would discuss affairs in Orkney, sometimes until dawn was silvering the high mountaintops in the northeast.

At the end of that summer, King Olaf took Earl Thorfinn to the royal shipyard. A magnificent vessel was lying in the stocks. The shipwrights were putting the final touches on her. The earl said he hadn't seen a finer vessel.

'She is yours,' said King Olaf. 'She'll be ready in a week, just about the time you're due to sail back to Caithness.'

Earl Thorfinn gave Thorkel the ship that he – the earl – had sailed to Norway in. Together, in great style, Thorfinn and Thorkel sailed home across the North Sea . . .

All this news was brought to Ranald Sigmundson in Breckness by skippers and merchants.

Ranald was specially pleased about the visit of Earl Thorfinn and Thorkel to Norway.

It seemed now that the dice were loaded against the mad earl. 'But yet events must move fast from now on, for Einar intends to make himself sole Earl of Orkney, and he will make his move before long.'

The word from Birsay was that Earl Brus sat in the palace there, playing chess much of the time on his ivory-and-silver inlaid board, and sometimes riding round the farms discussing farmwork and the best kind of seed to sow on such-and-such a soil, and whether the horses from Lothian were better than those from Brittany. But it was known that Brus had spies in the household of his brother Einar, and knew beforehand every move that Einar would make. He was more open with his brother Thorfinn over in Caithness, and messengers went freely back and fore between Birsay and Thurso.

Einar – it was said – was half afraid to go freely about the islands, lest some farmer he had made poor by his taxes should turn on him. He recruited more and more 'hard men' into his bodyguard. But even if he rode down to the shore in Rousay, some woman would come to the end of the house and rail at him for a murderer, extortioner, fool, coward. If one of the bodyguard stirred to silence the woman, Einar would say to her, 'Save your energy, my dear. Save your energy, for you will have to work a bit harder next year at your carding and spinning, because I am having to raise your man's taxes. Besides, you might be a widow soon. I'm thinking of taking your man south to Lewis and Ulster on my next war-cruise, and then, before long, you'll have a son and a greedy daughter-in-law to contend with over occupancy of the farm. So I'd keep my mouth sweet, my dear, if I were you, or you'll have a bleak future . . .'

Then the berserkers would laugh. As that company rode on down to the shore, the croft doors would be barred against them, one after the other.

8

But soon, good news reached Breckness. The three earls had reached some kind of concordat. Henceforward there would be peace in Orkney. Thorkel had returned to the farm at Skaill, which was his now that his father Amund – that good old man – had died. From Skaill

Thorkel would look after Earl Thorfinn's interests in Orkney.

Thorkel sent one of his men to Breckness, inviting Ranald to attend the great peace-feast at Skaill. There would in fact be two feasts, one at Skaill and one immediately after, at a big house belonging to Earl Einar in Rendall: all the guests would ride from Skaill to Rendall, stuffed as they might well be with food and drink, and there sit down at Earl Einar's table. 'There will be plenty of belching and whirling words by the time the second party is half-way through,' said Thorkel's messenger. 'Thorkel would very much like you to be there, at the first party, Ranald. I think you needn't worry overmuch about attending the second affair.'

'Well,' said Ranald, 'it will be a welcome sight, to see the three earls sitting down together at the high table, breaking the bread of peace – Brus and Einar and Thorfinn.'

'No,' said the messenger from Skaill, 'but there will be only one earl there, Einar. Earl Brus has sent word he can't come, his stomach is delicate, he daren't eat roast duck and whalemeat, and as for ale and mead, the very thought of it makes him yellow in the face. His doctor has advised him to stay beside the fire and the chessboard, the air at this time of year is bad for his lungs. But the earl in Birsay has sent word that he hopes the feast will be a great success, and of course the second feast also . . . As for Earl Thorfinn, he has so many urgent things to see to in Caithness – all those Scotsmen queueing up at his door, wanting this and that adjudication from the earl about lawsuits and inheritances and boundaries – that he can't see his way to be present, try as he may . . . And now good-day to you, Ranald Sigmundson. The feast at Skaill is on Wednesday first, at noon. Thorkel says, though there will be only one earl present out of three, he can promise you a very exciting day. By the way, bring an axe and a dagger.'

The horseman rode off, scattering a company of white geese in the courtyard.

Ranald thought there was something very strange about the whole affair. Why, at such an important event, should only one earl be present out of three? It seemed to Ranald that Brus wasn't all that delicate – last time he had sat at table with him he had washed the whalemeat down with strong ale, and seemed to enjoy it. As for weak lungs, last winter Ranald had seen Earl Brus haul up a fishing-boat on the noust out of a storm, and he had shouted to two men who had hurried down the sea-banks to help him that he would manage quite well, there was nothing he liked better than dragging a yole up a stormy beach.

That was strange, for one thing.

It seemed to Ranald, too, that surely Earl Thorfinn could spare a day away from his parchments and quill pens in Thurso, to be present at such a very important peace celebration. Ranald knew for a fact that Earl Thorfinn rarely spent more than half-an-hour a day in his office. He had a factor and scribes who saw to all those things.

That was strange, also.

Strangest of all was that Earl Einar should consent to come to Skaill at all, among lesser men, and not have a chance of speaking to his brothers.

The more Ranald thought about it, the more questionable the whole affair seemed. It had all the makings of a dark mystery.

Why had Thorkel's man told him (Ranald) to be sure to take his hand-axe with him and to put a dagger in his belt?

He decided to go to Skaill, and on the Wednesday morning he set out on horseback.

Thorkel was there to greet him, and also their friend Hallvard the Icelander. Both men were extremely cheerful. In the kitchen at Skaill preparations for the feast were well under way. One girl was scrubbing the long table, another girl was seeing to the fire in the centre of the hall, piling on peat and driftwood, for it was a cold morning.

'I think it will be a good day here at Skaill,' said Thorkel.

Presently there was a clatter of many hooves on the cobbles of the yard. Thorkel went out to meet Earl Einar. The 'hard-men', Einar's bodyguard, were there in force.

Thorkel brought the earl in to meet Ranald and Hallvard. The earl's bodyguard sat on benches at the far end of the hall, and began to throw dice. They called for ale.

Ranald had not seen Earl Einar for some time. He was shocked at the change in him. His eyes were sunken, and they shifted here and there in his head as if the man was not quite sure of himself.

Frightful it was to see him smiling – as of course a welcome guest at any feast should – for then Einar's mouth too shifted this way and that, in a sequence of grimacings.

'Let's hurry,' he said to Thorkel. 'Soon there will be a lasting peace between us two. I don't want to linger too long here at Skaill, for I don't eat much these days, and two heavy meals are too much for me.

Besides, I always feel more at ease in my own house. We will just eat a bit of your loch trout here, then we'll go on to Rendall. You'll get a feast today, Thorkel, such as you've never stomached in your life before. What you have in your kitchen here a man might buy himself any day at a horse fair in Firth or Sanday. We'll stay for a mouthful, and then ride on together.'

Ranald was struck too by Earl Einar's voice. It had lost its former resonance, and he spoke quickly, in low flat tones.

'Well,' said Thorkel, 'if we are to eat so little here in Skaill, the farm lasses will be pleased, they're always hungry for leftovers.'

'I'd be glad of a flagon or two of ale at the food bench,' said the earl. 'Ale helps me to sleep. I don't sleep well nowadays either. But you, Thorkel, I promise you this, after the hospitality you get from me later today, you'll have the longest deepest sleep you ever had.'

Then the serving men and girls arranged the bench at the high table, and Thorkel invited the earl to sit on the chair of honour.

The serving girls began to bring in broth in wooden bowls.

'I'll have a word with my men first,' said Earl Einar. He walked over to where his men were lounging at the fire, and spoke to them. At once six of them got up and left the hall.

Einar said, 'I've sent them on to say we'll be on our way soon. Certain preparations must be made. Take away this soup, it turns my stomach. You, ale man, fill my horn.'

Ranald thought he'd never sat at a more unlucky table, though there seemed to be laughter of a kind coursing through all the talk.

Thorkel bade all the guests put in their hands and eat.

The great dappled loch trout had been brought in and laid in platters on the table. 'Stinking fish!' said the earl. 'I'd like my ale mug filled again, and see if you can get some older stronger ale out of Thorkel's cellar.'

Thorkel took all those insults well. 'Nothing is too good for such an earl,' he said, and laughed. 'I doubt if even the mead of Valhalla would be to his taste. Ah well, we will all have to drink that nectar of heroes soon enough.'

Einar belched, and swivelled his eyes round here and there. 'You've always talked too much, Thorkel Amundson,' he said. 'All too soon there comes an end of words . . . I don't want your pig tripes, I'd be glad to get a head of froth on my ale, if it isn't too much to ask. Ditch-water has more life in it than the ale they brew here in Skaill.'

The serving man took away the platter of well seasoned haggis that he had set in front of the earl.

'It's a long ride on horseback between here and the hall in Rendall,' said Thorkel. 'Though the earl doesn't like our food, I advise you others to eat as much as you can here, for what man knows where and whether he'll get his next dinner?'

Then the great haunch of roasted ox was brought in, and a man began to carve it at the end of the table. 'How long was that horse dead and rotten before you hung it over the fire?' said Einar. The man with the ale pot stood at the earl's shoulder. 'Can't you see, you clod-hopper, that my mug has been empty for an hour and more!'

Earl Einar's men were making beasts of themselves at the fish platter and the roast platter, at their table between the fire and the door. They must have drunk half a barrel of ale before the meal was half over. Most of them were drunk. One staggered outside and the splash of his vomit could be heard at the high table.

'Try to eat some bread and honey, my lord,' said Thorkel, 'while I go and have a word with my factor.'

Thorkel rose up and left the table and spoke in a low voice to Prad his factor, who immediately went outside, and they heard the sound of Prad's horse on the cobbles riding out.

'We've stayed here at Skaill too long,' said Einar. 'We should have been on the road to the proper feast an hour ago and more.'

'We'll be ready soon enough,' said Thorkel. 'The pity is, the other two earls aren't here with us today.'

'Whether Brus and Thorfinn are here or not', said Einar, 'matters nothing. I am the earl that matters, I assure you. The day is coming soon when the brothers will be eating out of my hand – either that, or begging me for mercy. I am Einar, my own man. I don't need to go skulking across the sea to Norway, for the king to pat my head and put a mark or two in the palm of my hand, and then pack me off home in a warped ship. The King of Norway will know, and that before long, that Earl Einar of Orkney is a greater ruler than he in the councils of the west ... Honey is it you call this sticky stuff? Are you sure your gardener hasn't gathered snail-slime and put it in a pot? No, I want no more ale either. All I want is for you, Thorkel my friend, to ride with me at once to Rendall. Come, I am ready now.'

'Only fate knows', said Thorkel, dipping his bread into the honey pot, 'whether when a man sets out on a journey, he will ever get to the end of it. So it's better always to ride out with sweetness in the mouth of the horseman. This Sandwick honey, I assure your lordship, is the very best heather honey.'

Then Earl Einar put his head down on the table, and laughed. It seemed to Ranald like laughter from a tomb. 'It is true what you say, Thorkel, about fate and the last journey. Oh, that is very true. You never spoke a truer word.'

He raised his head from the table and his eyes went swivelling this way and that, and finally focused full in Thorkel's face – and Ranald had never seen such a look of malice and hatred on a man's face as that morning on Einar's.

Thorkel's grieve, Prad, had returned and stood in the doorway beckoning to Thorkel.

'My man wants a word with me,' said Thorkel. 'Your lordship should have one last flagon for the road.'

Thorkel and Prad spoke briefly together. Thorkel nodded. He turned and beckoned to Hallvard and Ranald. They left the table and went to the open door.

'Prad', said Thorkel, 'has been doing a little scouting for me. He wasn't long in discovering what I knew already. Here and there along the road to Rendall, Earl Einar has men lying in ambush for me. What should be done with such a man?'

'The man is mad,' said Hallvard. 'He should be turned out into the darkness, a poor shivering ghost. I am sure of one thing, Valhalla the house of heroes will have nothing to do with such a creature once he's dead. But the death should not be too long in coming.'

Ranald said he thought there might yet be a way of smoothing things over.

'Never forget,' said Hallvard, 'that you and I, Ranald, were meant to die in the ambush too.'

Thorkel took a cudgel and hid it in his tunic.

'We'll go and say a few last words about journeys to his lordship,' he said.

'What's keeping you!' cried Einar from the high bench. 'Are you ready? Are our horses saddled? We should have been up and off an hour ago. Where's the flagon you promised me for the road, Thorkel?'

'Here it is, the stirrup cup,' said Thorkel, and brought the cudgel down on Earl Einar's head, so that his skull cracked like a nut, and in a frenzy of ale and blood and vomit he toppled from his place and fell

146

into the great fire in the centre of the hall. Prad meantime had shut and barred both doors. The earl's bodyguards were too drunk and over-awed to do anything but gaze at the burning fringe of their lord's festive coat. One of them wept. 'I know it's a cold day', said Hallvard, 'but your lordship shouldn't hug the fire so tightly.' Hallvard had a great curving axe with a hook at one end. He put the hook round Einar's neck and heaved him out of the flames on to the platform where the festive table was. And there the earl lay, dead and smouldering. Girls from the kitchen came and stood in the door, their aprons up at their mouths or over their eyes, and they shrieked occasionally, more because a valedictory shriek was expected from women than for grief at the death of this man and this earl. The cellarman said, 'I'll have to put on another brew at once. He was some drinker, that Einar!'

'I'm glad I had my meal,' said Thorkel. 'I think there won't be that much to eat in Einar's hall tonight. As for Einar, he won't need to worry about wind-in-the-gut or hangovers any more.'

'All this has been well done,' said Hallvard. 'But you, Thorkel, have killed an earl, and earls in general take a poor view of earl-murder. My advice to you is, go back at once to the only earl who will thank you for this day's work, young Earl Thorfinn over in Caithness. Earl Brus might not be all that pleased.'

Thorkel allowed Earl Einar's bodyguard to ride away from Skaill unmolested. A disordered company of wretches they looked as they clattered out through the courtyard gate.

Then Thorkel gave orders to his grieve Prad about the running of the household; Prad was to see that a priest was sent for so that Einar could have an honourable burial.

Then Thorkel shook hands warmly with all the household, even the kitchen girls and the man who tended the pigsty. A few of the kitchen girls wept again, but this time out of love for their master.

Ranald stayed on for much of that day. The events of the morning had shocked him, and he was torn between his old friendship for Thorkel and abhorrence at the murder Thorkel had committed. 'It wasn't a clean killing,' said Ranald to Hallvard, 'like in hand-to-hand combat, but Thorkel struck him down in cold blood. I don't like that. Besides, Earl Einar was a guest in Thorkel's house. It seems to me that when a man involves himself too much in dealings with earls and kings, his nature coarsens and a shadow comes into his spirit. When we were young men, Thorkel would not have acted in that way.'

But Hallvard the Icelander laughed. 'There had to be a death today,' he said. 'It was one or the other of them. Thorkel killed Einar in self-defence. Besides, Orkney and the whole world is well rid of a mad dog like Einar.'

Ranald could see that a great many stores were being stowed into the *Skua*, Thorkel's ship.

Early in the afternoon two men rode to Skaill from the Hall in Birsay, six miles away.

'Word travels quickly,' said Hallvard. 'I wonder what Earl Brus has to say about this?'

One of the horsemen was a monk from the monastery at Brough, a small steep island off the Birsay shore. The monk said that Einar should have the kind of burial befitting an earl – that was Earl Brus's demand – and Brus would see to it that his dead brother was carried across to Einar's domain in the island of Rousay and buried there.

Thorkel agreed at once to that. His own men would carry the body to Birsay. After that Brus could do with it what he liked.

The other horseman was Brus's treasurer, Frith. Frith was the kind of man who uses different words to a farmer – even to an important farmer like Thorkel – than to earls and kings. 'I see you're getting your ship ready,' he said to Thorkel. 'That's wise of you. It's no light thing to kill an earl who also happens to be an earl's brother. You'd better have that ship under way before nightfall. I must tell you that Earl Brus doesn't want you hanging about in Orkney, after what's happened here this morning. When you get to Caithness, tell Earl Thorfinn this, that now Earl Brus will take over Einar's share of the earldom. Tell Thorfinn this too – Earl Brus will buy him out of his third share. "For", says he, "it is better that Orkney should have one earl only, a single strong earl quite independent of Norway". . . .'

Thorkel thanked Frith for taking the trouble to so much as speak to a poor farmer like him, and an earl-killer too, and an outcast from the islands. 'But in my opinion,' said Thorkel, 'a farmer whose hands are crusted with mud from the ploughing is as good a man as a creeper and a crawler in high places who washes his hands in the silver and gold of unjust taxes. Such a sycophant should keep a civil tongue in his head, speaking to an honest farmer.'

'Maybe so,' said Frith, 'but there are set ways of talking to a man whose hands are crusted with murder. Be on that ship before the sun is down, Thorkel Amundson, or it will be the worse for you.'

Then Frith the treasurer turned his horse's head about and rode off north to Birsay.

The monk was inside, saying a prayer over the body of Einar. The candle he had lit shone brighter as the first shadows came down. The sun smouldered like a closed forge on the horizon.

Presently farmworkers came with a litter and Earl Einar's body was placed on it, and the pall-bearers set out for Brus's hall in Birsay, the monk going on in front, uttering from time to time some Latin words.

Now the last of the stores was on board *Skua*.

Thorkel stood on the shore and took leave of his friends.

Hallvard thanked Thorkel for such a good feast. 'I think I've never been at a better,' he said. 'But I think I'd better not stay on in Orkney. Brus might not be too pleased. As soon as I get a ship to Iceland, I'll set out for home . . .'

Then Hallvard embraced Thorkel and walked up to the farm.

Thorkel turned to Ranald. 'Old friend,' he said, 'what do you think of today's happenings? You haven't said much all day.'

Ranald said he had been sickened by everything that had happened that day – the drunkenness, the insults and the threats, the plotting and counter-plotting, and most of all by the murder of an unarmed man, who had been also a guest of the murderer, and an earl to whom courtesy is due even in the worst circumstances. An earl, if he had to die, was due the courtesy of a clean dagger death, not to be bludgeoned like a rat in a cess-pit, as had happened to Earl Einar.

'Well,' said Thorkel, 'I am sorry you think that way, Ranald. I thought we would be friends forever.'

'Give my regards to Earl Thorfinn,' said Ranald. 'I agree with Frith. It would be better for the peace of Orkney if that young man sold his third part of the islands to Brus, and contented himself with Caithness and Sutherland. Surely there is enough land across the Pentland Firth to keep him busy. He can't be the King of Scotland's man and the King of Norway's man too. That's a farmer's advice to Earl Thorfinn. Tell him when you see him in the morning.'

Thorkel said he would be seeing King Olaf before he saw his foster-son Thorfinn. He wasn't quite sure, he said, how Thorfinn would take this killing of Einar. The killing of an earl, however foolish and wicked that earl had been, was different from the killing of common man. Earl-murder must always be frowned on, in case men made a habit of it . . . Earl Thorfinn might well look on matters in that way. He intended to sail to Norway at sunrise. He thought King Olaf would not be ill-pleased with the news he brought from Orkney.

Then Thorkel stepped forward to embrace his old friend Ranald, but Ranald turned away from him and walked up from the shore to the stable where he had left his horse Thundercloud.

Ranald turned once on the sea-banks and said, 'Go in peace, Thorkel.'

Then he rode home under the stars.

Ragna his wife, and Thora his mother, and all the Breckness household were waiting to hear news of the feast at Skaill.

'I am sick at heart,' said Ranald. 'Don't ask me about it. They were wild animals I had dealings with today, not breakers of bread.'

He wrapped himself in his coat and lay down at the fire and went to sleep at once.

The good folk at Breckness were greatly troubled.

After an hour Ranald woke up and the black cloud seemed to have left him.

'Well,' he said, 'is there no supper in Breckness for a traveller? I haven't eaten a bite since noon.'

Ragna hastened to bring him a bowl of soup and some new-baked bread.

As he ate, Ranald told them what had happened at Skaill that day. They listened, enthralled.

Even the two eldest children, Sumarlid and Solveig, crept out of their cots and heard how a great lord had been killed, caught in the web of his own dark plotting.

9

The next day, Ranald Sigmundson decided that he would take no more part in the politics of Orkney. He would not even ride to the annual assembly of the chief men at Tingvoe. 'No,' said Ranald, 'I will give all my wits and all my attention to the running of the farm at Breckness. That's the best thing for a man like me. I might take a share in a merchant ship, but no more sailing – I want nothing to do with that great enchantress, the sea.'

The farm prospered. True, there were one or two bad harvests, and poorish harvests, caused by rough weather in late summer, or the sowing of poor seed in spring, but for upwards of a decade bad harvests were general all over the north, from Shetland to Ross, and provident farmers like Ranald always saw to it that the households round about had plenty to eat through the long winter and spring.

In the few years of bad harvest, the islands would be aswarm with beggarmen, a few of them small crofters who had been ruined by the black worm in the corn or a sudden tempest from the east. Then some neighbouring farmer would step in and take over the few acres of the unfortunate crofter for a song, sometimes not even letting them stay in their cottages. Then another family would be on the roads, begging. But in general the big farms allowed the dispossessed crofters to go on living under their own meagre roofs, and they would take them and their wives on as farm-servants – ploughmen, makers of cheese and butter in the kitchens of the big farm.

In the early spring of one year, following a very bad harvest, three crofters from the ridge above Breckness knocked at Ranald's door.

They were, all three, honest hardworking glebemen, and it hurt their pride very much to say what they had now to say to Ranald. 'We are down to our last sack of meal, and as you know we had to kill our cow in December. It will be a hard thing for us and for our families if we have to take to the roads, Ranald, and build shelters for ourselves in this quarry or that. We have no skill at begging. And so, Ranald, there's nothing for it but that we must sell our crofts. As you are the only farmer hereabout that could buy them, now we offer them to you at whatever price you will give. You know we are good ploughmen and horsemen and shepherds, so we'd be glad if you did us the further favour of employing us here at Breckness as labourers.'

Ranald said he was sorry that it had come to this pass with them. The bad harvest had all but ruined his income too. He told the three crofters from Don and Liffea and Creya that he would think about it. Let them come back to Breckness the next day, and then he would give them his decision.

Ranald's mother Thora and his wife Ragna had been listening to this painful dialogue, each from her own end of the house (for nowadays the two women rarely met). As the three crofters were leaving, Ragna came out of the barn with three little sacks of oatmeal, and she put three segments of white crumbly cheese into the sacks, and offered them to the crofters.

The crofter of Don said, 'We're not beggars yet, Ragna.'

151

Ragna said it was a gift, so that the children could eat their porridge on such cold mornings, and have a bite of cheese before they went to bed.

There was such kindness and openness about Ragna that men could take charity from her without feeling shame.

The three crofters shouldered their sacks, and thanked Ragna and set off home across the snow.

Then Ragna went inside, to see to the blowing up of the fire and the baking of more bread.

Ranald stood at the main door of the farm, wondering what ought to be done about the crofters who were never rich at the best of times and were very poor this spring, and by summer might be on the roads begging. Earl Brus's tax-men would be visiting them before Easter, too.

He was aware that his mother Thora was standing right in front of him. 'Ranald,' she said, 'this is a golden opportunity for you to enlarge the farm. You could cultivate their crofts far better than those men. You could buy the land cheap. I know you have a conscience as tremulous as a butterfly or a piece of thistledown, but this purchase needn't trouble you. There will be no beggars, no thin blue-veined children crying in ditches. Some of the workers here at Breckness are old. We need young strong men for the ploughing and all the spring work. Very well, you can take on those crofters as hired men. They would be better off that way. And so everybody is happy.'

Ranald said he would think about it.

Thora raised her voice, so that what she said could be clearly heard inside the house. 'Our barns are not full to bursting, exactly. We might have to ration our own supplies within the next month. What foolishness, giving away our oatmeal and cheese for nothing! Next thing, all the poor folk of Orkney will come here in troops, once they get to know what a rich and prodigal farm Breckness is.'

Ranald said he was trying to riddle things out in his mind, and he couldn't think clearly with such a word-storm going on.

From inside the house, Ragna and the farm girls were singing as they blew up the fires and kneaded the dough.

Ragna was expecting a fifth child, and it seemed to Ranald that his wife had never been happier.

Thora went back to her own part of the house. Her face was glowing as if she had been out in a gale.

The three crofters of Don and Creya and Liffea stood next morning in the door of Breckness.

Ranald said to them, 'I know that you don't want to shrug off your crofts like threadbare coats. A farm, big or small, is like that some years. But most years, a croft is a thick coat that keeps the farmfolk warm and secure. We'll see a good harvest next year, I feel sure. The coats will renew themselves, they'll be green in high summer and then, at harvest-time, all heavy and gold. (Forgive me, friends, I sometimes speak ornate language – it comes from having the temperament of a poet without the poet's art and skill.) But now I'll be plain with you. I won't buy your crofts for a song, and I won't have good men turned into beggars because a black worm has gotten into the corn this past year. What I propose is, that I lend you enough money to see you through till next harvest. It will be a good harvest, I feel it in my bones.'

'It will be some time, Ranald Sigmundson, before we can pay you back,' said Per the crofter of Don.

'There's no hurry, no hurry in the world,' said Ranald. 'Take your time . . . How long, Per, have your people been crofting at Don?'

'I'm the fifth generation there,' said Per.

Kriv of Liffea said his great-grandfather had broken out the rough hill ground and drained it to make the croft of Liffea.

And Svelt of Creya said that Creya was the dowry that came with his wife Asa. But Asa's people had been there for a hundred years, and he and Asa had five sons, and now if all went well it seemed they might still be there a hundred years on.

'That's true,' said Ranald. 'That's the way it should be. Men are made of the dust they labour at, and in the end they go back to the same dust. That's the way it should be, always. Come into my room, where we'll be out of earshot and eyeshot of women.'

Ranald had been aware, since the coming of the three crofters to his door, of his mother's face peering from time to time round the end of the house.

Ranald unlocked his desk and unthonged a heavy bag and counted twelve silver coins into the hands of Per and Kriv and Svelt.

'We offer you our crofts as security,' said Per.

'There is no need,' said Ranald. 'There will be seven good harvests in a row, just like when Joseph was overseer in Egypt. Plenty and poverty often run in seven-year cycles, I've noticed. There is no need for signatures and seals when one is dealing with honest men.'

The crofters thanked Ranald and trudged through the snow with their little pokes of money.

Ragna came to the door and called after them to give her greetings to their wives. Per of Don turned and thanked her for the porridge and cheese they had enjoyed yesterday.

But Thora kept to her quarters for a week and would speak to no one. She even barred her door against Ranald.

10

The years passed. Ragna was combing Ranald's beard one morning when he noticed a silver hair among the russet hairs in the teeth of the comb. Ranald picked out the silver hair and looked at it ruefully.

'There's no running back when the wave of time breaks on a man's shoulder,' said Ragna. 'He must stand and endure it. Think what a wise old silver-headed man you'll be at the debates in Tingvoe, in ten years or in twenty years.'

'That's true enough,' said Ranald, 'there's no turning away from that wave. In the end it drowns us. When we were young men together, coursing hares at the Birsay links and racing our horses across Greenay hill, we were happy and thankless, and we didn't know just how precious youth was.'

Meantime their children were growing up on the farm, and the five young ones (for in the previous summer little Margaret had been born) were a constant delight to them, but sometimes – as in the case of Einhof the younger son – the joy was clouded with anxiety. Einhof would set out with his brother Sumarlid to the monastery where the Warbeth brothers instructed a dozen of the farmers' sons from all over the parish in Latin and arithmetic, and plainsong and scripture, but by mid-morning he would be seen wandering alone on the shore, picking shells and little crabs out of the rockpools, or sitting beside an upturned boat while a fisherman was caulking or tarring it for the imminent lobster fishing.

'Alas,' said Brother Cormac, 'the boy doesn't take kindly to the classroom, like his brother Sumarlid. There is no great harm in that. We can't all be scholars. But there is something else about the boy. Whenever he sits in the classroom it seems – I don't know how – as if the rhythm of the lesson is disrupted. The other boys pay less attention to their books whenever Einhof is here, there is a constant whispering and sniggering and general air of misbehaviour. I think, to tell the truth, Ranald, that it would be better for everyone concerned if you were to find Einhof, young as he is, employment at the farm. After all, how can a man give glory to God better than tilling the soil?'

Einhof had the gift of mimicry. He could imitate people in the district, their words and gestures and eccentricities, to perfection, so that the farmworkers and his fellow-pupils at the song-school and the family at the dinner table were made helpless sometimes with laughter; and even his grave father had to smile.

But Einhof was as negligent at his farm duties as at his lessons. Oh yes, he assured his father, he would round up those forty sheep on the far side of the Black Crag and bring them into the shearing pen – he would set out at once with the dog Bran . . . Evening came, there was no sign of boy or dog. Einhof would be found by lamplight in the weaver's hut a mile away on the flank of the ridge, listening to the weaver and the weaver's wife telling of the good times that used to be, in the days of Earl Sigurd, not like nowadays when his two sons Brus and Thorfinn were forever bickering and raising the taxes and following each other to Norway, to curry favour with the king there. 'Ah,' said the weaver, 'the best times have been. Orkney is like a tinkers' camp nowadays, nothing but squabbling and riot, and the place riddled with the King of Norway's spies and tax-men . . .'

Einhof laughed when he heard this, as if it was no immediate concern of his, though he had heard the same complaints many times from the farmworkers at Breckness. His father would not allow such rumours and speculations concerning the earldom and the King of Norway to be so much as whispered at his table and hearth. 'We are farmfolk,' he would always say, 'and a farm is a place of peace, not a slaughter-house . . .' Ranald Sigmundson seemed to forget, the many times he said that, how the pigs and sheep and cows were slaughtered regularly at the killing-stone at the end of the house, till the gutters ran red and the reek of blood was everywhere about Breckness . . . However, the family and all the household knew well enough the farmer's meaning. Politics and statecraft were not to be discussed within earshot of him.

In the countryside those things were discussed thoroughly, and often ignorantly, but taxes touch every man to the quick, especially when on top of the earl's tax there comes to the door a tax-man from the King of Norway. Such seemed to be the drift of affairs, Orkney was falling increasingly under the sway of the king in the east. 'He is our real master,' the people grumbled. 'Earl Thorfinn and Earl Brus are only his playthings.'

So the weaver and the weaver's wife were pouring out their complaints to the boy Einhof, and Einhof was listening and laughing as if it was a good well contrived story, when Grim the farm grieve arrived to ask why Einhof hadn't brought in the forty sheep to the shearing-pen, as he had promised to do that morning?

Einhof frowned. 'Sheep,' said he. 'What sheep? Oh those sheep on the other side of the hill, along near Yesnaby. Well, I looked for the sheep, the dog Bran and I, and we couldn't find them anywhere, though we searched high and low along the cliffs and up in the moor hills. I was tired, so I just dropped in here at the weaver's house for a cup of milk and a piece of cheese. And they've told me things my father never tells me, nor the monks either – just how things are in the earldom and in the kingdom of Norway. It is only right and fitting that a young fellow should understand such things, for he'll have to play a part in them some day, won't he?'

Grim answered that Einhof's father was angry. As for the sheep being lost, he himself – Grim – had found the flock grazing quietly on the slopes of Moosland, and they had come in quietly to the shearing-pen.

'My advice to you', said Grim to Einhof, 'is to go as quiet as a shadow to your bed. Your father is not in the best of moods tonight.'

Einhof bade the weaver and his wife goodnight, and went furtively back to the farm, and he was soon in bed and asleep.

Einhof had 'the gift of masks', of being able to assume a dozen kinds of personality in the course of a day. He was early at the breakfast table next morning, looking bright and eager. His mother put a wooden bowl of porridge and milk in front of him. Oh yes, he assured her, he was looking forward very much to going to the monks' school that day. Brother Colm had promised to teach them plainchant and how words and music interwove, each enriching the other, so that truly angelic sounds were produced . . . Einhof had, too, a faculty with language beyond his years, and a good voice for song as well as for mimicry.

His mother smiled. In many ways this boy was her favourite of all the children, in spite of his waywardness. Einhof went on to say that that kind of artistry interested him greatly – so much so, that in the end he might devote himself to poetry and harpsong.

Just then, Ranald appeared at the table with a cloud at his brow, but when he saw Ragna and Einhof engaged in such eager earnest talk, and about such a high serious matter as plainchant, he decided to say nothing about the lack of shepherding the day before.

'Good morning, father,' said Einhof, and stood respectfully until his father had sat down. 'Now I must be off,' he said. 'We are going to have an interesting day of it at school. I must get there as soon as I can.'

And he was off and through the door like a bird.

'Well,' said Ranald to his wife, 'I know it happens, a worthless boy can all at once change his ways. Didn't I change, myself, from a little trembling sea-coward to a competent enough sailor, almost overnight? I pray it may be the same with Einhof. Now I'm glad I didn't give him the tongue-lashing he deserved, for now that he seems set on a new tack, it might have driven him into stormier waters still.'

Sumarlid came and greeted his father and mother with little formal bows, and took his place at table. Ragna poured milk over his bowl of porridge. There was no more talk at the breakfast table. But Ranald looked at his son and heir with grave approval. Here was a young man who would see well to the farm when he himself was dust.

Then the two elder daughters, Solveig and Ingerth, came in, sleepy eyed, and they broke the silence of the breakfast table with their chatter, so that even their mother had to hold her finger up to her lips – a sign that their father was in one of his low moods.

Sumarlid set off to the monks' school a mile away.

Then the infant, Margaret, began to cry from her crib.

Ranald said he must go up the hill that morning. One of the wells had silted up and he must supervise the clearing of it.

While Ranald and two of the farmworkers were busy with the spades and buckets at the well, he paused and looked down at the beach. There was his son, Einhof, who was supposed to be deep in music notation and Latin psalms with Brother Colm that morning, wandering idly among the rockpools, kicking a stone now and then, or running among a furled flock of gulls to scatter them into a wild screaming cloud.

Then Einhof spread his wings like a bird and screamed like a gull and leapt once or twice like a bird preparing to take off. It was as if the boy was taking part in the existence of one of those sea-birds . . .

That afternoon a fisherman called at the farm, asking to speak to the master. 'Someone has been stealing my lobsters,' he said.

'Do you know who the thief is?' said Ranald.

'It has been going on for a month now, the thieving,' said the fisherman. 'I'm sorry to say that the thief is your son Einhof. I saw him taking two lobsters from my box this morning. I called to him. He ran away.'

Ranald's heart turned to stone inside him.

He knew that Einhof had lately taken over an old pigsty near the farm that was no longer in use, and often he stayed there for hours on end, acting out his fantasies and games in secret. Often enough Ranald had seen peat-smoke drifting from the open door of the sty. Now Ranald led the fisherman to the sty. A rusty iron pot hung over a burnt stone. Here and there across the filthy floor was a scattering of red empty lobster shells.

That day Einhof did not come home. Sumarlid said it was true, his brother had not attended the song-school, and Brother Cormac was ill-pleased about that.

Einhof's fish and bread got cold on the plate when the family rose from the dinner table. The thundercloud sat heavy on Ranald's brow. It was clear that there would be trouble when the truant came home at bedtime.

Ragna tried to smooth things over. 'Boys behave that way at a certain age, then when the first gold hairs are on their lip, they become good honest straightforward men, people the community couldn't do without. It's that way with our Einhof. Why, even you, Ranald, deserted from your father's ship in Iceland when you were Einhof's age, and are you the worse of it?'

Ranald said nothing.

The feeling of disquiet pervaded the whole household, so that even the infant Margaret cried in her cradle from time to time all through that day, though she was usually a happy child.

Einhof did not come home that night. His mother got up once or twice and lit a candle and stooped over the empty bed. 'Ah well,' she said to herself, 'there'll be a cold penitent boy standing at the door at sunrise.'

But Einhof didn't come home next morning, nor the following morning, nor any morning that week.

A search party went here and there looking for him. They combed the district thoroughly, looking into every cowshed and stable and ruin. The crofters and their people were questioned – no one had seen the boy. 'And I doubt,' said the weaver's wife in the wailing tones that she kept for the tax-man and for the gravedigger and for her man when he came home drunk, 'I doubt if we'll ever see Einhof again. Look in the quarries. Look along the shore under the cliffs. Tell the fishermen to be on the lookout for a body floating out west.'

In fact, after a week of fruitless searching, those desperate combings were made. But even a dead Einhof did not show up.

Then Ragna wept into her apron, but only once.

She dried her eyes soon and said, 'God will look after the boy, dead or alive.' And the work of the farm went on as before.

At the end of that month, Ragna combed many silver hairs out of her man's beard.

He began to complain of pains in his shoulder and thigh-bone – 'That comes', said he, 'from too many cold nights at sea in my youth.' He found it difficult to ride his horse Thundercloud, because then the jolting on the rough tracks made him bite on his lip with agony.

It was noticed how much milder and more affectionate he was now to his children. He would often lay his hand on Sumarlid's shoulder and take him aside and discuss with the young man the work he planned to do on the farm next year, and the year following, and even for a decade to come. 'You, Sumarlid, will be the farmer here in Breckness after me. I want you to know everything that is to be known about the keeping of horses and sheep and swine, and how a farmer must have respect for the land he tills, neither forcing it into premature fertility nor letting it revert to bog and rushes. The land and the farmer have a solemn bond with one another. This bond is not forged in a year or two – no merchant or skipper can suddenly say, *Now I'll buy a farm and work it*, for the land will not work for the stranger – but it takes generations for the land and the dust of a family (living or dead) to mingle well with one another. Now, as to this year's stock, we will require a new horse, for Thundercloud is no longer the horse he was, and there will have to be four young oxen for the ploughing in March . . .'

And Sumarlid would listen gravely to his father's land-wisdom, and nod from time to time, but sometimes he had a suggestion of his own to make, and that pleased Ranald, because now he knew for sure that Sumarlid loved the farm and would look after it well when he himself was howe-laid.

As for his three daughters, it was said throughout the parish that

Ranald spoiled them and yielded to them in everything. But occasionally, if he saw any signs of disobedience and waywardness in them, he could be suddenly stern and forbidding, and the second daughter Ingerth would be shaken with fear and sorrow on such occasions. The three girls had happy natures, and the eldest daughter Solveig was a great favourite in the district. She spoke her mind directly, but her innocence took the edge off what she had to say, so that even neighbours who might have been offended by her honesty smiled and praised her. Solveig could soon work about the farm as well as anyone. As she got older, her tongue lost none of its edge and often people were hurt by her speech. The youngest, Margaret, seemed to grow more beautiful with every month that passed, but as yet she was too young to be vain.

Thora and Ragna hardly saw each other. They minded their own business. Ranald went to see his mother at least once every day. To him she poured out all her complaints, that seemed to increase the more bent and writhen-mouthed she became. 'That boy Einhof,' she said, 'if I had had the bringing-up of him, he would still be here. He had the makings of a great man, Einhof. I'm sure he would have been an excellent skald. But that wife of yours didn't see the great qualities in the boy. No wonder Einhof ran away. Some time or other, maybe in ten years, maybe sooner, you'll hear word that the King of Sweden or the Duke of Normandy has a brilliant wit among his courtiers, a treasure by the name of Einhof. I predict this, though of course I won't live to see it. As for the way your wife brings up those girls, I think it's shameful, it is indeed. They're brought up like young ladies, not like a farmer's daughters at all . . .' (This was untrue – Solveig worked as hard as any farm lass.)

Ranald could hardly get a word in. When he did, he said he'd be glad if Thora did not mention the names of either Einhof or Ragna again. The former 'was out of the story'. As for his wife, he could wish for none better. Then they sat down together to taste Thora's bread and ale, and they talked for a while about other matters (which is to say, of any ten words uttered, Thora spoke nine). 'Thus and thus fate deals with a man,' said Ranald once, 'and so far fate has been not unkind to me, but who knows what fate has in store for any man?'

Two matters concerning Einhof Ranald did not tell his mother. Word had been brought to him a month after Einhof's disappearance that a troop of masquers had been recently in Orkney, going among the big

160

houses giving entertainments, songs and mimes and ballads. No one knew where they came from, those entertainers, they went as free as birds to any part of Scotland or Ireland or Scandinavia that they chose, and they were generally made welcome (though there were invariably one or two rogues in any given company, on whom a close eye had to be kept). Those troopers had even performed in the earl's court in Birsay, and Brus had been greatly taken with their masques and had entertained them lavishly. They were inordinate liars, but in a free-and-easy jovial way, so that no one took exception to their boasting. For example, they had just come, they said, from the court of King Malcolm in Inverness, and before that the twelve princes of Ireland had been delighted to be their patrons, and now they had urgent invitations from the King of Norway. The King in Bergen could hardly wait to have them sing and dance and juggle and joke in his great hall . . . All of this was nonsense, for they were all people from the ragged half-starved fringes of society. Only once they had got entry into a merchant's or a landowner's hall, they fared well enough for a weekend or even as long as ten days. Then, the very presence of the troop seemed to have an upsetting effect on the household, and the master would come and tell them firmly to move on.

This particular troop had sent word to Breckness that they were in Orkney, and 'they would consider it a high honour and privilege to display their universally acclaimed talents at the household of the renowned and generous patron of the arts, Ranald Sigmundson . . .' Ranald returned word that, if they crossed the border of his land, he would set the dogs on them. Einhof had got to know of the arrival of the troop in Orkney, and he had been very much excited by the news, but a stern word from his father sent the boy away to his room, glum and resentful. The very next day, the farm grieve happened to mention that the vagabonds had had the impudence to invite themselves to Breckness – they were actually on the way – but Ranald had sent Grim the steward to turn them back. There would be no nonsense of mouthings and masques and dancings and prancings in the barn of Breckness.

It was two days after that that Einhof had disappeared.

Word was brought to Ranald that the company of actors had embarked on a trading ship, the *Erne*, at Hamnavoe, Iceland bound. There had been six members of the troop when first they had come to Orkney. This bringer of news had counted *seven* embarking for

161

Iceland. One of them, a young man, was well scarfed about the face.

Ranald nodded, and listened.

Later that week, the newly imposed tax to the crown of Norway being due, Ranald had gone to his strong-box to take out the money. The lock had been forced, and two silver coins were missing.

'I feel sure', Ranald said to his wife that evening after dinner, when they were alone together, 'that our son Einhof is alive.'

But, as he said it, he looked none too pleased.

11

The years passed, and the farm at Breckness prospered. The crofts round about prospered too, in a more modest way. The country people learned from Ranald Sigmundson that they must provide, in good years, for the occasional lean year, and so there was never destitution in that part of Orkney.

Ranald kept away from politics and the assemblies at Tingvoe. But news of the earls' quarrels and manoeuvrings was brought to him from time to time.

It seemed to Ranald, watching this perilous jousting from his quiet corner of Orkney, that the King of Norway, anxious about the growing might of the Scottish crown and how Orkney must be kept within the orbit of the northern kingdom, had played his part with great skill.

First of all, Earl Thorfinn sent word to his brother Earl Brus that, after the death of Earl Einar, they should share the islands equally between them. No, Brus had answered, according to the terms of the earlier agreement, Einar's share fell to him. Therefore, he now ruled over two thirds of the earldom. Surely the younger brother had enough territory, a huge earldom in northern Scotland, and in addition a third of Orkney. He, Thorfinn, was secure in his possessions by virtue of his kinship with the King of Scotland. It was a difficult and a divisive thing, Brus suggested, to serve two masters: Norway as well as Scotland.

Brus knew well that he would not be able to stand against his able and arrogant and well-armed brother if Thorfinn moved against him.

'Why can't I be left to rule my lands in peace?' he said one night in Birsay. 'All I want to do, after a day's work in my office and down at the ships, is to have a game of chess beside the ale jar, and then sleep with an easy conscience. At my time of life, who wants to go on a long sea voyage? The day after tomorrow, all the same, I intend to sail east to Norway to see the king there.'

Brus turned to the skipper sitting beside him at the table. 'See to it, my friend,' he said. Then he turned to his wife Hilde and said, 'Our young child Rognvald will sail with me. The sooner a boy gets salt in his mouth, in this part of the world, the better his chances are. Besides, the innocence of the child may work better for me in the throne-room of Norway than the poor kind of rhetoric I can command . . .' So, Brus and his advisers and young Rognvald his son sailed east to Norway.

Brus explained the situation west in Orkney and Shetland and Caithness to King Olaf. From time to time the king turned and Thorkel Amundson would whisper behind his hand into the king's ear. The king said, 'There seems to be nothing but endless trouble in Orkney. It is not a question, Brus my friend, of your land and your brother Thorfinn's land. I am King of Orkney and Shetland too, you seem to forget that. The islands belong to me alone, as they belonged to my predecessors. I'll confirm you in your governance of two thirds of the earldom, on condition that you acknowledge me as your supreme overlord, entitled to a fair share of the islands' revenues. This is no idle whim that I thought up this morning over breakfast – the whole history of the north is proof that Norway has complete sovereignty over Orkney and Shetland. Brus my friend, either you agree with me in this matter, or else I abandon you to the ambitions of that young brother of yours, Thorfinn, a very fierce and a very able young man.'

Brus said he would have to think about it.

'And this is your boy, Rognvald,' said King Olaf. 'Well, Brus, if you've done little else on earth, you've fathered a marvellous young son.'

A trumpet sounded outside. A messenger entered. 'My Lord,' said the man to King Olaf, 'another ship out of the west has just anchored. Earl Thorfinn Sigurdson of Orkney and Caithness requests an audience.'

There were days then of comings and goings in the Norwegian court, and consultations open and secret. Thorkel Amundson played a prominent part in the drift of events. It was evident that King Olaf placed great importance on Thorkel's advice. Earl Thorfinn considered that his friend and foster-father Thorkel had behaved in an underhand manner, after the murder of Earl Einar – sailing east to Norway instead of seeking his friend Thorfinn's protection in Caithness. Often now, when Thorkel came to speak to him in the palace, Thorfinn would turn away from him and speak in a loud cheerful voice to some courtier of no importance. This ignoring of Thorkel by Earl Thorfinn was an insult almost as degrading as if the earl had spat on his coat.

At last the king, with Thorkel Amundson standing at the side of the throne, announced his decision – one third of Orkney to Brus, one third to Thorfinn, one third to the king himself, to be ruled over by whatever man he chose.

The earls took the oath of allegiance on a parchment roll of scripture.

The trumpet sounded.

The great conference was over.

Earl Thorfinn rose from his knee and seemed very cheerful. He even winked at Thorkel, as much as to say, 'Well, it's done now and it can't be undone, and I'm sorry to have lost your friendship.'

Earl Brus rose from his knee, and seemed downcast. He beckoned, his son Rognvald came running towards him, and Earl Brus embraced the boy fiercely, as though this that he was holding was the only treasure left to him on earth.

Earl Thorfinn asked the king for leave to sail next day – there was much to do out in the west – an earl shouldn't leave his land too long unguarded. And he thanked King Olaf for his hospitality and the royal wisdom. He shook hands heartily with his many Norwegian friends, and left the palace for his ship.

That night Thorkel had himself rowed out to Earl Thorfinn's ship in the harbour, and asked to become once more the earl's friend and adviser. The earl lifted the proud penitent's head from his knee. 'I could ask for nothing better, Thorkel,' he said.

In the morning Thorfinn's ship sailed west with a light breeze.

Earl Brus lingered on for another week at the court. It seemed to him that now the dice was loaded against him. The king and court treated him civilly enough, but there was an undertow of neglect all the same, as though Brus from now on was a man of small importance. Earl Brus was only cheerful when he walked out in the gardens with his son Rognvald, or sat with the boy in their chamber setting out the pieces on a chessboard. The child showed an amazing gift at the game for one so young.

A lackey came to Earl Brus's door one morning – not one of King Olaf's advisers, but some polisher of the royal boots, an altogether inferior messenger. 'The king will see you at once,' he said to Earl Brus. 'Bring the boy too.'

King Olaf said, 'Now, my friend, I want you to look after my third of Orkney. So the situation is as it was before you left home. It is a sign of my favour and friendship.'

Earl Brus thanked the king. He knew well that his situation was now very much weaker than it had been. He was now completely under the thumb of Norway, and he knew well that his brother Thorfinn would not stop before all the earldom was his own, utterly, from Unst in the north to Stroma in the south.

'I will do even more to please you, my friend,' said King Olaf. 'I have taken a great liking to your young son, Rognvald, so much so that I want him to remain here at my court when you leave tomorrow. A king can't honour a man more than to foster his son in his court.'

Earl Brus bent down to embrace his son, but Rognvald struggled free from his arms and stumbled up the steps of the throne and buried his face, laughing, in the king's brocade coat.

'You see how happy the boy will be with me,' said King Olaf.

The trumpet sounded. The audience was over.

Earl Brus went down to his ship, and closed himself in his cabin. The sailors heard him weeping bitterly for much of that night.

In the morning the *Ottar* raised anchor.

From far out at sea, the sailors saw a small boy on the headland, waving his cap . . .

These great events – among others of less note – were told to Ranald and his household by merchants and some of the bigger farmers who visited Breckness from time to time. As soon as the bringers of news opened their mouths, Ranald would raise his hand as if to plead for silence. But in the end he always listened, with downcast eyes. The household listened eagerly, they could not have enough of such 'saga-stuff', the turning of the pages of the book of fate.

Most of the stories now concerned the young Earl Thorfinn in Scotland. There had, it seemed, never in the north been a man like this black-headed hawk-eyed ugly young man. The heroics of his father Earl Sigurd had been puppet-dancing compared to the raids and depredations of Thorfinn, who once more had his headquarters in Caithness – though he had his men in Orkney too, supervising his third of the earldom there and collecting his rents.

Thorfinn's grandfather, King Malcolm of Scotland, died of old age, and a distant kinsman called Karl Hundason claimed the throne of Scotland, and at once set about putting the kingdom to rights. Among other matters Karl considered that he ought to tame this turbulent half-Norse Earl Thorfinn in the north. He sent a soldier called Maddad with a strong army against Thorfinn's keeps and castles, and Karl himself sailed up the east coast of Scotland with a formidable fleet. So, Thorfinn would be crushed between the land and the sea. Thorfinn laughed when he learned how he was to be held in this vice and smashed. He sent Thorkel – who was now fully restored to his favour – against Maddad; and Maddad's army – still lacking the soldiers from Ireland he had urgently sent for – was broken and scattered among the hills.

Meantime, Thorfinn in his own ships crossed the Pentland Firth to Deerness in Orkney, luring Karl's fleet to pursue him. Thorfinn knew the tides and surges on this part of the ocean well. There was so much fog on the sea that the ships seemed like ghost ships. Then suddenly Thorfinn turned and closed with the Scottish fleet, throwing grappling-irons on board as they came looming out of the fog, and seeming to be twice as big as they actually were. There followed a frightful slaughter on board the invading ships: if Thorfinn's men did not literally wade through blood, they slithered and slid along blood-splashed decks with axes and swords that rose and fell rhythmically, and at the end of the day they were splashed red from head to foot, like fearsome clowns in a fair. And none was so drunk with merriment and gore that day as Earl Thorfinn himself. The earl did not direct the battle from a place of safety, like many famous commanders. He took it ill if any sailor pressed further than himself into the thick of battle.

The Scottish ships turned and fled, but one or two of them burned in the sea-haar, like roses unpetalling after a tempest.

In the year or two following, Earl Thorfinn led small armies deep into the west and south of Scotland, laying siege to fortified keeps, but also attacking villages with flame and axe, pitilessly.

Those 'victories' made Earl Thorfinn famous as a battle-commander all through western Europe.

King Olaf in Bergen listened to the news gravely. 'I think', he said, 'I ought to have taken that young man Thorfinn more seriously. We will have trouble with him before long.'

Thorfinn was fortunate in that he had a court poet with him in those actions, a young man called Arnor. It seemed that Arnor's ability as a poet grew as his patron Earl Thorfinn's fame spread, so that the conquests and the songs-of-battle intertwined. Arnor was not one of those poets who sit at a fire at home writing about sieges and stormings with relish, while, if there is a creak in the woodwork at midnight as the logs sink, his spirit trembles as if a thief or a wolf were prowling about the house. No, Arnor the laureate was there on the fringe of the battle, heaving his axe, and if Thorfinn didn't allow him into the heart of the action, it was because he considered that, in reality, any battle was a charade and a shadow-play unless a poet carved the action deeply upon granite, so that men would remember the hero's achievements for many generations. These verses were a kind of passport to Valhalla.

So Arnor Laureate had a place of honour at the bench beside his lord.

News of the great victories of Thorfinn was brought to Breckness. And Ranald would say, as soon as the first splash of blood came upon the story, 'That's enough! I don't want to hear any more.' And he would go out of the room, but never for too long. At the end of the red swatches of history, Ranald would be seen leaning against the door-post, listening to the more homespun news.

The mistress of the farm, Ragna, wanted to know more about this poet Arnor. Where had he come from, this skald? Out of what ale-house had Earl Thorfinn plucked him? Was he an Irishman or a Norwegian? – for no bard of that name, Arnor, had ever been heard of in Orkney. Everyone she asked said Arnor must be an Icelander, for all the good poets came from Iceland in those years. Icelanders could not help speaking with golden tongues. And, Ragna went on, if his poems were so good, surely the welcome visitor would remember a line or two? It happened that one of them did know one or two of Arnor's poems, and he recited them, but so badly that the pewter pots on the shelf gave back dull echoes. 'But yet I assure you', said Skarf the skipper, 'when I heard Arnor himself recite them at the earl's house in Thurso, the room was enriched, as though it was an extension of Valhalla itself.'

Arnor's Song I

'Now', said the wolf, 'I am eating the red heart of him.'

'And I', said the eagle, 'will make me a nest of the yellow hair.'

'His hand', said the wolf, 'is inside me, his generous gold-giving hand.'

'I', said the eagle, 'have devoured the tongue that discoursed so variously with sweetheart, captain, merchant.'

The wolf said, 'Where is his foot now that went up past the mountain snow?'

'O sweetly his eye looked on the light of an April morning,' said the eagle. 'Never again.'

So howled wolf and eagle over the corpse on the moor, in Galloway.

Arnor's Song II

The stone of the battlement
Laid in the heather.

Loch water laves
The fallen white stone, the lintel.

Little walks through a Celtic keep now
But four gray winds.

Where is the harp,
Heart of the proud dance in winter?

Where the hearth, the round silver plate?
Where the ancient courtesy?

The last guests in this place
Were Thorfinn's soldiers.

Can the runes of verse
Celebrate victory, and restore
A broken stone web?

Ragna pressed the skipper about this mysterious poet – what did he look like? Was he tall or short? Fat or thin? Dark or fair?

'To tell the truth,' said Skarf, 'I was so engrossed with the verses that I didn't pay all that much attention to Arnor. He looked like a kind of nondescript man to me, you wouldn't give him a second look if you were to meet him at the Hamnavoe horse-fair . . .'

It so happened that while Thorfinn was winning those famous

victories by land and sea, south in Scotland, his brother Earl Brus was having a bad time of it. That autumn, in particular, the crews of viking ships were infesting Orkney, raiding farms and stealing sheep and cattle and molesting women all the way from Westray to Hoy. Those Norwegian vikings had had a poor summer in the shipping lanes of the Atlantic, between Ireland and Iceland. Normally, laden with booty, the viking longships sailed home before harvest, steering well to the north of Shetland. But this late summer they turned for home with poor pickings in the holds, and when one of the viking skippers suggested that it might be a good idea to gather in some surplus milk and honey from Orkney, they set their course more to the south, and fell on the islands just as the farmers were getting their scythes sharpened for harvest, and their oxen harnessed. The vikings came and left so suddenly and violently that to the Orkneymen it seemed only that a terrible tempest had broken over their steadings, and left ruin and desolation behind. And, in the days following, the farmers wanted to know what Earl Brus had done in the way of defending his people? Nothing; many of the earl's own cattle and swine had been driven off, though the vikings had known better than to attack the great Hall in Birsay – Brus's bodyguard was too formidable.

Earl Brus was covered with shame and sorrow. He wrote at once to King Olaf, telling him what the vikings had done in Orkney, and asking that they be punished with the utmost severity. 'For, sire, they are your subjects, and you are answerable for them . . .'

At the same time, Earl Brus wrote to his brother in Caithness. 'You, Thorfinn, are not slow to collect your taxes from that part of the Orkney earldom over which you have jurisdiction. I hear you are a famous warrior in Scotland now. The vikings may come again next year. Will you send some of your famous war-men to Orkney, with the revenues you get out of Orkney, so that my farmers and their families can sleep in their beds in peace?'

Within a week, a messenger from Caithness arrived in Birsay. 'I am grieved', Earl Thorfinn wrote, 'to learn of what the vikings have done in Orkney this summer. I know, brother, that you would sooner sit at your chessboard than recruit soldiers, and train them. It is, after all, work for a specialist. I have a suggestion that I hope will be agreeable to you. Let me take over Einar's share of the isles – that part which the tyrant over there in Norway has purloined for himself, to bestow at his discretion – and never forget, brother, that King Olaf claims to be your

169

overlord and mine too. I will defend the coasts of Orkney, never fear, those sea-tramps will not trouble you again. I promise this, solemnly. Only, I think it better that I take over two thirds of Orkney. May your games of chess be formidable and skilful and successful this coming winter, over there in Birsay, beside the fire with the jar of mead at your elbow. I trust you get good word concerning your young son Rognvald, kept a prisoner in Bergen.'

Wearily, Earl Brus agreed to Earl Thorfinn's proposal.

Men had noticed, in the last year or two, how the good earl seemed to lose all relish for life. This withering had begun soon after his return from Norway, having left his son Rognvald to be fostered by King Olaf. His handling of affairs at the annual assembly at Tingvoe was lacklustre. Even on good days he would not course the hares across the links at Birsay, or take his favourite hawk Cloudcleaver to Greenay Hill or Ravey Hill. He would even break off a game of chess, and excuse himself to his opponent, and go to his room (after telling the people in the kitchen not to prepare a place for him at dinner).

Earl Brus was well liked by the people. They grieved to see the shadows gathering about him. At the same time they were glad that from now on they were to have the protection of Earl Thorfinn.

When the news came of Earl Brus's death, drowned in shadows there on the great carved bed in the Hall, a silence went through the nine parishes in the west.

Old Madda, who sewed patches on the servants' coats, and swept the ashes on the hearth, went into the chapel and lit a candle for Earl Brus.

Later that night, a troop of boys came into the chapel and sang psalms; the night was touched with stillness and purity and beauty.

It was two days before the news of Earl Brus's death came to Breckness. Ranald said that no more work should be done that day. 'Let me tell you,' said Ranald, 'Brus was in every way a better man than this Thorfinn who has gotten so much fame for himself in battles and sieges.'

Next day, the Breckness folk saw a group of three sails sailing north from Caithness, along the west coast of 'the island of horses' to Birsay. The sails were black. They knew then that the mighty Thorfinn was on his way to the funeral of his gentle dead brother.

Ranald and his son Sumarlid rode north to Birsay for the funeral of Earl Brus.

In the church there all the wealthy farmers and merchants and skippers of Orkney stood among the candle-splashed shadows, while three monks recited the requiem for the dead, and choristers – farm boys from the parish – sang *De Profundis* and *Dominus Pascit Me*.

Two Norwegians were there, supposedly merchants, but they were thought to be spies, sent to keep the king informed as to the state of affairs in his western province. A constant stream of Norwegians passed through Orkney, as always.

Near the catafalque where the body of Earl Brus lay, Ranald saw the glimmering faces of Earl Thorfinn and Thorkel Amundson.

When the body had been borne out of the church, afloat it seemed on a sea of tapers and elegiac psalms, Earl Thorfinn approached the two Norwegians and said to them, 'Tell your king back home that now Thorfinn is taking over the whole earldom of Orkney.'

Thorkel raised his hand in greeting to Ranald and made his way through the company of mourners inside the church to greet his old friend.

Then Ranald turned his back on Thorkel, and took his son Sumarlid by the arm and they mounted their horses and rode south to Breckness. As they rode through Sandwick, Ranald said, 'I want nothing to do with those men of blood.'

A mile or two further on, at Yesnaby, Ranald said, 'Who was the man in the church with the hood over his head, who never moved far from Thorfinn? I couldn't see his face but there was something familiar about him.'

Sumarlid said, 'Someone told me that man is the famous poet Arnor. He is in high honour at Thorfinn's court. Thorfinn thinks that without this man and his poetry he might pass away like a shadow or a wind through grass.'

'There is little hope of that,' said Ranald. 'Earl Thorfinn has left hundreds of widows and orphans in the straths of Scotland. Blood-lettings and burnings all through the highlands. The curses of Alba and Strathclyde against Thorfinn will go on from one generation to the next.'

'And yet,' said Sumarlid, 'it will be best for us to come to terms with Thorfinn. I kept my ears open today. It seems that Thorfinn will settle in Orkney soon. He wants to build a new palace on the small steep isle off the Birsay coast. There's word too that he will build a church not far from the palace. He has even sent word to the Pope that he would like a bishop in Orkney soon. Then the church in Orkney won't be under the thumb of the Bishop of Nidaros in Norway.'

Ranald rode on in silence. It was a fine morning. They rode past the cliffs of Yesnaby, with the sea shifting in broken white surges against the reefs below, among wandering booms and echoes.

Sumarlid was usually a quiet young man, but his mouth was full of words that day, perhaps to lift the gloom lying so heavily on his father. 'I spoke to one of the Norwegians at the funeral,' he said. 'They are supposed to be here enquiring about the price of horses, but of course it's well known they are the king's men. The horse-dealer said it was a great pity that Earl Brus's son couldn't get to the funeral. "But you'll see him in Orkney soon enough," said the Norwegian. "I tell you this, Rognvald Brusison is much admired in Norway. He has all the makings of a great man. He speaks about Orkney all the time, this young man. He says he must have words soon with his uncle Earl Thorfinn, and come to some friendly agreement."'

By this time the two horsemen were on the high ridge called Black Crag, and the farm of Breckness lay below them, with the oat-field and the barley-field showing the first green of early summer.

'It would be better', said Ranald, 'if that son of Brus stays always in Norway. I can foresee the worst kind of trouble if he sails west.'

'But Rognvald is entitled to his father's inheritance, surely,' said Sumarlid.

'No,' said Ranald. 'Let there be one earl only in Orkney, even if it is the blood-splashed Thorfinn.'

They drew near to the farm-steading.

'The winters are beginning to lie heavy on me,' said Ranald. 'I no longer get up so cheerfully in the morning. Half-way along the seventh furrow, my arms steering the plough get suddenly tired. I notice, too, that at the fishing I've lost the skill of knowing where the fish are trekking. Last week, again and again, the hooks came up empty. As for my beard, your mother combs more silver hairs out of it now than bronze hairs. It will soon be time for me to sit in the chimney-corner. I will leave the running of the farm entirely to you, Sumarlid.'

Ranald's young daughter Margaret ran out of the house to greet them.

Ranald lifted her up and kissed her and ruffled her bright hair with his fingers.

The cloud of melancholy left his face. This youngest child was a pure delight to him. 'I hope', he said, 'you've been helping the kitchen girls to stir the soup-pot, and put in salt and fish. Sumarlid and I are very very hungry.'

The wind rose and went in deep surges through the corn-fields, and the waves of Holy Sound broke against the rocks at Braga.

The girl took her father's hand and they went together in at the door of Breckness, and Sumarlid saw to the unsaddling of the horses.

12

The beautiful child Margaret who had stood that day among the green barley shoots did not live to see their ripening and ingathering.

Soon after Ranald and Sumarlid returned from the earl's funeral, the girl complained of tiredness. No, she would not play with her pet lamb, perhaps tomorrow, today she was a bit tired. From time to time she was shaken with a cough, and though her mother put the cup of mulled mead to her lips at night – a good cure for a cold – the spasms of coughing got worse. It could be seen how thin her arms were, and how her brow gushed with sweat if she did the simplest thing, such as comb her hair or bend to thong up her sealskin shoes. There came a perpetual apple-flush on her cheeks. Her eyes grew large in her face, and glittered. No, whatever delicacies her mother and the kitchen girls prepared for her – soft white cheese and pieces of young trout and bread made with honey and dipped in milk – Margaret said she was not hungry. A cup of cold water from the torrent at Warbeth – that, she said, might ease her throat. For now something ailed the child's throat too, her lucent speech came gray and hoarse, and whenever she spoke more than half-a-dozen words the cough took possession of her and racked her so that she had to lie back on the pillow quite exhausted.

'She is young,' said Ragna, 'she'll get over this.'

But the girls standing behind Ragna looked down at the floor. And Ranald sent for one of the Warbeth monks, Malachi, who was said to have great knowledge of herbs and their curative properties. Malachi came, and looked, and blessed the child, and went away again, shaking his head.

Often Margaret wept, when for example she heard her pet lamb Bondi bleating at the end of the house. But soon afterwards she would be shaken with excitement and joy. She would be better soon, she declared in her husky voice. Never had the blackbirds sung so sweetly, never until now had she known how beautiful was the sound of the rain on the roof. And whenever her father came in to see her, which was often, she would girdle his wrist with her transparent hand. 'Nothing can touch me so long as you're with me, father,' she would say. And he would set his hand on her hair that was lank with sweat and sickness, until she dropped off into a brief unquiet sleep.

At last, in high summer, Ranald sat with her all night, and for many nights. And when he woke in his chair, the candle would be out and the first light of dawn flooding in over Hoy Sound.

'Tomorrow we'll go fishing,' Margaret said one night to her father. 'It's good, to have the salt on your lips, isn't it? I did not know it was so good, until now.'

And Ranald said that indeed, in the morning, they would hoist the sail and go west on the ebb.

Then Margaret said she had forgot to say her prayers. She would say her prayers, then she would sleep. 'God bless father, God bless mother. God bless Sumarlid. God bless Solveig and Ingerth. God bless Einhof. God bless all who work on this farm, the men and the girls. God bless Bondi my lamb. God bless King Olaf. God bless Earl Thorfinn . . .'

Her voice, those last few days, had shrunk to a whisper, but now her voice seemed to brighten a little at her sunset orisons.

At last she said, 'God bless me.'

She drifted off into sleep.

When her father woke up in his chair, Margaret was dead.

He lit a new candle. He bent and kissed the cold fingers and the cold face.

The household was asleep.

Ranald walked over the dew-heavy grass to the monks at Warbeth.

A lark was singing high over Garth.

13

After Margaret's death, her father largely left the supervising of the farmwork to Sumarlid.

He seemed to have no interest in affairs in general, especially about the manoeuvrings of the Orkney earl and the king in the east. In fact, nobody dared to raise these matters in Ranald's presence, at the dinner board or beside the fire, they roused such anger and impatience in him.

Now Sumarlid rather than his father rode each year to the assembly at Tingvoe, and Sumarlid was well thought of by the farmers and merchants. 'But', said Sven of Houton in Orphir parish, 'it seems your father has grown old before his time.'

The little parliaments at Tingvoe were now completely dominated by Earl Thorfinn. It soon became obvious to everyone there that the earl's will in nearly everything must be obeyed. He listened openly to their opinions, and smiled if they happened to coincide with his own, but he rode roughshod over any suggestions that he thought might not be for the good of the islands. The flash and thunders of his anger made those solid farmers cast down their eyes and turn aside. It could be seen then that he belonged in part to the same breed as his brother Earl Einar. But whereas Einar's rage had been rooted in an unsound mind, Thorfinn's was wholesome, and after it was vented on them, men could see that behind it lay a rare wisdom and foresight. They acknowledged, most of them, that Thorfinn had a mind deeper and wider than their own petty and on the whole selfish considerations, and all of them agreed in the booths after the day's debates were over that it was better by far for Orkney and Shetland to have one strong earl in charge of affairs, rather than two or three earls perpetually bickering, and sailing off eastwards to get comfort, gold, and arbitration from the King of Norway; to be followed in no long while by the rival earl; so that in the end there was no escape for either of them until Orkney was more firmly than before under the dominance of Norway, and the bonds sealed with solemn oaths.

It now appeared that oaths meant little to Thorfinn, if they had been sworn by him under duress.

The Norwegians who sailed to Orkney – even those merchants going about lawful business – were coldly received by the earl's stewards and chamberlain. An occasional envoy from the king was housed in the coldest room of the new palace in Birsay, and got the briefest of audiences from the earl before being dismissed. At the dinner table, the accredited envoy from Norway was set at that place furthest from Earl Thorfinn, beside the scrivener (it might be) or the falconer.

As for those easterners who seemed obviously spies, they were given short notice to quit the isles. If they stayed on beyond their three days' grace, Earl Thorfinn had them enrolled as oarsmen on his warships. Now he was claiming four earldoms in Scotland, and he had his eye on the Hebrides and Argyll besides. Those coasts had to be well patrolled by sea, and sailors were in short supply.

Year after year, the assembly men (including Sumarlid Ranaldson) would ride home, saying that their week in the debating booth at Tingvoe had been well spent on the whole – though this one and that who had carefully prepared a speech might voice his resentment in private at having the hard knot of his argument ruthlessly cut through by the biting sapient tongue of the young earl.

It pleased most of them that there was one earl sitting on the high chair – an able and an honest leader, for all his high-handedness.

Sumarlid rode home from one assembly with John Simonson of Cairston. 'It may be', said John Simonson, 'that our troubles aren't entirely over. Didn't Earl Brus leave a young son in the court at Bergen – Rognvald? That boy must be growing up now. Surely you saw me speaking to a stranger in our booth one night? He was one of those spies sent over the sea by the king from time to time. This man told me that Rognvald is held in the highest regard throughout Scandinavia. The young man has even been to Sweden, and some say he visited Novgorod and sailed down the Volga. The man told me too that King Olaf has bestowed the earldom of Orkney on Rognvald Brusison. I didn't tell any of this to Earl Thorfinn – you know what rages he can fly into – and in any case Thorfinn certainly knows it; he has his own merchants and skippers bringing him news all the time out of Norway. I hope this young Earl Rognvald Brusison finds plenty to occupy his energies and talents in Finland and Ukraine. It will be a return to the old bad times if he were to turn his face westwards, and order a dozen ships to be built, and sail across to claim his inheritance.'

In an ale-house in the fishing hamlet of Hamnavoe, John Simonson and Sumarlid Ranaldson lingered for a while, discussing this and that. Then Sumarlid rode on to Breckness. His mother and his two sisters were pleased to have him home again – so indeed were all the folk of Breckness – but there was no sign of his father still when the family sat down at the dinner table.

'Oh, he comes and goes like a tinker,' said Ragna. 'He spends most of the days down at the shore talking to the fishermen. He even gives them a hand to mend their lobster creels and bait their lines. He comes home with his shoes stiff with salt, and you have no idea how hard it is to get salt out of leather.'

Thora, Sumarlid's grandmother, was at the dinner that night – a thing that rarely happened, for, if anything, there was less sweetness than ever between the old woman and her daughter-in-law – but Thora liked to hear the news that Sumarlid brought every year from the bee's nest of gossip that went droning on at Tingvoe around the serious affairs of state. What marriages were afoot, the old one wanted to know, and had a dowry been mentioned? And was old Tibb still alive in Papay island, that she had learned embroidery with as a girl? And was it true what she had heard, that Thord Rolfson in Evie had taken a silver ring from his mother's arm while she was asleep and given it to some slut he had taken a fancy to, and now Thord and this girl were living in an upturned boat in Vementry in Shetland? So the old lady had heard from a passing tinker and she fully believed it . . . But now, today, Sumarlid must have even more exciting things to tell them.

But Sumarlid knew nothing about such trifling matters.

Sumarlid's younger sister, Ingerth, was betrothed to a farmer called Ramir Olafson in Sandwick, and they were to be married in the chapel at Warbeth after harvest. Sumarlid told the family that Ramir Olafson was well, and had enquired eagerly and often in the booths at Tingvoe about his bride-to-be. In Sumarlid's opinion, Ramir was a good prudent man, and entitled to a generous dowry. And Ingerth was lucky to be going to the farm in Tenston as wife and mistress.

At this, Ingerth cast her eyes down at her plate, but the family could see the smile that came and went on her face till the meal was ended.

Solveig, the eldest daughter, looked severely in front of her. Several young men of promise had visited Breckness in the course of the last five years, and had had words with Solveig and her mother, and more than one of them had slunk off over the fields like chidden dogs. Solveig had seen too much domestic upheaval, cruelty, unfaithfulness here and there in the parish to put overmuch trust in men, however handsome and well provided.

'She'll be well called a spinster, that one,' said her grandmother. 'There'll be no young ones wailing round Solveig's corpse, when her time comes.'

But the young spinster Solveig excelled at every kind of work about the farm both indoors and out in the fields. She had been known to drive a team of oxen into unbroken land, the plough stottering between the yoked beasts and the strong girl . . . A cow would drift from the herd across the pasture when she called its name . . . She would go into the dark barn where the fierce falcon Dawn sat on a beam, furled, and it would flutter down on to her gloved fist, in answer to one low sweet call. Then out, girl and falcon, into the wind and sun of morning, out and up to the hill above Garth, and the bird was flung from the farm girl's fist and hesitated in the wind, and then climbed high into the bright blue sweep of morning!

They sat at the table, the family, and the fish-bones were thrown sputtering into the fire, and a girl came in with a big heated platter of lamb.

Ragna said, 'Your father has missed his soup and haddock again today, and it looks as if he won't be getting any mutton chops either. Let's hope the fishermen down at the huts have given him a mug of hot fish soup. If he's still hungry when he comes in at last, there's a crust or two left from the morning's baking. Let him go to bed with that in him.'

Old Thora mumbled that that was a strange way for a wife to speak about her husband. She had known men who had half-killed their wives for daring to say half as much. But it was difficult to know now just what the grandmother was saying, for she had lost all her teeth and her mouth and her gums gave out no distinct message . . . But she looked severely across the table while she upbraided her daughter-in-law with fluttering lips.

Ragna let on not to understand what she was saying.

Solveig said, 'I'll see that father doesn't go hungry to bed.'

Ingerth said, 'He has not been the same since the death of our sister, Margaret. Another year and he'll be well again. He'll be there in the little chapel to hand me over to Ramir of Tenston, and the priest standing before us with the book and the ring, and the farm boys singing around.'

Ingerth had never said so many words at one time at the dinner table of Breckness. Now, half appalled at her loquacity, she bowed her flushed face over the plate of mutton in front of her.

Solveig put a cold look on her sister.

Old Thora said, 'That'll be your best day, granddaughter. Make the most of it. After that bridal day, sorrows come thick as snowflakes.'

'There's some old dog shaking himself at the door,' said Ragna.

But it was Ranald Sigmundson feeling for the latch in the falling darkness.

He came in, smelling of hooks and mussels. Solveig hastened to light a lamp. In the low enriching light, it could be seen how three or four years had changed Ranald. His hair and beard were a gray weave, his face a net of wrinkles, his shoulders were bowed, his eyes seemed half-sunk between his gray eye-bushes and his prominent cheek-bones.

'How many lobster pots did you patch today?' said Ragna.

Thora bade them goodnight and went through to her own part of the house, shuffling and mumbling still.

Ingerth hastened to prepare a place at the table for her father.

'No,' Ranald said, 'I've eaten with the fishermen.'

At last, Ranald and Sumarlid were alone, sitting on either side of the fire.

Sumarlid began to tell his father about the events at the Tingvoe assembly, but Ranald shook his head. 'I don't want to hear anything about what they're up to, the men of blood and violence. Let them dig deep pits for themselves.'

He asked whether any ships had come from the west lately. Had any of the skippers at Tingvoe mentioned Greenland and Vinland?

He wondered whether they ought to sow English barley in the shore field next spring – their own barley had been scant last harvest. Sumarlid ought to think about it. Also, they ought maybe to be getting horses from Scotland – the island horses, though strong, were too small and wild.

14

That summer a monk visited the brothers at Warbeth from Donegal in Ireland. Fergus was his name. He was on his way to the Faroe Islands to establish a small religious community there. 'But there's no hurry, no hurry in the world, this is a beautiful place you have here. I'll get to Faroe in God's good time.'

Brother Fergus entertained the monks with Irish stories – Sweeny who had defiled a sanctuary and so, changed into a bird, had to endure thorn and ice and a bitter exile from his human condition. Out of his pain, Sweeny gave utterance to the most beautiful poems and songs.

But most of all the Warbeth brothers urged Fergus to tell them, yet once more, the story of the voyage of Saint Brandon, who had sailed west in an ox-hide ship with twelve brothers from his monastery in Ireland in search of 'the earthly paradise', and of their many strange adventures on the western ocean – how in one island a dog had led them, sea-starved, to a lordly hall with overflowing board and a sleep-dowered dormitory – how the monks, hungry again in another part of the ocean, had prepared breakfast on the back of the terrible whale Jascoyne – how on an island further on the birds had discoursed to Saint Brandon in angelic voices, they being changed to birds for having been neutral in the great rebellion of Satan – how they had come at Christmas to an abbey of monks who neither spoke nor laboured, yet their cupboards and wine jars overflowed always, and their silence was lovelier by far than the sweetest music ever heard by human ears – how the west-faring monks had seen a man on a rock pitilessly flayed by wind and sea-spray and hail, and this man they took to be Judas – how they came to an island of ice and fire, and were in great danger, whereby two monks cast themselves into the biting sea and were lost – how they came to the island where Saint Paul the Irish hermit dwelt alone, who was fed daily by an otter that brought him a fish in its mouth – how in the end Saint Brandon and his sailor-monks had come to 'the island of the blessed', or 'the earthly paradise', and there they would gladly have stayed forever, it was so unutterably delightful there, with trees laden with ever-ripe fruit, and comely young folk coming and going among the green hills and beside quiet waters, and never a storm-cloud in the sky, and the very stones underfoot were uncut diamond and emerald. This, thought Brandon and the monks, must be heaven itself. But no, said the grave and pleasant youth who showed them the island, heaven was further west still, the gleam of it could be seen sometimes on the horizon, this island the monks had sailed to was the place Adam had lived in before the Fall. The monks (said the young man) should return to Ireland, and wait there until God summoned them, one by one, to the supreme felicity of heaven.

Ranald happened to be visiting the abbot one day when Brother Fergus told, yet once more, the story of the voyage of Saint Brandon. This was the first time he had heard it, and he was even more enchanted by the story than the monks of Warbeth.

'There was a poet at my farm one winter a while ago,' he said, 'and he had a poem on the same theme.'

Later that day he had a few words with the Irish monk. He told him how, as a boy, he had sailed west to Vinland, where no easterner had ever set foot before.

'Did it look like the Island of the Blessed to you?' asked Fergus.

'Vinland is very beautiful and very fertile,' said Ranald, 'but the Fall operates there too, alas. I saw greed and murder and treachery enough in Vinland.'

'Ah,' said Fergus, 'it is only the innocent heart that can find a way to the Earthly Paradise. I don't think I could ever get there myself. I'll have to content myself with Faroe and its people. As for heaven itself, we'll only get there by way of a charitable life and a holy death.'

At harvest, Ranald presented his daughter Ingerth in marriage to her young husband Ramir Olafson from Tenston in Sandwick. The farm-folk crowded into the chapel. The young farm boys sang like little angels on either side of the altar. 'They're anything but angels,' mumbled old Thora to her neighbour. 'I know them, they throw stones at my door on a winter night and then run off laughing. They torment the young dog. They leave rotten fish-heads on my windowsill, in the hot sun, I tell you I thought I was smelling my own death that day last summer . . .' The woman standing beside Thora told her to be silent, for now the abbot was raising his hand in blessing over the bent heads of Ramir and Ingerth.

There was great merriment that evening in the big barn of Breckness – the best of food and drink, harp-music and pipe-music, dancing on the swept floor, the old people on benches along the walls reminding themselves of parish events long before.

Ranald received every guest at the door. It was noticed that he was very silent that night. Ragna and Solveig saw to it that the platters on the long table were never empty, and that every ale horn had its beard of froth. The serving girls ran back and fore continually between kitchen and festive barn. The piper drank so much that the pipe faltered and fell from his fingers long before midnight, and also the harper's hand stumbled among the strings. Then the reels went on to old deep-mouthed choruses. An old fisherman came in and replenished a lamp here and there, from time to time, from a jar of fish oil.

Sumarlid was seen to be dancing often with Liv Johnsdaughter of Cairston, a dark-haired girl . . . 'He won't have his sorrows to seek with that one,' said old Thora. 'It's plain to see there's Pict blood in her, her great-grandmother was a trow from under the hill . . .' The grand-mother was enjoying the wedding feast. She even danced once with the old shepherd Vrem, and as she stamped her feet she vented barbarous cries like a seagull. Then round she dragged old Vrem in another circle; and the dance was urged on and on by the ballad chorus.

At midnight, Ranald kissed Ingerth and came away.

He had not danced all night, except with his wife Ragna at the first bridal dance, the processional.

Ranald's mother said, 'There's something far wrong with him. A cat would have eaten more than he's eaten all night . . . Yes, Vrem, bring me the tub of hot ale, it might give us strength for the next dance but one.'

Ranald did not sleep for hours that night for the sounds of music and revelry. Even at sunrise the dancing was going on.

15

The years passed.

Old Thora died one spring on the peat hill, thrusting up a heavy wet dark square with her spade into the sun. She had been digging peat on the high moor for days, with a small company of farmworkers. Then all at once she seemed to crumple, her knees gave way, the spade fell from her hands and she toppled into the peat bank. She was dead when the peat-cutters pulled her out.

Sumarlid got married by the priest in Cairston to Liv Johnsdaughter, and the bride rode over the hill to Breckness with Sumarlid next day.

They got a good welcome from Ranald and Ragna.

Sumarlid said that he and Liv should live now in Thora's empty quarters, after the farm carpenter had added a room or two.

But Ragna said no – Liv was now mistress at Breckness, and she ought to have the running of the house. She herself – Ragna – would go and live in the dead grandmother's quarters. 'And', she said, 'there's room enough there too for the farmer himself, any time he wants to stay there . . .'

The truth is, Ranald for the past year had hardly stayed in Breckness at all. It was plain to everyone that something ailed him. He wandered for days across the hills, or crossed the ridge to the little hamlet of Hamnavoe. There was a boat-builder in Hamnavoe called Lodd, who made fishing-boats for the villagers, but fishermen from all over Orkney sent orders to him for sixearns and yoles. Often Ranald would spend a whole morning in Lodd's shed, and as Lodd chopped and hammered, he and Ranald talked together in their slow voices, that seemed to have the rhythm and sound of quiet seas in them. Often they would sit in silence for a whole morning. Then Lodd would break off to eat, and he would ask Ranald up to his house, and his young wife brought cheese and bread and a jar of ale to the table.

Lodd's wife Mart was proud to entertain one of the gentry, and a man who had been famous since his youth. She went from door to door in Hamnavoe, telling the women of the guest she and Lodd were entertaining. And some of the Hamnavoe women sneered, and others smiled, but mostly they just shook their heads. It must be an ill wind that brought one of the gentry among them – it boded no good.

One day, in the boat-shed, Ranald asked Lodd if he was not tired of building small boats – would he not like to try his hand at building a bigger boat, one that might cruise out into the Atlantic?

'Why,' said Lodd, taking a nail from between his teeth, 'you're not thinking, sir, of turning pirate in your old age? Is it a viking longship you want me to build?'

Boat-builder and farmer laughed together.

'No, Lodd,' said Ranald, 'but it's thirty years now since I set foot on ship, and I have a fancy to make one last voyage before I die.'

'I'm sorry I won't be able to oblige you,' said Lodd. 'I've been building fishing-boats since I was an apprentice to my father. Sixearns and yoles are the only kind of boats I can build. Besides, as you see, I haven't got room in my shed here for anything bigger. I would need to have half-a-dozen men working for me, to make the kind of ship you're thinking of. A fine botch it would be, when finished! No, sir, I doubt you'll have to send to More in Norway, or Ullapool in Scotland, if you want to order a ship of that kind. They have yards there, and swarms of shipwrights.'

'Think no more of it,' said Ranald.

'I'm sorry, sir,' said Lodd.

'Don't call me "sir" either,' said Ranald. 'You're as good a man as I am. You can call me Ranald if you like.'

'I will then.'

'When I passed the ale-house on my way here,' said Ranald, 'I heard one half-slewed man say to his neighbour, "There he goes again, the old dottled farmer from out at Breckness..." There's nothing wrong with my ears, Lodd, I heard it distinctly. Twenty years ago I'd have gone into that ale-house and clashed their heads together. But now I don't mind what people say about me ... You can call me an old dottled clodhopper to the neighbours if you like, Lodd.'

'I would never do that,' said Lodd. 'You're my friend, Ranald.'

Then Lodd's wife came into the shed and said. 'The fish and bread are on the table.'

Ranald got off the fish-box where he had been sitting, and made a broken step or two (for all this past winter he had had pain and stiffness in his knees). Then Mart steadied him, and they went together all three up the steps to Lodd's house . . .

On his way home that afternoon, Ranald called at the monastery at Warbeth. He thought it might divert the abbot to tell him how he had almost given Lodd the boat-builder an order to build a big ship that would unlock the western horizon for him. 'It was a passing whim, a fancy,' said Ranald to the monks. 'Who knows where such idle ideas come from? And yet the image, once I had put it into words, seemed more real and solid to me than any ship I had ever sailed in. The older I grow, brothers, louder and more wonderful the summons of the sea comes to me. I must close my ears to it, but it is not and it never will be easy.'

The abbot and the brothers smiled. A bell rang. They drifted towards the chapel to sing their vespers.

A few days later, Ranald was gone from breakfast time one morning till late the next afternoon.

Ragna asked him where he had been. She had gone down to the shore but the fishermen hadn't seen him for days.

'I was with the two shepherds,' said Ranald.

Then Ragna began to rail at him, so that the whole district resounded with her rage. (The young girls in the milk-house paused among the cheese and butter they were making.) 'Is there anything wrong with us here at Breckness?' cried Ragna. 'Aren't you well enough looked after, in the way of food and fire and comforting? What does an old wealthy farmer like you want with servants and labouring men and monks? What's so special about them, I'd like to know? You went out yesterday in a new woven coat, and here you are with an old filthy rag on your back. Don't tell me – I know you gave that coat to some tramp you met on the road – it isn't the first time. Oh, man, man, why did I ever come to live in such a crazy place as Breckness!'

Ranald said that he and the shepherds were going to repair the ruined bothy on the side of the Black Crag. That was where his mother had lived for a time when Harald Thorn had taken possession of

Breckness a long time ago when he, Ranald, was on the sea between Norway and Orkney.

Ragna, her rage guttering out, listened silently.

'Now,' said Ranald, 'I'm getting to be an old man, Ragna, and it's time for me to make preparations for the last voyage. For that, I need silence and a place where I can meditate alone from time to time. I mean no insult to you – you've been a loyal wife to me. If I'm not seen for a couple of days, or a whole week maybe, you may know that I'm up there in my cell, trying to work out some hard problems that have troubled me greatly this long while.'

When Ragna looked out of the door later, she saw the shepherd and his son putting a new thatch on the roof of the bothy.

'Well, God go with you, you poor old man,' said Ragna to her husband who was nodding asleep in his deep straw chair. 'I did not think it would come to this, with one who was so famous and far-travelled in his youth.'

Ranald and Peter the abbot talked many times about fate, and evil and good, and free will. Again and again they turned their minds to the shadow of fate that had hung from – it seemed – the beginning of things upon the minds and actions of the northern peoples. 'And I myself', said Ranald, 'am still convinced that things can't be other than they are, individual men and tribes behave as they do because their history was written down for them from before the beginning. Believing this – it is in the very marrow of our bones, it is carved deep in our hearts – bestows a kind of wild freedom. Let us wring what we can out of the tight fist of fate. Then we can go down with a certain carelessness, even with laughter, into the invisible dust . . .'

'But so,' said the abbot, 'the cruel man and the unjust man are but confirmed in their evil. "We see that there are other ways of living," they may say, "but fate has cast us in our parts, no use trying to tear ourselves from the web that fate has thrown about us." I grant this, Ranald Sigmundson, there seems to be an inevitability about life and history and time – this action, this thought, proceeds inexorably from the action and thought that have preceded it, right back into the dream of childhood, all the way forward into the mists of old age – Omnipotence-and-Omniscience cannot have it otherwise, and so, surely, that majestic all-compassing prime mover is no different from fate itself. But there is a mystery in all this that is, I think, beyond the power of our minds to understand – there is freedom, the possibility at every moment of our lives to choose either this or that. It can be objected that it is fate, not the man himself, that chooses in the end. But every man born is aware, now and then in the course of his life, of what you have just called a wild sweet freedom when all seems to be possible and good. No matter what mask he wears, this Everyman – earl or beggar – he finds himself, mind and spirit and body, possessed with a joy that he cannot explain or comprehend – sometimes only once or twice in his life, sometimes often, and I have known men who seem to have that pure light on their faces always. Some say, this garden is lost somewhere in the dream of childhood – some say, it is only when a man falls in love truly for the first time – some say, it is far on in a man's life, when his sun has set and he sits content at his fire. Yet I think that, apart from such natural gleams, the whole of a man's life is pervaded by sweetnesses that have no physical or mental source, they touch his mind and heart and spirit even in places of stone and thorn. Often enough he denies them, when he is in pain and misery. But a day or a week or a month or a year further on, the enchantment touches him again. It need not, for us contemplatives, be a matter of accident, this grace-fall – a man can summon it at any time by prayer and meditation and the offering to the Infinite of what he has to offer, whether it is joy or suffering or work or simply the prayer itself . . . The prayer will not be answered if it is rooted in selfishness – "I want this . . . Give me that . . ." – but the man must beseech for the good of all humanity and indeed of all creation. Here, on this ground, there seems to be a state beyond the dark operatings of fate, a place of light and peace. Imagine, my friend, a great grim keep, in which we wake up and are told "This is the House of Life – here you must do what you are given to do, told to do, for the time that is allotted to you, and you will obey the rules of the House to the uttermost letter, and there is no appeal, but there will be a measure of enjoyment for you from time to time, if you have the wit and the cunning and the strength to seize what this place has to offer. Even as the animals out there pursue inexorable ways, so must you, but you are creatures of intelligence and memory and foresight, and so your pleasure in the chase and the kill, so to speak, will be so much the more vivid and meaningful and heightened. Obey the rules of the House, and you will learn acceptance and a kind of peace. Seize the opportunities the House allows, and you may get fame and wealth and power. Now be stirring, man, there are many things for you to do, you will come soon enough to the last dark door . . ." One day, in the seemingly endless strict corridors and stairs and closets of this castle, going about his round of duties, the man finds himself looking out of a little casement upon a garden of great beauty and delight. He is enthralled by the flowers and fountains and statues and sundials, the streams and trees and the innocent creatures. The garden is not another world, he sees, it is a part of the great grim House, for the high wall of the House encloses the garden too, the House and the garden belong to each other. "I wasn't told about the garden," he says. "I think it must be a dream only, it doesn't exist, or if it exists it is for the great hidden powers who rule in this House, and their favourites, to enjoy, certainly not for a house-thrall like me . . ." He looks and sees that the door into the garden is unlatched, not fettered like the hundred other doors of the House. Perhaps he will be punished if he intrudes into the garden. The rules of the House have said nothing about a garden like this, only about the transient satisfactions of cunning and gain and glut. He opens the door and goes into the garden and takes a flower from a tree and returns with it to his cell. Then, somewhat fearfully after this moment of freedom and – it might be – lawlessness, he goes back to the daily drudgery and returns worn out with broking and bargaining and getting what he can, according to the laws of the House, from the other dwellers in it, and when he lies down on his bed at last he is convinced that the garden was a dream and a delusion. But when he wakes in the first gray of dawn, the man sees the apple blossom on the pallet of his bed . . . How shall the life of the man be changed after that, even though he spends months and years looking for the corridor that leads to the garden, and perhaps never finds it? After a day or two, the flower has shrivelled to dust, the last faint fragrance is lost in the stale air. He might happen to tell his experience to a friend. The friend will say, "Where is the evidence? Where is the apple blossom you plucked?" The only answer is silence, or a song – but in those noisy times silence and song have small meaning. Still the man is convinced he has known that one moment of freedom, its sweetness and purity are a part of him always, a seal and a promise, and nothing can be the same to him again . . . Sometimes, as he grows older, the man mentions the garden to this one or that that he thinks might be interested. Mostly, they give him cold looks, but now and then a face smiles, transfigured for a moment before the old shadows of getting and spending fall again, the adamantine duties of the House. In the end, all the same, the man gets to know

– or thinks he does – among all the throngs of people he has dealings with in the market-place or counting-house those who have experience of the garden, by the merest chance look or gesture. Others will insist, "Our lives are full to overflowing with all kinds of good worthwhile experience, we have had a full measure of the good things life has to offer . . ." And yet, since his visit to the garden, the man can tell by a deadness in the eye or in the voice when "the enjoyers of life" are deceiving themselves – and at the same time there is a wistfulness in their boasting as if they know that their "good things" are but a shadow of a more perdurable hoard . . . Often the man, all doubts and despondency about the garden after years of sterility, will turn a corner in his daily round, and there, unexpectedly, the unseen fragrances are all about him. Or he will chance to meet someone in the great keep – quite an ordinary person, seemingly – and the stranger's coat, as they brush sleeves in passing, gives out the enchanting subtleties of tall grass, dew, rose blossom and honeycombs . . . Ranald Sigmundson, we monks have a faith and a hope that the garden exists all right, and we think that we can go out among the birdsong and the blossoms more often, perhaps, than other men – though we belong like all others to the House of Life, and are thirled until we die to its laws and its rules.'

Ranald said he would have to think about what his friend had said.

'Do you not think', said the abbot, 'that man would have made a shambles and a burnt-out ruin of this earth, given his intelligence and ruthlessness, if he was only a superior beast? There will always be the possibility of that – what saves us, so far, is the unsullied vision. We have seen those earls of Orkney destroying each other with a cunning and a viciousness far more cruel than the necessary predation of animals. I think this is possible, that some day in the grim Hall in Birsay, an earl might lay aside the burdensome coat-of-state and ask for a white coat to be woven for him on the looms. For he has been summoned to come to a place of stone and thorns. It is time, says this earl, for that cruel place to undergo transfiguration.'

'I don't follow you,' said Ranald. 'The only earl now is Thorfinn. Is it possible that such cruelty and ruthlessness can in time to come beget sanctity?'

'With God, all things are possible,' said Peter the abbot. (It came to pass, in the fullness of time, that the grandson of Earl Thorfinn Sigurdson was Earl Magnus of Orkney, whom we know today as Saint Magnus the martyr.)

One Sunday the abbot preached to the people in the chapel at Warbeth.

Vanity of vanities, all is vanity . . . What profit hath a man of all his labour which he taketh under the sun? One generation passeth away, and another generation cometh . . . All is vanity and vexation of spirit . . .

'We see that many evil things are done under the sun, piracy and house-burning and murder and thieving and the destruction of what is innocent and beautiful. Then we are inclined to think, Man is truly an evil creature and only evil things proceed from his hands and his heart and mind. Even if he is well inclined towards his neighbour and all men everywhere, can he work a lasting good under the sun? It seems not: for the good things he accomplishes soon pass away and are forgotten, even as he himself ends in dust. Vanity of vanities, all is vanity.

'In our short span of life, we see little to cheer us in the estate of man. Year follows year, and there is hard labour in the fields and in the fishing-boats, and women weep in secret (for here in the north we think shame to show our sorrow on the shore or on the hillside – and this is perhaps in us a stubbornness of spirit that keeps us from a measure at least of heart-ease).

'But, hidden grief or communal grief, a man loses the brief delights of youth, he grows old and dies, and we hide his body away from the sun that was in the end too much of a burden to him.

'Here, in the north, not even "the mourners go about the streets". Those who loved him in his life weep – if at all – in secret corners.

'Was the light of the sun created for no more than this short sorrowful story?

'The great lamp of the sun lightens the whole earth and sea, and it may be that a man is distracted by the multitudinous things that go on between dawn and the going down of the sun. The estate of man is too much for him – he is lost and bewildered – in the end he sees only the wickedness and the vanity done under the sun – for evil shows itself always in bolder manifestations than the truth, and delights to noise itself abroad in the highways and byways.

'But always, at night, a good man may lie down at peace with himself and sleep.

'Yet, even so, he may think, searching his conscience before sleep, "I have wrought no evil on earth today as far as I know, and I have helped my neighbour in this small matter and that, but does it matter in the end? This sleep that will soon fall on me at midnight is a foreshadowing of death, the last endless sleep. Then it will be as if a poor crofter or fisherman like me had never lived. I might indeed have lived more comfortably nowadays with my wife and children if I had gone viking in the days of my strength, and gotten fame and gold . . ." But the good man knows indeed that, though he is poor, it is a better treasure to lie down at night with an unburdened heart. He may still believe that he will wake to vanity and a bleak death-faring, when next morning he opens his eyes to the light of the sun.

'The good man may not be aware that somewhere on earth, while he slept, other men were seeking the true light, and meditating upon it, and this light that I speak of is the Light behind the light, the same that kindled the sun and moon and stars in the beginning. And this Light, "the light of the world", is what every man born is seeking all the days of his earthly life, whether he knows it or not.

'I will mention the feeblest of all lights, the candle that burns all night in a cold cell of this monastery. The monks here are all frail creatures like the men of the plough-share and the net, and given to error, but now and then, here and there in cell and sanctuary all over the world, a great company of minds and hearts is set on a quest for the ultimate meaning of things, for that goodness and truth and beauty that are at the heart of life.

'The world is wrapped in night and sleep. The solitary sits at his candle, and his spirit is abroad on the ocean of God's love.

'Presently the night-watcher is aware that the flame of his candle is so thin as to be invisible. The sun, new risen, is flooding through his window. It is not the sun of all vanity, but the sun of holy wisdom, and under it wonderful things are done, day after day till the end of time.

'These truths are not given only to a solitary here and there in the long watches of the night.

'They ought to be a part of every man and woman and child. If we are true to that light, we shall know – on our last day on earth, if not before – that life is a thing of beauty beyond price.

'The piece of the light that we tend and trim in our hearts will outlast the darkness and the dust of death . . .

'And so, dear children of the light, go out in peace to your fields and your fishing-boats.'

VI

Tir-nan-og

1

Ranald moved into the hut on the side of the Black Crag after the
spring ploughing. Sometimes he stayed there for a few nights only,
sometimes for as long as a month.

'He must have fallen out with his wife,' said the farmworkers and the
crofters round about.

But Ragna went up to the hut every day with food for her husband in
a basket, and they gave each other a good greeting in the door, though
Ragna was rarely asked inside, only if the rain was falling in buckets or
if a gale from the sea was blowing Ragna helter-skelter about the high
moor.

The hut had the simplest furnishing, only a chair and a table and a
bed. There was a lamp on a shelf and a small hearth for burning peat.
The farmworkers of Breckness saw to it that their master never lacked
peat, especially as the cold weather came on.

But Ranald would only stay in his hermitage for a few days, or it
might be for a single night or for a whole summer month.

One winter there was a sudden storm from the northwest when the
fishing-boats were broken on the rocks all the way from Yesnaby to
Hellyan, but all the fishermen managed to scramble ashore through
smothers of foam and broken water. One of the boats was close
inshore, off Braga reef, and the two fishermen – a father and son – were
trying desperately to keep their boat off the skerry. But there was no
way of saving the boat. There was a thin splintering of strakes heard
among the crashings of the sea, and both men were in the cold whirls.
All the watchers could see were two heads, one black and one gray,

sundered by another great wave. The young man managed to drag his sea-heavy body ashore, and hands dragged him high up the beach. There seemed to be no hope or help for the old man, even though a new wave lifted him and threw him among the rocks under the monastery. Then the folk saw someone in the sea, wading out into the gale and the cold spindrift. The man took the wrecked fisherman by the hair and dragged him out of the surgings on to the seaweed and the sand. The man bent, as if listening for a heart-beat, then he hoisted the half-drowned fisherman on his back and made along the shore towards Breckness, staggering under his burden from time to time as the tempest rallied and fell away again.

The people said, 'It's old Ranald the laird!'

Ranald opened the door of Breckness and he called, 'Ragna, here's a man needs fire and food.' He didn't stay to warm himself at the hearth, but climbed at once up to his hut on the steep moor. (He had been at his meditating for three days now.)

The old fisherman seemed to recover from the attentions of Ragna and Solveig. But suddenly, while he was supping broth and telling them he knew it had been a folly going out fishing on such a morning, with all those bad weather signs in the sky and the moon waning – 'But it's no good talking to boys, they think they know everything about the sea' – just when he was saying that, the horn spoon clattered out of his hand on to the flagstone and the old man slumped. Solveig caught him by the shoulders before he fell, but he was dead already.

'I'd better go now and see how things are with the old hero in his hut,' said Solveig. (Solveig spoke contemptuously about men, especially those who liked to fight in the ale-houses and show off in front of women and boast of the great things they had done on the western sea or east in Jutland or Lithuania.) Those loud-mouths were often wounded by her tongue, more severely than if someone had struck them with a clenched fist. So, men tended to fall silent whenever Solveig Ranaldsdaughter was present.

The door of Ranald's hut was almost torn from its hinges by the wind when she opened it.

Ranald was boiling an egg in a little kettle. His sea-drenched coat was hanging over a beam, and he had stuffed his long boots with straw to dry them.

'Father,' said Solveig, 'you're about the only man I know that I could sit with for an hour and be at peace.'

'Not today, Solveig,' said Ranald. 'The abbot gave me a scroll yesterday with a chapter of *Ecclesiastes* on it. There's wise things in it. I'll be all day – and for a few days to come – trying to work it out. So leave me in peace now, Solveig.'

Solveig said the old fisherman he had rescued had died, after all.

'Then it's well with the man,' said Ranald.

Solveig kissed her father on the cheek – she tended to be very miserly with her kisses – and went away.

'Tell your mother and brother and the farm girls I ask for them,' said Ranald mildly.

2

Sumarlid visited his father at once whenever he rode home from an assembly at Tingvoe. He could hardly wait, one year, to stable his horse. Ranald was staying at the farm that spring.

'Let me sit on your bed,' said Sumarlid. 'There are so many things to tell.'

'They may not seem so important to some people,' said his father.

Extraordinary things had been happening in Orkney, and in Norway and Scotland too. To Sumarlid and to most Orkneymen it seemed they were living in exciting times, and in dangerous times too, for no farmer or merchant could feel secure on his steading or in his ship with all the shifting violence that was abroad.

'If you've come here, Sumarlid, to tell me about those blood-splashed men in high places, and about their plots and counter-plots, I don't want to hear. Go in to your wife and tell her. The children might enjoy bed-time stories like that.' (Now Sumarlid and his wife had two handsome young sons, Thorstein and Thorbiorn.)

And Ranald made as if to cover his ears from Sumarlid's eager tongue.

But in the end he always listened.

First, King Olaf was dead in Norway, and King Magnus ruled there now. King Magnus had been a close friend of young Rognvald Brusison since childhood. They had shared adventures and dangers together, and it was said that Rognvald had saved Magnus's life.

When Rognvald arrived suddenly in Orkney with a fleet of ships, he carried with him a royal scroll appointing him Earl of Orkney – over that third of it that he inherited by right from his father Brus, and also the third that was at the free disposal of the king in the east.

There was only a token rejection of him by Earl Thorfinn's stewards in Orkney. But in the end even they were won over by the comeliness and courtesy of the young man who had last seen Orkney in his infancy. Rognvald had long golden hair, it was 'like a bright waterfall', the court poet Arnor said, 'his eyes are like ice on the edge of a loch in winter'. Those eyes of the new earl often brimmed with laughter at the dinner board, among the ale cups when he sat with his friends, but when he was discussing policy or finance with his advisers, over chart or ledger, there would be the wintry ice in them until a solution to any difficulty was found, generally by Rognvald himself, and his forehead 'would clear like a summer dawn', as the poet said in his fanciful language . . . Sometimes a man would come on Earl Rognvald standing alone in a corridor of the hall, and the blunderer would be surprised at the cold ruthless dream on the face of the solitary lord.

Earl Thorfinn could do little, to begin with, about this sudden usurpation. He was too busy with his army – half freebooters and half regular troops, in the north and west of Scotland. He claimed now to rule over nine earldoms in Scotland, stretching from Caithness to Argyll and Galloway, but if he was earl of those places he had not carved *Pax* on their great houses, but he left them smouldering ruins, and a shepherd would find his flock scattered at dawn by those sea-borne brigands from the north, and broken boats littered the western seaboards.

When word came to Thorfinn that his nephew had taken over two thirds of Orkney, and – if reports were true – the remaining third trembled like a ripe apple for the plucking, so popular and capable was the young man, Earl Thorfinn laughed. He sent a token messenger north to Orkney to protest. Earl Rognvald received the envoy graciously and sent him back again with a letter to Thorfinn. 'I inherit by right my father's share of Orkney, and King Magnus of Norway has granted me the third which is in his gift. I will collect your revenues and taxes and rents, in your name, and I will arrange for the defence of the islands, since you seem to be over busy at the moment with your swords and horses and ships in southern places. I hope, Earl Thorfinn, that in the end those matters will be peacefully arranged between us . . .'

'Here we go again,' said Earl Thorfinn when he had read the letter. 'The old scar open and bleeding again – two earls in Orkney, and

Norway setting them against each other like two mastiffs in a dog-pit. I would put pen to parchment to write all this to Rognvald, but what's the use? I need the strength in my hand for war, not for letter-writing. As soon as this campaign is over, I sail north to Orkney. My nephew is right about this; I want peace in Orkney every bit as much as he does, but I may have a different way of bringing peace about.'

All those forays and raids deep into Scotland – they could scarcely be called skirmishes, far less battles – were celebrated resoundingly by Earl Thorfinn's poet, Arnor the laureate, in the hall of a captured keep, while the clan chief sought shelter in some corrie from the snow.

'There will come a fearful end to all this,' said Ranald one day, a year later, after Sumarlid had ridden home from the assembly at Tingvoe. 'All those heroes and war-men and pirates! What's needed in Orkney is a saint. But I don't know how a people like us could ever produce a saint.'

Sumarlid mentioned the little communities of monks in Birsay and Eynhallow and Papay and Stronsay and Warbeth. The song of peace went up from their choirs continually, all through the day and night.

'That's true,' said Ranald. 'Who knows how many saints there are among those poor humble men? Not only in the little churches either, but in the crofts and in the fishing-bothies there are men and women of great goodness, though their lives are often hard. Fate, it seems, hands out good and evil in equal measure. I am thinking, now, rather of a saint who will confront those men of blood and compel them to beat their swords into plough-shares. He will walk through the islands in a coat of light, when he comes at last, this saint. People will come to him gladly with their sick minds and bodies. He will set the seal of peace on our cruel history. Cruelty and scheming and violence will go on, for that is ingrained in human nature, but against the doors of the saint's house the war-men will batter in vain. So, at any rate, Abbot Peter believes, and I follow him so far, but I am overshadowed always, in the end, by the ancestors.'

Meantime, life went on much as before at Breckness farm and on the crofts round about. Sumarlid was a good farmer. Occasionally there would be a poor harvest, but Ranald had long ago taught the crofters to make provision for the dark years, and besides, if there was any hardship on a croft, help was willingly lent from the well stocked barns at Breckness.

195

One winter old Eyvind the steward died, and Ranald was there to close his eyes. Even Ragna came in to kiss the cold face, for he had been a faithful and wise old man. The two small sons of Sumarlid went out and called in the falling snow, their voices clear as bells, 'Eyvind the steward is dead!' – as if it was wonderful news, this death.

Solveig said, 'The monks are building a little yard at the end of their chapel. They say all the dead of the district, high and low, should be buried there, not in any family mound. I've told them to dig a grave there for Eyvind.'

They all agreed that Solveig had acted well in this matter. But Ranald said she should have consulted him first.

Solveig's voice was loud on the hillside all the year round. If the ducks were laying less eggs than expected, she would chide the woman whose business it was to see to the fowls. 'Rotten water!' she would shout at some crofter who was known to be rather lazy. 'Of course you'll draw up rotten water if you don't clear out your well from time to time. Nobody will drink your ale, man. Not only that, your children will be ill in their guts, maybe they'll die. Get out your spade and bucket this very day, you slugabed!'

And Solveig would say to some farm lass, 'What, tears? For a man? What man? Oh, Wald from the Loons, is that who you're grieving for? Of course, even the best of them go smiling and smirking into the faces of other girls. From time to time they do that, no matter how faithful and good you are to them. Let me tell you, there's not a man on this earth worth shedding a tear for. Wald'll come back, never fear, once that slut sees through him. Only, if he does come to your door, I'd put the dog on him . . .' Then Solveig would tell stories about other men in the island, with such drollness and mimicry that the deserted farm lass would laugh.

It was not that Solveig hated men. There was a young skipper in Hamnavoe who carried modest cargoes between Shetland and Caithness – his name was Ljot – and he and Solveig were friends for some years. She would see his ship *Falcon* rounding the Kame of Hoy. An hour later she was on horseback, riding down to meet Ljot when he came ashore at Hamnavoe. Often Ljot came to Breckness, and then he and Solveig would speak together in a quiet candlelit corner of the big chamber, while all about them spinning-wheels hummed and the shuttle clashed in the loom, and Sumarlid and the farm labourers came and went. There was little privacy for courtship, even on a big farm.

Word got out somehow – certainly Solveig never let it be known even to her parents – that she and the bronze-bearded young skipper were betrothed. If any forward person stopped Solveig in the days following and said (for example), 'This is a good thing you're going to do, you and Ljot from Hamnavoe', Solveig would say coldly, 'What are you talking about, woman? Get about your tasks.' Or another would call from a corner of a field, 'You'll be building a little house of your own, you and Ljot. Where, I wonder?' She might as well have been a seagull, that inquisitive woman, for all the answer Solveig gave her.

But it is known that Ljot had spoken privately with Ranald and Ragna. That same day, going home, he had stopped at the monastery for a word with Peter the abbot.

But in the end it all came to nothing. *Falcon* did not return from a voyage to Mey in Caithness. A few oars and broken thwarts were thrown up on the beaches of Brims and Ronaldsay.

Solveig stayed indoors for one day, then next morning she took her hawk to the hill above Garth, and flung him free into the wind. The hawk went up and up and was lost in a cloud.

After that Solveig only spoke to men in the way of business.

3

Ingerth Ranaldsdaughter lived at Tenston in Sandwick with her husband Ramir Olafson. They lived contentedly at the farm there, and had six children. They were quiet people and little is reported of that family for a while. Ramir Olafson admired Earl Rognvald when he came from Norway, and soon they became friends. Sometimes Ramir rode to Breckness, both to do business in the way of farmstock and to exchange family news. Ramir kept telling Sumarlid what a great man Earl Rognvald Brusison was, and Sumarlid agreed that it would be a good thing if only Earl Rognvald took over the islands completely.

Ranald was always courteous but otherwise had little to say to his son-in-law Ramir. 'Ramir talks about little except this marvellous new earl from the east. I am sick of earls and their dark crooked manoeuvrings. But I give my blessing to Ramir and Ingerth and their children. As for farming, let Ramir talk to Sumarlid about that . . .'

One day Ramir rode over from Tenston, very crestfallen. Earl Thorfinn had suddenly come to Orkney with a strong fleet of ships and had forced Earl Rognvald to leave the islands. No doubt, said Ramir, Rognvald had sailed east to get succour and supplies and advice from King Magnus in Norway. In the meantime things were faring badly with the Orkneymen who had supported the defeated earl. Ramir himself had been visited by three of Thorfinn's men. He had been informed brusquely that, as from today, the tax he owed the earldom was to be trebled. 'If you are not satisfied with that,' Thorfinn's man had said, 'maybe Rognvald Brusison in Norway will give you a job to clean out his byres.'

Ingerth had begun to cry at the loud coarse voices in the yard outside, but the elder children had run out to look at the strangers.

The spokesman of Earl Thorfinn took a coin out of his purse and gave it to the eldest boy, Rolf. 'Here, take this, boy, you may need it to buy a loaf of bread for your father soon.' Ramir snatched the coin from Rolf's small cold hand and threw it into the farm midden. 'Tell Earl Thorfinn', he said to the three horsemen, 'that I pay taxes to Earl Rognvald only and to the king in Norway.'

'You know what happens to defaulters,' said the spokesman. 'One night, somehow or other, there is a fire in their thatch.'

And they rode off laughing.

Sumarlid told his piece of news to his father. Ranald said, 'It is an unfair burden. Still, Ramir should have paid Earl Thorfinn's tax. We would help him with the money.'

Sumarlid said Ramir was too proud to accept a gift, or even a loan.

All these power-changes and power-shifts had little effect on life at Breckness or the scattered crofts round about. Their taxes were unchanged – no doubt because those quiet people had kept at home and not gone dancing at Earl Rognvald's midsummer festival on the Ward Hill of Wideford.

No news came from Tenston for some months.

Then Ramir rode again over the hill. Even before he dismounted, Sumarlid could see how flushed with excitement he was. 'Wonderful news!' he cried, one foot in the stirrup still. 'Our true earl is back again. Earl Rognvald is home in the great Hall at Birsay! Thorfinn is dead. Hawkface is dead, the witch's son, he's a burnt cinder over there in Orphir.'

When Sumarlid summoned the household, Ramir Olafson sat at the fire with an ale mug in his hand and told the story.

It seemed that Earl Thorfinn had a farm in Orphir where he stayed sometimes with his wife Ingibiorg and some of his men. 'She is a very beautiful woman, that Ingibiorg,' said Ramir. 'I am truly sorry that she is a handful of ashes too.'

Two nights previously, Thorfinn and Ingibiorg had a great supper prepared and all the important people in Orphir and Stenness and Scapa were invited. The yard of the house was dappled with torches as the guests dismounted and the horses were led away to the stables.

Inside, it had all the makings of a great feast. Earl Thorfinn had brought his best musicians, the mead bowl was going round for the third time, from the kitchen came the smells of broth and fish and roasting pork. Arnor the earl's poet was there. He had recently recorded the victories of his lord in resounding verses – a long sequence of alliterated kennings – but the Orkneymen had not heard that new poetry yet, it was to be chanted after dinner. (Some people said that Arnor's poems were not as good as the claims made for them. They were mostly chanted when men were half drunk and sleepy, and in that condition everything seems to be better than it actually is.) But those slanders were put about by the enemies of Thorfinn and his poet, and especially by other poets who were jealous of the fame of Arnor the laureate. The fact that Earl Rognvald Brusison, a man knowledgeable about verse, thought Arnor to be a very good poet, was ample warrant that his fame was well deserved. Ramir himself had once spoken to Arnor, in Birsay, at the Hall there, and Arnor had mentioned Breckness and its folk, and how he meant to visit there some day.

'I long to hear the sea breaking on Braga,' Arnor had said to Ramir. And furthermore he had said, 'And I'm told that you, Ramir, are the husband of Ingerth Ranaldsdaughter of Breckness. I hope you're a good man to her, for though Ingerth is nothing much to look at, she's a good-hearted woman . . .'

The fact that Arnor the laureate seemed to know Breckness and its folk caused a brief wonderment that day at the fireside. Ragna looked thoughtful for most of the afternoon, and didn't seem to take in much of the wonderful story Ramir now told.

While Earl Thorfinn and his guests were taking their places at the bench, Earl Thorfinn sniffed the air and said, 'I think I'm smelling more than the savour of broth . . .' Then one of the guests began to choke and cough. Another said, 'It isn't usual to have such a fog inside a house – I can hardly see the lady Ingibiorg at the far end of the table . . .' Then the cook's boy ran out of the kitchen screaming that the roof was burning! The entire end of the house was on fire.

'I think', said Earl Thorfinn, 'we may be having a visit from my nephew Rognvald. But I didn't invite him.'

Women began to scream and tear their hair. For now the thatch over their head was a mass of flames, and burning thatch-straw began to fall on the dinner table, and smoke was everywhere.

Ingibiorg said to the boy who tended the fires, 'You won't need to carry in any more logs tonight!' Then she bent and kissed the boy.

The child began to cry.

'We'll go out through the main door,' said Thorfinn. 'But go quietly and in some sort of order, not like hens in a burning hen-house.'

Earl Thorfinn laughed. 'I must say,' he said, 'my nephew Rognvald is an able man. He knows his moment to strike. Who would expect him to come at the start of winter? Summer is the time for great blows to be struck under the sun.'

When they tried to unlatch the door, it would not open. It had been barred from the outside.

Then the house servants ran hither and thither in the smoke and flames, coughing and crying out.

Then they heard a loud voice outside. 'Servants and house-thralls are free to leave. Let them come out of the window one by one. Only Thorfinn Sigurdson and his henchmen are to stay indoors and enjoy the fire this cold night. Let none of Thorfinn's heroes try to escape. We will know their faces by our torches.'

Earl Thorfinn said to Ingibiorg, 'You are free to leave. They won't harm a woman.'

But Ingibiorg said, 'I will rather choose to die with you, man.'

(All these things were reported to Ramir by those still inside the house at the time of the burning.)

An old man had been sleeping on a bench while this was going on. One of Thorfinn's men roused this old man, who had long been in the service of the household and now did odd jobs repairing harness and fishing gear. He had to shake the old man for a while before he woke. 'Go outside,' Thorfinn said, 'you'll be safe there.'

'It's a pitiful thing,' said the old man, 'to drive me out of sleep into the cold night. I'm near enough to death as it is.' But Thorfinn's man thrust this ancient out through the window, coughing and complaining. And he was the last of the household to leave the burning house.

The window was barred, and the fire roared up against the stars. It was said that the glow in the sky could be seen in Kirkvoe and Hamnavoe. Some far-watchers said it must be the northern-lights, but others said, 'No, the northern-lights are beautiful, but this glow is man-made.'

Earl Rognvald and his men lingered about the place till sunrise. The fire was guttering out. The ruins were still too hot to examine closely, but they saw the charred corpses of many men. 'It's a pity', Rognvald said, 'that a beautiful lady like Ingibiorg should end this way.'

But then he and the burners rode laughing away towards Kirkvoe.

That was the great story that Ramir Olafson told at the Breckness hearth.

Later that day Sumarlid visited his father who was spending the day mending nets with the fishermen.

Ranald shook his head. 'Nothing good or lasting will come of such a deed. He who wounds his enemy in the night wakes up to find blood in his own mouth and eyes. I think we haven't heard the end of this story.'

4

The fact that Orkney had Rognvald Brusison as earl once more made little difference at Breckness or the crofts.

But the same three tax-men who had bullied silver out of Ramir the year before now returned, with pleasant faces. 'Earl Rognvald Brusison sends greetings to you, Ramir. He values your friendship more than ever. He will be pleased to see you at Kirkvoe anytime. Earl Rognvald intends to rule from Kirkvoe rather than Birsay from now on. The earl has looked through the rent-rolls, and considers you are being over-taxed. From now on, you will only pay a third . . .'

One day Solveig met her father on a sheep-path driving some ewes. Solveig was living now in a little house she had built for herself on the ridge the previous year. She liked living there, among winds and clouds, rather than in the chamber of the women of Breckness, brimming from dawn to sunset with chatter and gossip and the song of the spinning-wheel. If she wanted company, Solveig would go to the smithy – she did not mind the din of hammer on iron or the shouts of the men above the noise, and they treated her as one of themselves. Or she would go to the stables to talk to the horsemen, and stroke the silken neck of some horse who would (apart from Solveig) only allow

Keld the master horseman near him. If Solveig heard that there was trouble in some croft, especially a crofter ill-treating his wife, she was soon at the door. Usually she had only to look at the crofter. But sometimes she would say hard words and the man had nothing to say for himself then, or else he would mumble that he had lost his temper this once but it wouldn't happen again – no, he wouldn't so much as lift a finger to his Ruth as long as he lived. But if Solveig saw that she had a surly dangerous hound of a man to deal with, a mean bully, she would take him by the scruff of the neck and beat his head against the bedpost, till he yelled for mercy and the poor young croft woman covered her mouth with her hands. Then Solveig would say, 'Let me hear word once more that you are bad to Ruth, you miserable wretch, and I'll throw you into the burn. Make no mistake about it!'

But this day Solveig went to the hut on the hill. She sat quietly on her father's stool and she said, 'Why are you so thin? Why do you let Ragna's food grow cold outside your door? You're not eating enough.'

Ranald said, 'Old men get thin. Old men lose their appetite. An oatcake and a bit of cheese in the middle of the day, and I want no more.'

Solveig said, 'I see you trudging across the fields to the fishermen's bothy most mornings early. It's cold then and you don't have a proper coat.'

Ranald said he liked to be out early, among the dew and larksong. 'God tempers the wind to the shorn lamb and to the ruckle of bones that an old man is.'

Solveig saw that her father had a parchment on his table with marks and measurements on it.

'What plan is that?' she said. 'Do you have a fine new farmhouse in mind, to make John of Cairston jealous?'

Ranald said he was making the plan of a ship. He had sailed in many ships in his youth, he said, and most of the ships had had something to recommend them, some in fact had been very good vessels indeed. But in every ship there was an imperfection, a flaw somewhere, a bow that didn't make a pure cleave in the water, a clumsiness in the hull so that, however favourable the wind and tide, the ship never really danced in the sea, the way a good ship should. 'So here I sit, Solveig, an old man, drawing the plan of a perfect ship. This is strange, isn't it, for I have no intention of ever going to sea again. In fact, it's so long since I spoke to the Hamnavoe skippers, and discussed this and that on the piers, that

I've forgotten what a merchant ship looks like, and as you know there are always new styles and new designs. So I expect any skipper that I showed this plan to would have a good laugh. I'm just designing a ship for the fun of it, Solveig. It passes the time between now and my death.'

Solveig said she would bring him a honeycomb next time she came to see him. 'Mix some honey with your mulled ale at night,' she said. 'That'll get you through the winter. A mouse would starve on the amount of cheese and oatcake you eat. Besides, the honey and ale will help you to sleep.'

Ranald said he sent his good greetings to Ragna his wife.

'Tell Ragna, I'll be back at the farm the day after tomorrow. Tell her to have my fireside chair ready.'

He said, 'Tell your brother Sumarlid I'm always glad to see him. Well, once a week or so. But tell Sumarlid I don't want to hear anything about earls or kings or vikings.'

5

Next winter, one day soon after Christmas, a horseman was seen crossing the ridge and riding slowly down between the fields to Breckness.

That bleak winter morning the horseman looked so forlorn that Sumarlid's wife Liv bade the house girls blow up the fire and put on some broth to heat. 'Not ale,' she said. 'I know these ale-drinkers. They get drunk in the morning and then they're at it all day – a trouble to everybody – and they don't sober up, some of them, till the new moon . . .'

The horseman drew near, and they saw it was Ramir Olafson, of Tenston.

When Ragna and Liv saw how pale and wretched he looked, they told the girls not to bother with the soup-pot, but instead look for a flagon of the oldest strongest ale.

It was a while before Ramir could say anything. They set him down in a deep chair beside the fire. By now Sumarlid had come in from the barn, and Solveig had come down from the hill. Ranald was working in the sheepfold that day.

'Some harm has come to Ingerth and the children,' said Ragna.

'It is worse even than that, I think,' said Solveig.

After he had gulped a few mouthfuls of ale, Ramir was able to speak.

'Our earl is dead,' he said. 'Our good Earl Rognvald has been murdered in the island of Papa Stronsay.'

For a while he could say no more. His face worked, his eyes focused upon misery.

'I hope there will be no eye-water, no weeping and wailing,' said Solveig. 'That's a miserable thing, especially in a man. If Ramir starts crying, I won't stay here.'

'I won't cry,' said Ramir. 'There aren't enough tears in me, or in any man, to express the horror.'

He took a few more sips of Ragna's strong ale, and then he was able to tell the story.

Earl Rognvald Brusison was living in Kirkvoe, the village between the two seas of Scapa Flow and Wide Firth. He had built himself a fine house there – he intended to let the old earl's palace in Birsay fall into ruin. Kirkvoe had a deep lagoon that was a perfect shelter for ships.

There had been good times all that year in Rognvald's new house in Kirkvoe. Landowners and merchants and skippers had come flocking to see the fortunate young man from all over Orkney, and from Shetland and Sutherland and Lewis too. Now that Rognvald was sole undisputed Earl of Orkney, it was plain to everyone that they would be well and wisely governed. The man who had out-manoeuvred Thorfinn must be a great man indeed.

The young women of Orkney had completely lost their hearts to the handsome earl. One of those women had presented Earl Rognvald with a little lap-dog, a creature with soft affectionate melting eyes that seemed to take to the earl at once, and whenever it was separated from its master it gave a series of sharp shrill barks, so that the big hunting hounds and the guard dogs growled deep in their throats and, but for their chains, would have made short work of Asa (that was the lap-dog's name).

What made the Orkney farmers and merchants happiest of all was that now King Magnus of Norway was their friend and ultimate protector. There would be no more of that double rule that, in the past, had wrought so much havoc in the affairs of the islanders.

To secure Earl Rognvald in his realm, the King of Norway had sent over a score of young chosen men. No harm would come to the earl with that loyal guard around him. Most of the Orkneymen would have preferred to see the Norwegians sailing back home, because they were spendthrifts and inclined to throw their weight around and the girls seemed to like them more than the local men.

It was noticed – but only in passing – that few men from Caithness had crossed the Pentland Firth to offer congratulations and loyalty to Earl Rognvald. Caithness had long been the base of Earl Thorfinn, from the time of his childhood even, and he had many friends there. 'Think nothing of it,' said Earl Rognvald. 'It will take some time for them to get used to the idea of Earl Thorfinn's death. The men of Caithness will come, give them time.'

Earl Rognvald was most particular about food and drink. He had been daintily reared in the Norwegian royal court, and though he could eat hard tack with the roughest and toughest in times of war, it almost turned his stomach to see how the Orkneymen gnawed bones at his table, and ate raw oysters with one throb of the Adam's apple, and often swilled sour ale.

It was brought to the earl's attention that the best malt-maker in Orkney lived in a small northern island called Papa Stronsay. This malt-maker was a farmer, but he would only malt the barley of farmers who he thought would appreciate the excellence of it. So barley was ferried to Papa Stronsay from nearly all the big farms.

'Let the others drink their own swill at their own troughs,' said this farmer, whose name was Ord.

'Well,' Rognvald had said, 'tell this famous malt-man the Earl of Orkney will pay him a good price for a dozen sacks of his malt . . .'

It was winter, and the days were short and cold, and everywhere in Kirkvoe and beyond the women were beginning to brew the Yule ale in their vats.

Earl Rognvald must have been thinking more about the famous malt-maker in Papa Stronsay. One day he said to Per, the skipper of his ship *Hound of the Gale*, 'I am sailing with you to Papa Stronsay in the morning. I have never been to that island. An earl should know every part of his earldom, I think. I hear there is a community of Irish monks there. We could hear some good Advent plainchant. We will stay the night with the famous malt-maker – he won't take it ill, having an earl stay overnight in his house. Then next morning we'll sail back among the islands to Kirkvoe.'

A few of the Kirkvoe merchants advised against this, saying that now in early December was a bad time to set sail, even on such a brief voyage and with the sheltering islands all about. There were still a few friends and adherents of the late Earl Thorfinn skulking in the remote islands. It might be better for the earl to sit in comfort in his new town house, and not to shiver over a wretched fire in a bare island, and pass the night on a stone floor.

And the young women – there seemed to be more and more of them in the earl's house as the days passed – made dove-eyes and dove-complaints all about the earl. 'Dear lord, don't leave us in winter-time . . .' 'I had a dream about you, my lord. In the dream you were a priest and you were being torn to pieces by a hound . . .' 'We women have intuitions – you ought to stay at home . . .' 'We have been making Yule gifts for you, they aren't finished yet – a white linen coat, and a comb to comb out your golden hair . . .'

But the more his courtiers objected to the little homely voyage for the purchase of malt, the more Earl Rognvald was set on the idea.

'No harm will come to you,' he said to the girls. 'The Norwegian bodyguard will be here in Kirkvoe, to keep you company and see off any trouble. Tell the servants to get the ale vats scrubbed. There will be a Yule feast in Orkney better than any feast outside Valhalla.'

The next morning with Per Arnison at the helm, the *Hound of the Gale* left Kirkvoe and in a short time the keel grounded on the shelving beach of Papa Stronsay.

The farmer didn't seem to be overjoyed that the Earl of Orkney – 'a young scented whipper-snapper' he called him – wanted to buy his malt. But the farmer's wife and sister and mother ran here and there like hens. They blew up the fire into golden sheets of flame, and killed a pig and threw trotters and head into a huge black pot over the fire, and trundled in a barrel of ale – even the fumes that rose from that barrel, unbunged, caused a drowsiness and a contentment. More and more peats were brought in from the peat-stack outside.

'I don't know if I have enough malt to sell you,' said the farmer. Earl Rognvald took a gold coin from his purse and set it on the table. 'Follow me out to the barn and we'll see,' said the farmer. 'Who did you say you were, Earl Rognvald? I thought Thorfinn was the name of our earl. It's all one to me, what the earl's name is. They tax me plenty, that's all I know. Mister earl, I wouldn't let that miserable little dog of yours run about in the farmyard yapping like that – my dogs could finish the creature off in a couple of gulps . . . Yes, here's my malt-store. Taste it.'

Earl Rognvald seemed to be pleased at the surliness of the farmer.

He took a little malt on the tip of his forefinger and sniffed it and touched it to his tongue.

'I'll have a score of bags,' he said. 'Put them on the ship at once.'

'Steady on,' said the farmer. 'I have other customers besides you. This malt belongs to all the big farmers from Sanday to Rinansay. They'll be coming any day. A dozen sacks you'll get, no more. Take it or leave it.'

By now a lantern was lit in the barn and the stars were coming out.

'Stay the night?' said the farmer. 'There's no beds for you. There's hardly room on the floor for you and your men to stretch out. I have plenty of peats. You'd better sit around the fire till morning. I don't keep an inn here, so it's a poor breakfast you'll get.'

Now the little dog was barking furiously at a ship that seemed to linger, darkling, in the Sound.

Then they all went in to supper.

It was a splendid meal for a small farm in a lonely island – bacon broth and a pig's head and trotters and great wedges of ham, and new-baked bread, and cheese, and such good ale that everyone seemed to be happy.

(Even the surly farmer smiled once or twice, but that might have been when he happened to glimpse the gold coin on the windowsill.)

The lap-dog Asa gnawed on a swine-bone for a while and then went to sleep beside the fire.

The farmer got to his feet and said he would go and sleep on straw in the byre. 'See you cover the hearth before you lie down,' he said to Earl Rognvald.

The ale and the warmth were making the earl and his men sleepy. The old stories came slowly from them, with stumblings and hesitations.

The dog Asa slept at the earl's feet.

The ale butt was still half-full. 'Help yourselves,' said the old woman. 'We're off to bed in the barn.'

'Why do I suddenly feel so cold?' said Per the skipper. He told the ship's boy to throw more peats on the fire.

'We'll be old enough by the time this fire is out,' said Earl Rognvald ... He startled and shook himself like a man coming out of a dream. 'That's strange,' he said, 'I meant to say, "We'll be *cold* when the fire is out." I said, "We'll be *old*". A slip of the tongue like that is no accident. I think it is a warning and a prophecy. My tongue was tolling a death-bell in my skull. I think Thorfinn may still be alive.'

A few wisps of burning straw fell from the thatch on to the floor.

Earl Thorfinn's voice hailed them from the door, outside. 'Yes, Rognvald, Thorfinn is still alive and well. I hope you and your men enjoyed your supper, for you won't be eating breakfast. You can't get out. The door is fastened.'

Then one end of the house burst into flame.

'At least the farmer and his womenfolk should be spared,' said Earl Rognvald.

'They're in the barn,' said Earl Thorfinn. 'I'll have to compensate them for the burning of their house. We'll pay for that out of your estate, Rognvald.'

Rognvald was wearing that night a fine white linen coat that the women of his court had made for him.

Now the voices of the men could hardly be heard through the noise of burning woodwork and thatch.

Per the skipper shouted, 'There's the priest in here. He ought to go free.' Then Per could speak no more for the smoke got into his throat and he was shaken with coughing.

The ship's boy said, 'I was never at a bigger fire.' Then his voice guttered out in coughings and chokings.

Earl Thorfinn said, 'I'll open the top half of the door. The priest can come out.'

The rush of air through the half-door made the fire burn more fiercely still.

Earl Rognvald put his hand on the lower half of the door and vaulted over the heads of the burners and disappeared into the darkness.

'He had a priest-coat on all right,' said Earl Thorfinn. 'But nobody could make such a leap but Rognvald Brusison.'

Earl Thorfinn told half-a-dozen men to comb the island for Rognvald.

Now there were no more sounds from inside the house but the low cracklings and chucklings of the lessening fire. The farm was a smouldering ruin.

'You scoundrels!' shouted the farmer from the end of his barley-field. 'I'm a ruined man. The womenfolk will have to sing at the fairs for pennies. You've made us all beggars.'

'Hold your tongue,' said Thorfinn, 'or I might change my mind about you. I'm thinking of making you my head brewer in Birsay. But you'll have to keep a civil tongue in your head.'

The farmer's sister said, 'We should all be thankful our lives were spared.'

The farmer's mother said, 'What came of the boy they had with them? There was such a bonny boy sailed here on the ship with them.'

The farmer said, 'I'm glad I put that gold coin in my purse, anyway.'

The old granny said, 'Whoever thought we'd have a Yule like this in Papa Stronsay!'

Earl Thorfinn said to the farmer, 'Do you have a fishing-boat on the beach? I wouldn't put it past Rognvald to get away on it.'

Meantime the searchers returned and said they had searched every inch of the island but there was no sign of the man in the white coat.

'Yes,' said the farmer, 'of course I have a fishing-boat. Am I to lose that too?'

Then they heard shrill frantic barking from the boat-noust.

Earl Thorfinn said, 'I think you should look where that little dog is making such a noise.'

They found Earl Rognvald sitting on the stern thwart of the farmer's boat, trying to still the lap-dog with soothing words. They killed him with daggers at once. His body lay sprawled on the seaweed. 'I think we'll send this creature after his master,' said one of Thorfinn's men. So they despatched the dog Asa too . . .

In the morning the twenty sacks of malt were stowed on board the ship *Hound of the Gale*, and Earl Thorfinn gave orders for the sail to be raised.

In the chapel the Irish monks were singing a requiem for the dead. The body of Earl Rognvald Brusison lay before the altar.

Before the ship set sail, Earl Thorfinn gave the farmer another gold piece. 'Am I supposed to be grateful for this?' said Ord the farmer. 'My great-grandfather built this farm and ploughed it out.'

'Pay no attention to him,' said the farmer's wife. 'We're very honoured to have the great Earl Thorfinn visiting us, and you must forgive this man of mine, he's very hasty with his tongue.'

'Two earls in one day in Papa Stronsay!' cried the farmer's sister. 'Whoever would have thought it!'

'One of them's quiet enough,' said the farmer's mother, and nodded towards the chapel where the dark music was going on and on.

But the farmer kept on grumbling about the grinders of the faces of the poor.

'I told you,' said Earl Thorfinn, 'from now on you're to be my chief brewer in Birsay. You don't need to worry about this farm any more. You can take your women folk with you if you want.'

But the farmer said he would make no malt and brew no ale for murderers and fire-raisers, no matter if they were earls or abbots or kings.

In the end, however, he sailed back to Kirkvoe in the ship with Earl Thorfinn. He said he would be glad if his womenfolk stayed behind in Papa Stronsay. He had grown tired of them this long while.

As they sailed among the islands of Kirkvoe, Earl Thorfinn told his men to lie along the bottom of the ship with their axes beside them. No more heads were to be seen than had left Kirkvoe the day before.

Earl Rognvald's Norwegian auxiliaries had come down to the shore of Kirkvoe to greet the malt-bearers, and they were unarmed.

Suddenly *Hound of the Gale* erupted with armed men, and the young Norwegians were killed on the shore, one after the other. Only one was spared.

So Earl Thorfinn became sole ruler of Orkney.

Later that day he summoned all the chief men of Kirkvoe and told them what had happened. Some of them looked sorrowful, for the dead earl had been well liked by the people. Most of them listened, nodding – thus and thus fate works, and it is no use being either glad or sorry at the pattern as it unfolds. The faces of a few were wreathed in smiles, and they hunched their shoulders obsequiously, and stuck out their necks like willing oxen at yoke-time, and those men said how glad they were to welcome the great Earl Thorfinn back to his undoubted inheritance.

Earl Thorfinn put cold looks on them, and said that he did not intend to have his capital in Kirkvoe. As soon as things could be arranged, he would move with his court to his half-finished palace in Birsay.

The young Norwegian whose life had been spared was led into the hall. The guardsman looked Earl Thorfinn gravely in the face. The earl said to him, 'There's a cargo ship leaving for Norway tomorrow. You, my friend, will be on that ship. I want you to tell King Magnus in Bergen that his man Rognvald Brusison is dead, and that Earl Thorfinn the true earl is now in full command here in Orkney, and he intends from now on to keep the revenues of Orkney in his own hands, and that Norway has no jurisdiction in Orkney any more.'

The young Norwegian was taken down to the ship. One of the

Kirkvoe merchants said, 'How was it, Earl Thorfinn, that you escaped from the fire in Orphir?' Earl Thorfinn laughed. 'There's a lot of smoke at a house-burning,' he said. 'I took my wife Ingibiorg in my arms and I ran out through a burning breach in the wall. No one saw us in the smoke. There was a great deal of confusion. It was a dark night. I carried Ingibiorg down to the shore where there were fishing-boats. I launched one and rowed across the Pentland Firth to Caithness. I have many friends in Caithness. Ingibiorg and I got shelter there. Nearly every day we got news of Rognvald's movements. When I heard, three days ago, that he was going to Papa Stronsay for malt, I thought that would be a good time for Rognvald and Thorfinn to meet again . . .'

So, at the farmhouse of Breckness, Ramir Olafson told the story of how Earl Thorfinn had turned the tables on Earl Rognvald, Ramir's friend and companion.

But that was by no means the end of the story as far as Ramir and his farm and family were concerned.

A week or so after the return of Thorfinn, the three horsemen who had come that first time to Tenston with unfriendly words had come back, riding on horses from Birsay. They wasted no words this time. 'You are Ramir Olafson? Of course you are Ramir, no use denying it. This farm belongs to Earl Thorfinn, and he has a tenant that he wishes to rent the farm to. Please arrange to be out of Tenston by the end of the month, you and all your people and all your beasts.'

'The farm belongs to me,' Ramir said. 'It has been in my family for five generations.'

'It now belongs to Earl Thorfinn,' said one of the horsemen.

'And Earl Thorfinn is turning you out,' said another horseman.

'We will come back,' said the third horseman, 'and collect taxes and rents due, before the end of the month.'

Then they turned the horses' heads and rode back in the direction of Birsay.

'So here I am,' said Ramir, 'a homeless man, and certainly Thorfinn won't rent me any other farm in Orkney.'

Sumarlid said, 'This is what comes of hobnobbing with princes and powers. Don't lose heart, Ramir. Egil, the old crofter of Heatherbraes, died recently. You could move in there, you and Ingerth and the children. It is not a fertile place like Tenston, and the winter wind blows loud and cold on the ridge up there. But you'll have a roof over your head, and I think my father won't ask too much rent.'

At the end of the month Ramir herded his family and his cattle and horses and sheep to Heatherbraes, and the household was well settled in before the worst of the winter began.

6

Now Thorfinn Sigurdson was Earl of Orkney and Shetland, in addition to the territories in the north and west of Scotland that he had won for himself in war.

The Orkney farmers and merchants, after a time, were glad to have a single strong ruler like Thorfinn over them. After Thorfinn had wreaked vengeance on some of those men who had too openly supported his nephew, like Ramir Olafson, he turned a mild face on the others and suggested that after all their troubles they ought now to establish together peace and prosperity in the islands.

To unite the people, the earl (whose black beard now had threads of silver in it) visited every island and parish, by horse and row-boat, with a small company of his courtiers, among whom was the famous war-poet, Arnor the laureate.

In due course, the earl's company arrived at Breckness, and was courteously received in the yard by Sumarlid and Liv and Ragna.

Ramir and his family shut themselves up in Heatherbraes that day, he barred the door and shuttered the window. The children were eager to see the great earl they had heard so much about, but Ramir ordered them sternly to remain inside. The eldest boy managed to climb out through the thatch and he was there at the edge of the crowd of farmworkers and crofters who had gathered to see Earl Thorfinn and Sumarlid greeting one another.

In Thorfinn's company was a man who was hooded and kept the collar of his coat well over his face.

Now Ragna and Solveig came out to be presented to the earl. Thorfinn was in a happy mood that morning. One by one he introduced his courtiers to the chief people at Breckness. The last one to be presented was the man whose face was muffled so that only his eyes could be seen. 'This is my poet Arnor,' said Earl Thorfinn. 'The flaming words he beats out on the anvil of his art are of more consequence than the earldoms I have hewn out for myself with my sword. Or rather, my story would vanish like smoke in the wind if it weren't for Arnor's ringing verses.'

Ragna said, 'It's a hard thing if a mother can't recognize her own son. Einhof, have you come here to return the coins you took from your father's strong-box the day you slunk away from home like a cur?'

Then Arnor the poet laughed. He threw back his head and dismounted and embraced his mother.

His brother Sumarlid gave him a colder greeting.

'Why did you have to go changing your name?' said Ragna. 'Einhof you were called at the christening font at Warbeth.'

Einhof was looking eagerly at the farm and the hills and the sea below. 'How small everything has become!' he said. 'The byre and the sheepfold and the well . . .' He recognized a few of the older farmworkers, and shook them warmly by the hand, and said they must have a drink together before it was time for Earl Thorfinn to leave. 'I think this is the happiest day of my life,' he said.

Then Ragna kissed Einhof-Arnor. This was thought to be too extravagant a show of affection. Solveig looked embarrassed. The farmworkers shuffled their feet. Sumarlid said, 'Welcome, brother,' and shook him firmly, but still a little coldly, by the hand. Now Ragna invited Thorfinn and his company indoors. If she had known they were coming, she said, she would have made a proper feast for them. As things were, she could offer them passable refreshment, her cupboard was not quite bare. Earl Thorfinn thanked her. He said they had many farms in Stromness parish to visit that day, and if they ate and drank at every table they would have bellies on them like hogsheads. 'I came here in particular', said the earl, 'to greet Ranald Sigmundson, the farmer of Breckness. I hope he is still alive?' Ragna said that her husband was living at present in that hut up there on the side of Black Crag, and rarely came out except to waste the time of shepherds and horsemen and fishermen. He was well enough in his health, Ragna said, except for stangs of rheumatism in his hands and feet, but his hair and his beard were white as wool or sea-spume. 'Tell Ranald I would be glad to see him again,' said Earl Thorfinn. 'He once visited my father Sigurd in our Hall at Birsay, when I was a small boy. I will never forget the story he told of his Vinland voyage. He is a good man, Ranald Sigmundson, and I would be happy to meet him now.'

Then Ragna told Solveig to go up to her father's hut and tell him that the earl had called at Breckness and wanted to see him. Earl Thorfinn had not dismounted from his horse. It pranced here and there on the cobbled yard, sending out sparks. A girl came out with a tray of mugs of the best ale and went round Earl Thorfinn's men. The earl snatched a mug and frothed his beard with it and swallowed the ale in two gulps. Then Solveig returned from the hut and said her father would not see Earl Thorfinn. Tell the earl, Ranald had said, that he would be better visiting the abbot at Warbeth, to get absolution for the evil he had wrought upon the earth. Earl Thorfinn, sitting on his horse, looked thunderstruck.

Then he laughed.

'Tell Ranald,' he said, 'I'll be going a bit further than Warbeth about spiritual matters. Next spring I'm going to see the Pope in Rome, myself and my cousin King Macbeth of Scotland. We'll sail to Normandy, and then we'll ride across the Alps into Italy . . . Tell Ranald that.'

Then Earl Thorfinn signed to his men that it was time for them to visit the next big farm, Cairston.

Ragna looked confused. She hoped, she said, the earl would not hold it against them that her husband had sent down such a discourteous message.

'No,' said Earl Thorfinn, 'I like plain speaking. You see all this crowd of fawners and flatterers I have to travel around with. There's not an honest tongue in their heads.'

Ragna asked her son Einhof who struck out warlike verses under the name of Arnor the laureate, whether he wouldn't stay for a day or two longer at Breckness?

But Einhof-Arnor said that, as the chief fawner and flatterer, it was his duty to be always at his lord's side. 'What I'd like to do very much is to see the old cracked flagstone at the end of the house where I scratched out a chessboard once and played all summer against myself, with shells and stones for bishops and kings.'

Earl Thorfinn laughed again, and made his chestnut horse prance on the cobbles.

'You, Solveig,' he said, 'I hear you're a great falconer. You must take your hawk to Greenay hill in Birsay. I'll walk with you into the big wind and we'll throw our cruel curves up among the clouds.'

Solveig said she much preferred to do her own falconry from the top of Ernefea.

Thorfinn laughed and asked for another cup of ale. 'They are their

214

own folk here at Breckness, I see,' he said. 'Still, Solveig, I think it's high time you got yourself a husband, to knock some civility into you.'

Ragna looked downcast. 'An earl deserves better answers than the answers he has gotten here at Breckness,' she said.

'I've enjoyed this visit more than any other farms I've been to since I set out,' Thorfinn said.

Now all his company were astride their horses.

Einhof kissed his mother on both cheeks before he got into the stirrup. He had offered his sister the same farewell, but she had quelled him with a cold look.

Sumarlid took his brother warmly by the hand.

Then the earl and his men rode off, and the farmworkers cheered. And Ramir-and-Ingerth's son, Rolf, went home by a roundabout way.

Solveig ordered the men back to their work. 'We've wasted a whole morning. Can't you see there's ploughing to be done?'

Word came later that year that the earl's stone-masons were busy working at a little cathedral on the island off Birsay called the Brough. A young cleric who had studied in Paris was coming north to be the first Bishop of Orkney. His name was William.

Ranald Sigmundson was in poor health much of that year.

But as soon as summer came he got stronger. His health seemed to ebb and flow like the sea. He was able to walk to the shepherds' bothy on the side of the hill, but now he had a stick, and one of the farm dogs ran on before him.

The fishermen felt slighted that he didn't visit them at the shore so much, but spent much of that summer with the shepherds.

The old man would grit his teeth going past the smithy if the hammer was ringing on the anvil. 'It reminds me of war,' he said.

The only sounds that seemed to please him were wind and rain, and the sheep and the cows and wild birds passing overhead. He even looked bad-tempered sometimes if Ragna or Sumarlid or Solveig stopped at his door to greet him, if he chanced to be reading fragments of *Ecclesiastes* out of the monk's scroll, or working on the drawings of his ship.

On his way back from the sheepfold, he would stop from time to time and look out over the ocean. A look of yearning came on him, especially if he saw a ship off the Kame of Hoy, sailing west. He would linger for a long time, leaning on his stick. Then the dog Bran, running on before, would summon him home with its barking.

His son Sumarlid visited him once a week at least, to let him know how things stood with the big farm. The old man seemed most times to give him only half his attention. 'All right, all right,' he would say. 'If those two horses fight in the stable, sell the awkward one and buy another . . .' 'Do what seems best. I have other things to think about . . .' 'The harvest was good, the men want more wages? Don't bother me with such nonsense . . .' 'You're riding to the assembly at Tingvoe next week, are you? Understand this, Sumarlid, – I don't want to hear a thing about what goes on there. Vanity of vanities. All that speech-making, all that scheming in dark corners. Go there, by all means, but listen and don't say anything and come away as soon as you can . . . And now leave me alone, I have a scroll here that the abbot gave me, about a man called Job who lived a long while ago. I'm having a happier old age than Job had, the poor man.'

Solveig would throw open her father's door with a crash and go in. 'That Ramir, he's getting above himself, ordering the hill-crofters about. "This is my ditch," he tells them. "Can't you see the boundary-stone – the patch you're pasturing your goat on belongs to me, man. See to it . . ." All this because he's your son-in-law. I gave him a piece of my mind. "You came here a beggar and an outcast," I told him this morning, "and now you're trying to cheat the hill-crofters out of the few acres they've had for generations. I know you, Ramir. Don't let me hear any more of that kind of nonsense." And there was my sister Ingerth standing in the door of Heatherbraes, holding her apron up to her eyes. That Ramir Olafson was red in the face by the time I left him . . .'

Ranald always listened patiently to Solveig, and in the end he would say, 'Solveig, speak to your brother Sumarlid about it. The management of the estate is in his hands – surely you know that. At least let there be peace here in Breckness.'

Often Solveig would go fishing in the sixearns, rowing with the fishermen far beyond Hoy. The fishermen didn't mind having Solveig in the boat – she worked hard at the fishing lines and she could speak the same rough language as themselves. If there were haddocks to spare, and her father was in his hut, she would throw open his door and leave a couple on his floor. 'You have a knife,' she would say, 'clean them yourself. You should try to do something useful every day. All that reading and thinking is bad for a person . . .' At the end of a week the smell of rotten fish in Ranald's hut was disgusting, and when the old man wakened on the night he would see the glow of them on the hearth-stone . . . At last a shepherd would scoop them up and throw them to the gulls.

This happened often in Ranald's last year.

Yet he always thanked Solveig for the fish when she brought them up, smelling of the sea for an hour.

7

Sumarlid rode back from Tingvoe one afternoon in spring. He left the unsaddling and stabling of his horse to the stable-boy, then he went hot-foot up to his father's hut. He knocked at the door, louder than usual.

'Come in,' said Ranald.

'I've just ridden back from the assembly,' said Sumarlid. 'I don't believe there has ever been an assembly like it. Earl Thorfinn is an astonishing man.'

'I don't want to hear anything about it,' said Ranald.

But in the end, as always, the old man listened to what his son had to say.

It was well known (Sumarlid said) how furious King Magnus had been when he heard how his well-loved Earl Rognvald had been murdered in Orkney, among the rocks and seaweed of Papa Stronsay, and how the élite guardsmen he had lent to the earl had been slaughtered on the shore of Kirkvoe next morning – all but one, who had been despatched with Earl Thorfinn's compliments to acquaint the king with the new situation. The king had sworn most bitter vengeance, but it was hard to see how he could ever get near Earl Thorfinn now, because Thorfinn ruled absolutely in Orkney and in great areas of Scotland besides – he was the absolute ruler in his domain, as powerful as the King of Scotland. Nor was Thorfinn the kind of man who could be tricked a second time, as when his house in Orphir had been surrounded and set on fire. To preclude such irruptions on his peace, Earl Thorfinn had his palace – not yet quite completed – on a small steep island off the northwest coast of Birsay, called the Brough of Birsay: this island could only be approached by land at ebb tide. Besides, Earl Thorfinn was building a small cathedral kirk on the same islet, to show forth to the whole world that he was more than a secular tyrant.

King Magnus of Norway spent many a sleepless night scheming how to get at this enemy in Orkney, but there seemed to be little hope of achieving anything. It was not as in the old days when Orkney was aswarm with Norwegian spies and informers. Nowadays every ship from Norway that landed in Orkney was strictly examined, and a time-schedule was set for the skipper and merchant to do their business and depart again. No sail broke the horizon eastward but word of it was brought to the earl or his advisers at once.

One Norwegian merchant was coerced, against his will, to ride north to Birsay. The man thought his last day had come, when the two horsemen who rode with him said that Earl Thorfinn wanted words with him. 'What have I done wrong?' he said on the road to Birsay. 'I'm a simple merchant, I wish your earl well, I hope he won't do me any harm, I'm newly married and I'm building a house in More and I'm trying to establish a business in timber and walrus tusks.'

The earl's two horsemen said nothing, and that made the peaceable Norwegian even more afraid.

The tide was out. They were able to walk among the rockpools to the palace where workmen were busy with ladders and scaffolding and mortar buckets.

The Norwegian got a friendly reception from Earl Thorfinn. 'What's wrong with you, man?' said the earl. 'No need for you to shake like that. Here, fill this good man's ale cup and bring him some bread and smoked lamb. You'll be back in your ship before sunset. You're very welcome. All I want to know is, how are affairs in the kingdoms of the east – in Denmark, Sweden and Norway? I've had no news from there this long while.'

The merchant answered that Norway was at war with Denmark, and the ships of Norway were gathering off the Sel Isles, and they would soon attack the coasts of Denmark. The shipyards of Norway were busy night and day building great deep-draughted warships. He had seen two or three of the splendid ships being launched.

'And the ships are to assemble at the Sel Isles at last?' said the earl. 'You are sure of that?'

'It's well known,' said the merchant.

'Well now,' said Earl Thorfinn, 'you'll just have time to get off the Brough before the tide comes in. Your horse is waiting for you on the

218

Birsay shore. I hope you do good business in your trading booth at Kirkvoe. Have a safe voyage home to More.'

The earl gave the merchant a silver ring. The merchant rode all the way to Kirkvoe as though his horse was fetlocked with wings.

Within days Earl Thorfinn had two fast ships fitted out and manned, and he sailed east to Norway.

At the Sel Isles the ships were gathering fast now from all the provinces of Norway for the attack on Denmark. King Magnus saw two strange ships sailing from the west, and they did not seem to bear the design of his battle fleet, though they were both long lithe powerful vessels. The strange ships sailed in close to the king's ship, and one of the sailors vaulted the gap between his own ship and the king's ship. 'Well, mess-mate,' said the stranger to the king, 'here I am with my ships and men, ready to sail in your battle fleet whenever you give the word.'

The sailors on the royal ship gaped at the stranger. 'Mess-mate' – a skipper nobody had seen before calling His Majesty the King mess-mate! The man, whoever he was, must be mad. Yet they could not but admire the man's courage. He seemed to them like a man who would tug death by the beard – indeed, death might quail before those sombre powerful eyes.

Nor was the king insulted at being called mess-mate, it seemed. He invited the strange skipper to sit on the bench beside him. The king was having a light midday meal of bread and ale.

The stranger put in his hand and broke a piece from the king's loaf and ate it. 'Now,' he said, 'let that be a sign of friendship between us.'

King Magnus said, 'Still you haven't told me your name.'

'I think', said the king's guest, 'if I were to tell you my name all at once, you wouldn't be too pleased. Still, you'll have to know it before we finish this ale jar. My name is Thorfinn Sigurdson, Earl of Orkney.'

There was silence for a while on the ship.

The king said at last, 'I had sworn, Thorfinn Sigurdson, that if ever we met you would pay with your life for killing the earl I had placed over Orkney, my dear friend Earl Rognvald Brusison. That was a cruel death you gave him, among the seaweed and the rockpools in Papa Stronsay.'

'It is fate that is cruel, not me,' said Earl Thorfinn. 'The same Rognvald thought he had burned me and my wife Ingibiorg in a house in Orphir earlier that winter. I admired my nephew Rognvald and I

219

think he had more than a passing regard for me. Yet fate dashed us together, fire against a wave of the sea. I alone came out of that clash of the elements – so fate willed it. And now I put myself in your hands, King Magnus. I offer you my total allegiance – apart, that is, from the allegiance that I owe to the King of Scotland.'

News of Earl Thorfinn's arrival had spread, and now the king's advisers and the skippers of the war fleet had climbed on board the royal ship and stood clustered all round the bench where the king and the earl were sitting. They wondered what kind of punishment King Magnus would devise for the earl in the west.

For a while King Magnus said not a word. He was holding the ale jar in his hands, and his knuckles were white.

Suddenly the king thrust the ale jar into the earl's hands and said, 'Drink, my friend. I'm glad you have come to see me. Such frankness and openness to a king is rarer than diamonds. It may be we will get on well enough in the end.'

Earl Thorfinn took the jar, and drained it. 'I will go with you wherever you want,' he said.

The courtiers and the skippers went back to their ships. It seemed to them that King Magnus and Earl Thorfinn had taken to each other at once, and would now be life-long friends.

The king told Thorfinn the situation as between Norway and Denmark. Norway was at war with Denmark. The Norwegian fleet had mustered here at the isles of Sel, awaiting the arrival of more ships from the shipyards. Those new-built ships should have arrived at the rendezvous more than a week ago. That was vexing. The King of Norway dared not sail against Denmark with a small fleet. But once the ships of the northern earls arrived, there was every promise of a great victory at sea.

Earl Thorfinn offered his two ships to add to the Norwegian fleet. 'They are good sailors and good fighting men,' said the earl. 'I don't think they will let you down.'

The king thanked the earl. They spoke together till the sun went down. From time to time, the seamen heard laughter from the poop-deck where Magnus and Thorfinn were sitting.

The king had a black boy who stood always at his shoulder, as still as if he was carved out of ebony. The boy had been captured during a raid on the coast of Morocco the previous summer. From time to time there was a kindling in his mulberry eyes, or he flicked his thick lips with his tongue, or the gold ring in his ear gave a small chime.

This black boy seemed to understand the king's lightest gesture. After the sun went down the king raised a finger and the boy went away and returned with two bearskin cloaks which he put on the shoulders of the king and the earl, for now it was growing cold. Then he went away again and returned with a lantern which he set on the bench. The light threw golden shadows across their faces, but the face of the black boy himself seemed to be lost in the darker shadows beyond the wavering circle of lantern light. The boy went away again and returned with a jar of hot mead, and a plate of bread and fish new caught from the sea and lightly simmered in wine.

'Bring the chessboard,' said the king, after the supper was over. They heard the small chime of ear-rings as the black boy came and went, and returned, and set out the chess pieces.

After the game of chess, which Thorfinn won, king and earl sat till beyond midnight, speaking earnestly about affairs in Scandinavia and Scotland and Ireland.

Then Earl Thorfinn took his leave.

'In the morning', said King Magnus, 'we will see the ships of the northern earls black against the dawn. Then it will be time to sail against Denmark.'

'Goodnight, Your Majesty,' said Thorfinn.

'Goodnight, my friend,' said the king. 'I am very glad because of this day.'

The black boy lighted the earl out of the royal ship into the small boat that was to row him back to his own ship. The lantern, held high, broke the sea into a hundred dancing coins.

Next morning the northern fleet had still not come.

King Magnus sent word for Earl Thorfinn to keep him company that day again. 'Now that we know each other,' said the king, 'it seems there have been too many years of mistrust between us. We have a great deal to make up in the way of friendship and good company.'

Indeed all through that day the seamen on the royal ship could hear laughter and the quoting of old resonant verses from the poop-deck. They had not heard their king in such high good humour for years.

The black boy stood at the king's shoulder, merely showing by an eye-blink or the flick of a tongue or the little chime of his ear-ring that he was a living boy. But let the king make a slight gesture with a finger, and then the boy understood at once what was wanted – a napkin for

221

the king to wipe his mouth – a wine skin and two silver goblets – the chessboard and the chesspieces.

'You play a good game of chess,' said the king, 'and you always beat me. I wonder why that should be. I am thought to be skilful enough at the chessboard.'

'It is luck,' said Thorfinn. 'Luck runs in full flood for a man for a time, then it turns all of a sudden, and the man is left making heavy weather of his days.'

A sailor was stationed always at the prow of the king's ship, to report at once the first sighting of the northern ships. Sailor after sailor kept watch all through that day. There was no sign of the fleet promised by the earls of the north.

'This is becoming vexatious,' said the king. 'You would think their ships were stuck in ice. We will have one more game of chess. Then at sunset we'll see their great black shadows moving down from the north.'

They played again, and this time King Magnus had an easy victory.

'My luck may have turned,' said Thorfinn.

It was sunset. The ocean westward was ablaze with light, gules and scattered gold and torn scarlet.

A young man in a red coat vaulted from ship to ship – so close were the ships drawn together – and at last he vaulted on to the king's ship. Two sailors tried to prevent him – he thrust them aside and came with long strides to the king's cabin.

'I could have you killed for this,' said the king.

'I am your loyal servant,' said the man in the red coat, 'and I always will be. It is this man that I want a word with . . .' He pointed a finger at Earl Thorfinn.

Earl Thorfinn said nothing.

'I want to know', said the man, 'when you intend to pay compensation for murdering my brother.'

Thorfinn said he had, of necessity, killed a number of men in his time, but he never killed a man for the joy of it, and if he had killed this discourteous man's brother, then the dead man must have richly deserved his death.

'Not so,' said the stranger. 'You won't have forgotten, earl, the day you sailed back from Papa Stronsay, after murdering Earl Rognvald there, the king's man. Full of triumph and guile your heart was that day, earl. Down at the shore of Kirkvoe a company of the king's

222

Norwegian guard was waiting, thinking the ship to be Earl Rognvald's ship laden with malt for the Yuletide brewing. Little did they know, those loyal Norwegians, that their good earl was lying cold among rockpools, northwards, red with blood and seaweed. You can't have forgotten that, earl.'

'I remember it well,' said Thorfinn.

'Then', said the stranger, 'your armed ruffians who were crouched along the bottom-boards of the ship rose up and leapt ashore and killed those young unarmed Norwegians one after another.'

'I remember that too,' said Thorfinn, 'with pleasure.'

'Well,' said the man, 'one of those Norwegians, a loyal servant of King Magnus here, was slaughtered along with his comrades. I am here, earl, to ask for compensation for the death of my brother.'

Earl Thorfinn said nothing for a while. Then he said, 'I have never paid compensation for the death of a man in my life. I don't intend to start now, even if your brother was one of the king's men.'

King Magnus had been looking thoughtful all through this dialogue. Now his face flashed crimson. He could not speak. It was as though he had bitten on the root of his tongue.

'Look closer at me,' said the man. 'It may be that you recognize me.'

Earl Thorfinn said he was not in the habit of remembering every ill-mannered ruffian he came across.

'But at least you'll remember this,' said the man. 'You spared one of those young Norwegians, so that he could return to Bergen and tell the king what had happened, and how the great Thorfinn could rule in his earldom without any need of Norway's protection and friendship. Do you remember putting that man on a ship bound for Norway?'

'I remember it well,' said Thorfinn.

'I am the man you spared. I am the messenger you sent east to King Magnus on that ship.'

'Well,' said Thorfinn, 'so be it. I was a fool to have spared you. But it would have been the spoiling of a great story, not to have sent you east with that news to the king . . . Now I see it's wrong to spare a man – it is, I think, the cause of my own undoing here in the Sel Isles.'

Still the king could not speak. He sat there balancing his head on his fist, looking into nothingness.

Dark waves lapped the ship's hull now.

'Black boy,' said Earl Thorfinn, 'would you light me over to the ship's side with the lantern? I think I may not be welcome here any more.'

But the black boy set down the lantern on a chest and he touched the king's bowed head with a gentle hand.

'I will find my own way in the dark,' said Thorfinn.

He turned then and spoke to the young man in the red coat. 'It is the storm of fate that blows through the world forever, and makes the swords rise and fall. I will not pay you any compensation. It was fate that struck your brother, not I. It was fate, not I, that spared you that day. Now may you have a long and happy life.'

The gentlest of moans came from the lips of the black boy, and the golden circle in his ear rang, so quietly that it could hardly be heard above the movement of the dark starless waters.

8

Year followed year at the farm of Breckness. The harvests were adequate most years, for Sumarlid was a good farmer. Sometimes they were abundant. Sometimes they were poor, either on account of stormy weather in late summer, or because the worm had gotten into the early crop.

But nobody ever starved in that district, because Sumarlid had inherited the wise husbandry taught him by his father, and the crofters round about took account of that old wisdom of the earth.

Earl Thorfinn sent his tax-men through the islands, but his taxes and rents were thought to be fair on the whole.

The people considered that they were well governed. They were glad to be rid of the old times, when earl struggled with earl for mastery, and the coat-of-state was rent over and over again, and the earls trooped one by one with the rags they had managed to keep to the king in the east, for Norway to apply some kind of patching, on condition however that he was acknowledged to be supreme lord of Orkney and Shetland.

Earl Thorfinn now sent no treasury ship to Bergen, with a chest in the hold heavy with gold of taxation. Instead he had more and more dealings with Scotland, and not as a vassal either, but as an equal of the king of Scots, to whom he was related by ties of kinship.

At that time the King of Scotland was Macbeth. Earl Thorfinn got on well with Macbeth, a strong ruler and a man of courage and foresight.

He had hacked his way to the throne of Scotland with a certain ruthlessness, but no milksop or dreamer ever won a kingdom in the west of Europe in those days. King Macbeth and Earl Thorfinn met from time to time, generally at one of the royal keeps near Inverness. They agreed at one of their meetings that they would set aside a year to make a pilgrimage to Rome.

'Look at those hands of mine,' said the King of Scotland, 'they're reeking with blood . . .' He showed Earl Thorfinn his powerful hands.

'They look clean enough to me,' said Thorfinn. 'In fact they smell like a woman's hands.'

'That's because Queen Gruath puts essence-of-rose in my washbasin. She is not well, my queen. On her account, as well as for the black deeds I've done in my time, I've decided to ride to Rome before I'm too old for the journey and the penance. Either that, or some young puppy who thinks he should be king will get an army of cut-throats from the King of England and lay siege to me here, and I might have trouble getting out of their clutches.'

Earl Thorfinn put his sea-smelling hand into the scented hand of King Macbeth, and they agreed that the following year, after the ploughing and seed-time, they would ride together over the Alps to see Rome and the other cities of France and Italy.

A frail figure drifted into the throne-room, and looked at Thorfinn, and shook her head and went out again quietly.

'That is Queen Gruath,' said Macbeth. 'She is not well.'

Thorfinn could hardly believe that the worn wraith of a woman was the queen who, a few years since, had read the future of Scotland on the foreheads of the princes and noblemen, and coldly instructed her man the way he must take to the throne of Scotland, not by devious twistings and turnings, but by one swift ruthless stride, and a single daggerstroke in the night.

Gruath had left a phial now on the windowsill. 'It is my attar-of-roses,' said Macbeth. 'It comes from Syria. It is for me to rub into my fingers and beard, to drown the smell of blood. But I'd rather smell of the ocean, like you, my good friend, or of the Alpine snows.'

And so Thorfinn sailed home to Orkney.

News of that meeting, in Dunsinane, was brought to Ranald by Sumarlid, after a springtide assembly at Tingvoe.

'Well, I'm glad to hear that,' said old Ranald. 'Earl Thorfinn is beginning to realize that he won't live for ever.'

225

Nowadays Ranald could no longer read the scroll with the ship-drawing on it, or some piece of parchment the abbot had lent him, his eyesight was failing so fast.

His grandson, Ingerth's oldest boy, Rolf, came every morning early and led Ranald sometimes to the sheepfold, sometimes to the smithy, sometimes to the fishing-bothy. The dog Bran ran barking in front as the old man and the boy walked together through the fields.

The old man's greatest joy was when Ingerth's six children visited him, either in the farm or in the 'place of meditation'. Sumarlid's two boys kept away; they had heard his stories of Vinland and Greenland and Norway too often. Thorstein and Thorbiorn were more interested in going with Solveig and her hawk to the hill, or sitting with the fishermen while they baited their creels, or standing in the clamorous smithy.

But Ingerth's children could not have enough of their grandfather's stories: how he had stowed away in Iceland on Leif Ericson's ship; how he had walked under the great trees with the skraeling boy; how he had won the horse-race in Greenland; how he had sat at the king's table in Bergen and drunk overmuch mead; how he had bargained with Earl Sigurd's merchants in Kirkwall for walrus tusks and timber; how he had taken back the farm of Breckness from the viking Harald Thorn; how he had played chess with the sons of Earl Sigurd at Birsay, and seen his future wife sewing a patch on a coat, but didn't know then that the girl Ragna would one day be his wife ('And I daresay', said Ranald, 'your grandmother has rued the day that she left Birsay and came here to Breckness, for she never got much happiness from me, that's the truth, and she's a good woman, bless her, Ragna . . .'); how he had sailed with hundreds of young men to the terrible battle at Clontarf in Ireland one Good Friday, and escaped from that warp-and-weft of war with only a scratch on his knuckle; how he had ridden to the assemblies at Tingvoe year after year, and listened to the open debates and the secret intrigues, and a deep disgust had entered into his heart at human folly and cruelty, his own included; and how he had seen that power drives men mad, and how Earl Einar of the Twisted Mouth had fallen into his own web-of-treachery at Skaill in Sandwick; and how he had decided to wash his hands of politics and violence and attend only to the farm of Breckness and the farmworkers there and the crofters round about, so that all should be protected and treated with fairness, as far as he, Ranald, could mingle fairness with firmness and generosity; and of how an Irish monk who had stayed for a while with the brothers at Warbeth had told him the marvellous tale of the voyages of Saint Brandon who had sailed out to find the Island of the Blessed in the western sea; and of how, at last, he had thought it best to come occasionally and live in this hut by himself, so that he could solve the riddle of fate and freedom; and so make preparations for his last voyage upon the waters of the end.

Ingerth's children, whenever it was raining so hard that they couldn't play in the burn or on the hill, would go to Ranald's hut, and sit so long that often they would not hear their mother's voice calling across the fields. 'Where are you? Time for supper and bed . . .' And they would wheedle another story out of their grandfather, and sometimes Ramir would come looking for them with a lantern.

Then Ranald would say goodnight to them, and the grandchildren would kiss him on his withered cheek one after the other, and follow their father into the lantern-splashed darkness.

Sometimes the two shepherds would come to see Ranald, and they would talk for an hour about the hardships of lambing in the late snow, or the abundance or paucity of fleeces that summer.

Now Ranald lived more in the hut than at home.

Solveig came once a week or so. She, rather than her brother Sumarlid, was at last the real superintendent of the farm, telling the farmfolk what they must do, and rebuking them severely for any foolish or perverse behaviour, whether in the furrows and pastures or in their own households. A strong man might tremble when he saw Solveig coming to his door; but as often as not it might be to give him a word of encouragement and praise. Nobody had qualms when Sumarlid came on a visit – Sumarlid was liked by all the people.

Solveig visited her father one evening just before Easter. 'The earl has gone to visit the King of Scotland,' said Solveig. 'They're making a pilgrimage to Rome. It'll take the Pope the best part of a day to hear the confession of that pair of beauties.'

Ranald said nothing. He did not appear to know that Solveig was in the hut. He sat, with his head on one side, as if listening.

There had been a week-long gale from the west, that had sent the breakers crashing into the base of Black Crag and among the rocks of Braga ('the place of the thunderous waters'.) Now the storm had quieted, but the Atlantic was full of noises still – surgings, cries, whisperings, gluttings, moans, sounds of lulling and longing and summoning, little bell-like sounds and occasionally, far off, a thunderous growl.

'It will soon be time for me to set sail,' said Ranald.

'You're all right where you are,' said Solveig. 'Put plenty of peat on your fire. It gets cold on March nights.'

Then Solveig left the hut.

When she went back the next day, her father was still speaking about the sea and voyaging.

'Where are you setting out for?' said Solveig. 'Is it Ireland? Is it Norway? You're on the old side for sailing now, father.'

'Tell your mother,' said Ranald, 'I'll need a sheepskin coat. It gets cold out on the Atlantic. Tell Ragna to brew a cask of good ale. Tell her I'll be needing a store of smoked fish and smoked mutton. Oatcakes keep best. It's going to be a long voyage.'

Solveig went away, shaking her head. Her father was beginning to be confused in his mind.

She told Sumarlid that he must look in from time to time every day to see how their father was. She thought it better not to say anything to Ragna.

Sumarlid called on his father, and saw the change in him. He didn't know what to say. His father didn't seem to recognize him. At last Sumarlid said, 'I got a good price for the two young mares at the mart in Kirkvoe.'

The old man looked annoyed. 'What are you talking about?' he said. 'I don't want to hear about the price of horses or cows. Oh, it's you, Sumarlid . . . Tell me, how are they getting on with the ship I ordered? Lodd in Hamnavoe is building a ship for me. Well, if course you know that. He should be putting the finishing touches to it now, that ship. He's a good shipwright, Lodd.'

'Lodd has been dead for six years,' said Sumarlid.

'Next time you're in Hamnavoe,' said Ranald, 'tell Lodd to get Dag in Scapa to make the sail. Dag makes the best sails of all.'

Sumarlid went away, shaking his head.

Ingerth came to see him with her children. 'Well,' Ranald said, 'it'll be many a long day till I see you again. There'll be a few seed-times and harvests before you can sail to visit me in the island.'

Ranald said earnestly to Rolf his grandson, 'Never go on a viking cruise, boy. They'll hold out promises of gold and silver to you, those skippers. Have nothing to do with them.'

228

Gunn, his granddaughter, touched the few frail silver strands of his hair.

'Marry a farmer, Gunn,' said Ranald. 'The sea is too cruel. The sea is more cruel to the women who wait on the shore than to the men that get salt in their beards.'

Then he said to the boy Hallgren, 'Have nothing to do with kings and earls, boy. They build desolate places for themselves. Pay the taxes twice a year. Beyond that, have nothing to do with the two earls.'

'But there's only one earl,' said Ingerth. 'Earl Thorfinn in Birsay. He's a good strong ruler, Thorfinn. The islands have never been so well governed.'

'Oh no,' said Ranald. 'There are always two earls, sometimes three. They tear Orkney in pieces like a coat. One runs with half the coat to the tyrant in Norway, the other takes his useless ornate rag to the tyrant in Scotland. It should be a rich beautiful coat-of-state, laid up there in a chest in the great Hall in Birsay.'

'But Earl Thorfinn wears the coat-of-state alone now,' said Ingerth. 'He's beholden to no one for protection, Norway or Scotland. They daren't touch him. He's as powerful, Thorfinn, as any king in Christendom.'

'Does Thorfinn have sons?' said Ranald.

'Oh yes,' said Ingerth, 'he has two fine sons, Paul and Erlend. I saw them once, riding across from Orphir. They called to see Sumarlid. They wanted to see you, but you sent word they were to keep their distance. Ragna was angry with you that day! Still, she was pleased that the earl's sons had done us the honour of calling at Breckness.'

Ranald laughed, if a sound like the rapid rustling of ripe barley in a stir of wind can be called laughter. 'Sent them away, did I?' he said. 'I was right, surely. Each of those two young gentlemen will want to lay the coat-of-state about his shoulders, once their scheming old rogue of a father is dead. Then the trouble will start again, roof trees on fire all over the north, the gutters running red. Mark my words.'

'Oh no,' cried Ingerth, 'I never saw such gentle courteous young men. They're very fond of one another, Paul and Erlend, that much was plain. They'll never be at one another's throats.'

'Mark my words,' said Ranald. 'Riches and power drive men mad, even good honourable young men.'

Then Ingerth got ready to leave with the children.

'How does it go with you and Ramir Olafson up at Heatherbraes?' said Ranald.

Ingerth said it went well with them.

'Things are told me,' said Ranald. 'Why are there often tear-marks on your face, Ingerth, when you come to see me? I know that Ramir is a lazy man and spends more time in the ale-houses than he does in his barn. I suppose it broke his spirit, being harried out of his farm in Tenston. So you are poor, I know that.'

Ingerth turned her head aside and said nothing.

'It's better to be poor than wealthy,' said Ranald. 'Your brother and sister will see that you and the children never go hungry.'

Ingerth turned to go.

'Next time you're in Hamnavoe with butter and cheese to sell,' said Ranald, 'you might have a look at Lodd Person's boatyard. He should be well advanced now with the ship he's building for me.'

The next day Solveig came to visit her father from brushing the horses in the stable. (Solveig rode faster and further than any man.) 'Are you still on about the ship you're having built? The shipwright is dead, and anyway Lodd Person built only fishing-boats. Ingerth came to me weeping last night, the ninny, about you and your talk of a ship you're having built. Where are you going in this new ship, tell me that? Is it Vinland?'

Ranald said that the voyage was a matter that concerned himself alone. His eyes brightened at the mention of Vinland. 'I'd very much like to go there,' he said. 'I'd like to make my peace with that skraeling lad before I die . . . But I'm not sailing to Vinland. The island lies away beyond Vinland. I have it all mapped in my head.'

'And who', said Solveig, 'is going to sail with you on this famous voyage?'

Ranald said nothing. Then his eye brightened again and he said that maybe a few old Orkney folk might be eager to sail with him. But they would have to be old. It would be a sorrowful thing to have a young man, or a child, on the ship.

Solveig said to Sumarlid, that evening, 'It's a lie, the saying that old age brings wisdom. Our father's mind is thin and cold as a washed-out shell.'

'No, but he seems gentle and happy,' said Sumarlid. 'I haven't known him so contented. And yet there's an eagerness in him, too.'

One day Ranald told Sumarlid he wanted a word with Abbot Peter.

The abbot came under the first star and stayed till the sky was thick with midnight stars.

The next morning Ranald went to an early Mass in the chapel. His grandson Rolf led him by the sleeve of his coat. The young dog ran on ahead barking. The fields were glittering with dew.

More and more often Ragna came back in the evening from the doorstep of the hut with the morning jug and the plate of food untasted.

But one day Ranald must have heard her laboured breath outside, and the sound of the ale jug being set on the doorstep, for he opened the door and took her by the hand.

'You've been a good woman in Breckness,' he said. 'I thank you for that.'

'I can't say the same about you this long while past,' said Ragna. 'You were a good enough husband in your early days.'

'I won't be needing any more of your ale and cheese,' said Ranald. 'Next time you're in Hamnavoe, I want you to pay Lodd Person for the ship. He's putting the finishing touches to it now. Listen carefully, Ragna. On the west gable of the farm, three courses up, you'll find a loose stone. Behind the stone there's a gold coin, a Danish crown piece. I set it there a while ago, when I came back from Norway on the *Laxoy*. I was very young then. I want you to take the gold coin and give it to the shipwright – it's the money I owe him.'

Then Ranald kissed his wife on the cheek.

And Ragna stumbled down the hill, her face streaming with tears.

Next morning was a fine April day, Easter Monday and a holiday. The ploughing was finished and the horsemen were sitting idle at the end of the barn. They were drinking ale in the sun. They saw Ranald Sigmundson leaving his hut, and toiling slowly on his stick down to the shore. Sumarlid came to speak to him, with the young dog Kame at his heels, but Ranald waved him away. He walked on slowly to the sea-banks. The abbot Peter and two novices were gathering whelks from the rockpools at the beach called Billiacroo. The abbot straightened himself and came over the wet seaweed to greet Ranald. Ranald and Peter spoke together. It seemed to the ploughmen and the fishermen at the shore that Ranald was inviting the old abbot to come with him. The abbot shook his head and blessed Ranald and went back to gather whelks from the rockpools.

Then Ranald walked along the shore, making, it seemed, for the

231

hamlet of Hamnavoe two miles away. Once or twice he lost his balance and stumbled in the seaweed. The fishermen had not launched their boats, for it was Easter Monday, but they were getting their lines ready for the haddock fishing on the next day. They looked at each other and three of them set off in pursuit of the old man.

Just below the little monastery at Warbeth, Ranald Sigmundson fell and did not get up again.

When the fishermen reached the place, an Irish monk Niall was administering the last rites.

Soon afterwards Ranald died on the greensward above the shore.

The fishermen carried his body into the chapel.

The monks lit candles at his head and at his feet.

The chapel was shaped like a little stone ship.

At sunset they sang in the choir.

Song of the Monks

Christ of the workbench, be thy strength and timberwit in the long, powerful keel.

Be thou in the well-made strakes.

Be thou in the tall mast.

Be thou in the thwarts and rowlocks.

Be thou in the bending oars when they break the water and the under-water breaks the blades into fragments, till each comes together solid and dripping, over another and another and yet another wave-crest.

Be thou in the bread and wine of the seamen, hidden in the sea chest.

Be thou, Lord, at the helm, when at last the voyager turns his face to the west . . .

Next day Ragna gave the gold coin to the abbot.

They buried Ranald on the following day.

On the third day, the monks sang a requiem for him.